GCSE
Physical Education

It's not easy to rack up a high score in Grade 9-1 GCSE PE, but luckily this fantastic CGP book has everything you need to prepare for the exams.

Each topic is explained in clear, straightforward language, and there are plenty of warm-up and exam-style questions to make sure you've mastered it all.

We've even included a free Online Edition to read on your PC, Mac or tablet!

How to access your free Online Edition

This book includes a free Online Edition to read on your PC, Mac or tablet.
You'll just need to go to **cgpbooks.co.uk/extras** and enter this code:

4176 8200 7935 2084

By the way, this code only works for one person. If somebody else has used this book before you, they might have already claimed the Online Edition.

Complete
Revision & Practice
Everything you need to pass the exams!

Contents

Answering Exam Questions 1

Section One — Anatomy and Physiology

The Skeletal System 4

The Muscular System 8

Warm-Up and Worked Exam Questions 12

Exam Questions 13

The Cardiovascular System 14

The Respiratory System 16

Spirometers 18

Warm-Up and Worked Exam Questions 19

Exam Questions 20

Aerobic and Anaerobic Exercise 21

Short-Term Effects of Exercise 22

Long-Term Effects of Exercise 25

Warm-Up and Worked Exam Questions 26

Exam Questions 27

Revision Questions for Section One 29

Section Two — Movement Analysis

Lever Systems 30

Planes and Axes of Movement 32

Warm-Up and Worked Exam Questions 33

Exam Questions 34

Revision Questions for Section Two 35

Section Three — Physical Training

Health and Fitness 36

Components of Fitness 37

Fitness Testing 41

Warm-Up and Worked Exam Questions 47

Exam Questions 48

Principles of Training 50

Training Target Zones 52

Warm-Up and Worked Exam Questions 53

Exam Questions 54

Training Methods 55

Warm-Up and Worked Exam Questions 60

Exam Questions 61

Preventing Injuries 63

Injuries and Treatment 66

Performance-Enhancing Drugs 68

Warm-Up and Worked Exam Questions 69

Exam Questions 70

Revision Questions for Section Three 71

Throughout this book you'll see grade stamps like these: Grade 1-3   Grade 3-5   Grade 5-7   Grade 7-9

These grade stamps help to show how difficult the questions are.
Remember — to get a top grade you need to be able to answer **all** the questions, not just the hardest ones.

On the question pages of this book, extended writing questions are marked like this: 1

Contents

Section Four — Health, Fitness and Well-Being

Health, Fitness and Well-being	72
Lifestyle Choices	74
Sedentary Lifestyle	75
Warm-Up and Worked Exam Questions	76
Exam Questions	77
Diet and Nutrition	79
Diet, Nutrition and Performance	81
Somatotypes	82
Optimum Weight	83
Warm-Up and Worked Exam Questions	84
Exam Questions	85
Revision Questions for Section Four	87

Section Five — Sport Psychology

Learning Skills	88
Skill Classification	89
Practising Skills	90
Goal Setting	91
Warm-Up and Worked Exam Questions	92
Exam Questions	93
Guidance and Feedback	94
Using Feedback	95
Mental Preparation	96
Emotion and Personality	97
Warm-Up and Worked Exam Questions	98
Exam Questions	99
Revision Questions for Section Five	100

Section Six — Sport, Society and Culture

Influences on Participation	101
Warm-Up and Worked Exam Questions	105
Exam Questions	106
Commercialisation of Sport	107
Technology in Sport	110
Sporting Behaviour	111
Spectator Behaviour	113
Warm-Up and Worked Exam Questions	114
Exam Questions	115
Revision Questions for Section Six	116

Section Seven — Using Data

Using Data	117
Warm-Up and Worked Exam Questions	122
Exam Questions	123
Revision Questions for Section Seven	124

Practice Papers

Practice Paper 1	125
Practice Paper 2	139
Answers	151
Glossary	159
Index	163

Published by CGP

Editors:
Chris Corrall, Joanna Daniels and Alison Palin.

Contributors:
Dee Gannon and Paddy Gannon.

With thanks to Simon Little for the proofreading.

With thanks to Ana Pungartnik for the copyright research.

Acknowledgements:

Definitions from Edexcel specifications used with the permission of Pearson Education.

With thanks to iStock.com for permission to use the images on pages 13, 128, 131 & 133.

Definition of health on page 36 is from the preamble to the Constitution of the World Health Organization, as adopted by the International Health Conference, New York, 19 June - 22 July 1946; signed on 22 July 1946 by the representatives of 61 States (Official Records of the World Health Organization, no. 2, p.100), and entered into force on 7 April 1948.

Normative data table for grip dynamometer test on pages 46 & 48 was published in 'Physical Education and the Study of Sport' 4th ed, 2002, Davis ed, p.123, 1 table ('Normative data table for grip strength test' for 16 to 19 year olds), Copyright Elsevier (2016).

Data about obesity rates on pages 75 & 122 copyright © 2015, Health and Social Care Information Centre. All rights reserved.

Graphs on pages 78 & 141 contain public sector information licensed under the Open Government Licence v3.0.
http://www.nationalarchives.gov.uk/doc/open-government-licence/version/3/

Graphs on pages 104, 106 & 146 based on data from Sport England.

Source for the data about shirt sponsorship in the Premier League on pages 107 & 122: sportingintelligence.com.

Normative data for vertical jump test on page 127 from ARKINSTALL, M et al. (2010) VCE Physical Education 2. Malaysia: Macmillan. p.248. © Reproduced by permission of Macmillan Education Australia.

ISBN: 978 1 78294 531 4
Printed by Elanders Ltd, Newcastle upon Tyne.
Clipart from Corel®

Text, design, layout and original illustrations © Coordination Group Publications Ltd. (CGP) 2016
All rights reserved.

Based on the classic CGP style created by Richard Parsons.

Photocopying more than one chapter of this book is not permitted. Extra copies are available from CGP.
0800 1712 712 • www.cgpbooks.co.uk

Answering Exam Questions

Before you get on with your PE revision, here are some handy tips about what to expect in your exams. There's also some advice on how to get top marks in all the different types of PE exam question, which you can put into practice as you work through this book.

Here's what to Expect in the Exams

The way your exams are structured depends on the exam board you're with.

Edexcel
1) You'll sit two exams.
2) Paper 1 will test you on component 1 — 'Fitness and Body Systems'. It'll be worth 90 marks and will last 1 hour 45 minutes.
3) You'll find the topics for component 1 in sections 1-3 and section 7 of this book.
4) Paper 2 will test you on component 2 — 'Health and Performance'. It'll be worth 70 marks and will last 1 hour 15 minutes.
5) You'll find the topics for component 2 in sections 4-7 of this book.

AQA
1) You'll sit two exams. Each paper will be worth 78 marks and will last 1 hour 15 minutes.
2) Paper 1 will test you on 'The human body and movement in physical activity and sport'.
3) You'll find the topics for paper 1 in sections 1-3 and section 7 of this book. APP MA PT UcD
4) Paper 2 will test you on 'Socio-cultural influences and well-being in physical activity and sport'.
5) You'll find the topics for paper 2 in sections 4-7 of this book.

> For the AQA and OCR courses, the stuff on page 68 in section 3 will be tested in paper 2 — not paper 1.

OCR
1) You'll sit two exams. Each paper will be worth 60 marks and will last 1 hour.
2) Paper 1 will test you on component 1 — 'Physical factors affecting performance'.
3) You'll find the topics for paper 1 in sections 1-3 and section 7 of this book.
4) Paper 2 will test you on component 2 — 'Socio-cultural issues and sports psychology'.
5) You'll find the topics for paper 2 in sections 4-7 of this book.
6) Each paper will be split into two sections (section A and section B), and each section will be worth 30 marks.

Eduqas
1) You'll only sit one exam called 'Introduction to physical education'.
2) It will be worth 120 marks and will last 2 hours.
3) You'll find all the topics you need for the exam in sections 1-7 of this book.

In total, your exams (or exam) will make up 60% of your GCSE mark.

Read the Questions and Don't Panic

1) Read every question carefully.
2) The number of marks each question is worth is shown next to it in brackets, or at the bottom of the answer lines. This can be a good guide to the number of points you need to make and how long your answer should be.
3) Make sure your answers are clear and easy to read. If the examiner can't read your handwriting, they won't be able to give you any marks.
4) Don't panic — if you get stuck on a question, just move on to the next one. You can come back to it if you have time at the end.

> The number of answer lines given in a question can also be a good guide to how much to write.

Answering Exam Questions

There are **Three** Different Types of PE Question

Multiple-Choice — **Cross** the Right Box

1) Multiple-choice questions give you a choice of four or five possible answers to the question. All you need to do is choose one option that you think is the correct answer. They're worth one mark each.
2) In the exam, it will tell you on your paper how to answer the question — you'll either have to put a cross or tick in a box, or shade a circle next to the correct answer.
3) Make sure you only choose one answer — if you pick more than one you won't get the mark.
4) Don't worry if you make a mistake and mark the wrong answer in the real exam — there'll be instructions on how to change an answer if you need to.
5) If you don't know the answer to a question, guess. You don't lose marks for putting a wrong answer — if you guess, you've at least got a chance of getting it right.

Short-Answer Questions

1) Short-answer questions are usually worth between one and five marks.
2) Make sure you read the question carefully. If you're asked for two influences, make sure you give two.
3) To get the marks, you need to show your PE knowledge, apply it to a situation, or use it to analyse or evaluate something. In questions worth more marks, you might need to do a combination of these.

Extended Writing Questions

Each extended writing question on the question pages in this book has a grey box around the question number.

1) Extended writing questions are worth between six and ten marks.
2) For these questions, as well as showing and applying your PE knowledge, you need to write about the advantages and disadvantages of something, or analyse how or why something happens.
3) At the end of your answer, you might need to write a conclusion where you make a judgement.
4) Even if a question looks tricky, give it a go — you'll get a few marks just for doing some of it.

You get **Marks** for Meeting Different **Assessment Objectives**

1) Assessment objectives (AOs) are the things you need to do to get marks for your answers.
2) Questions can test you on three AOs:

Assessment objective 1 (AO1) is all about demonstrating knowledge and understanding of a topic.
  1) Questions that test AO1 usually ask you to state, define, describe or identify something.
  2) They could also get you to label a diagram or complete a table or sentence.

Assessment objective 2 (AO2) is about applying knowledge and understanding of a topic to a context.
  1) Questions that assess AO2 might ask you to explain why or how something happens.
  2) You'll sometimes need to give examples to back up your points.

Assessment objective 3 (AO3) is about analysing and evaluating.
  1) Questions that test AO3 often start with words like analyse, evaluate, assess, discuss or justify.
  2) Analysing just means breaking something down into parts or stages to explain it. This can include analysing data to explain what it shows.
  3) To evaluate, assess or discuss something, you need to weigh up its advantages and disadvantages in the context given in the question.
  4) Justifying something means giving reasons why it's sensible.

3) A lot of questions will test more than one assessment objective — for example, if a question tells you to evaluate something (AO3), you'll also need to demonstrate your knowledge of the topic (AO1) and apply it to the situation in the question (AO2).

Answering Exam Questions

Answering Exam Questions

Don't Forget to Watch Your Spelling and Grammar

1) As well as your amazing PE knowledge, some questions will test your written communication skills (otherwise known as 'how well you can write your answer').
2) The questions where you get marks for your communication skills are the longer ones that are worth at least 6 marks.
3) In the OCR exams, any questions that assess the quality of your writing will have an asterisk (*) next to the question number (or letter) inside the paper.
4) You can pick up some easy marks just by making sure that you do these things:

   1) Make sure you answer the question being asked — stay focused on the topic you're asked about, and don't waffle about anything that's not relevant.
   2) Make sure your answer is organised. It's a really good idea to have a think about what you're going to cover in your answer, and jot it down in a quick plan before you start writing it. That way you can make sure you structure your answer well, and cover all the points you want to.
   3) Write in full sentences and use correct spelling, grammar and punctuation.
   4) Use the correct PE terminology.

Have a look at this Example Question and Answer

This example exam answer will show you how you might answer one of the extended writing questions.

15 Evaluate the use of continuous training and plyometric training to improve performance in cycling.

> Continuous training involves exercising aerobically for at least twenty minutes, and helps to improve both muscular endurance and cardiovascular fitness. Good muscular endurance would help to prevent muscle fatigue when cycling long distances, and a high level of cardiovascular fitness would allow a cyclist to cycle continuously for long periods. Continuous training can also be included as part of a normal cycling training session, allowing a cyclist to practise their overall technique.
>
> However, the steady-state exercise involved in continuous training would not prepare a cyclist for the differing intensities involved in the sport, for example, when cycling on steep gradients, or during a sprint finish in a race.
>
> Plyometric training involves exercises such as jumping, to improve power in the legs. Power is an important component of fitness in cycling, as it is used to pedal forcefully and quickly, helping a cyclist to maintain a high speed. It also allows a cyclist to accelerate quickly, so they can overtake other riders in a race. However, plyometric training alone is not the most suitable training method for a cyclist, as it does not provide practice of sport-specific actions, such as pedalling technique.
>
> In conclusion, a combination of continuous and plyometric training would be very useful for a cyclist wishing to improve their performance. Using both training methods would help to improve a cyclist's muscular endurance, cardiovascular fitness and power, all of which would lead to improved cycling performance. However, a cyclist wishing to improve their performance further might also use interval training, which would improve their ability to exercise at high intensities.

Annotations:
- This applies knowledge of continuous training to the cyclist by saying what impact it will have on their performance.
- This shows good knowledge of continuous training by talking about the components of fitness that it improves.
- This looks at the disadvantages of continuous training by talking about aspects of cycling performance that it doesn't improve.
- This shows good application of knowledge by giving specific examples from cycling.
- This shows knowledge of plyometric training and applies it to the cyclist's performance.
- This paragraph outlines the disadvantages of plyometric training for a cyclist.
- This bit shows that the training methods are being evaluated by making a judgement about their usefulness.
- You could really show off by bringing a different training method into your conclusion.

Total for Question 15 = 9 marks

Answering Exam Questions

Section One — Anatomy and Physiology

The Skeletal System

Welcome to the GCSE PE fun bus — first stop is the skeleton. It gives the body its shape and has loads of jobs to do. It's made up of various kinds of bones, all with their own function. Here we go...

The Skeleton has Different Functions

The skeleton does more than you might think to help your performance in sport. Its main functions are:

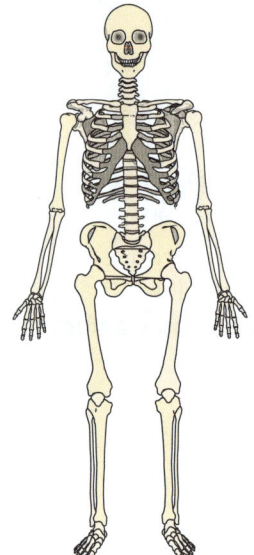

① SUPPORT/SHAPE:
1) The skeleton is a rigid bone frame for the rest of the body. Our shape is mainly due to our skeleton.
2) The skeleton supports the soft tissues like skin and muscle.
3) This helps you to have good posture, which is essential in loads of sports.
4) E.g. good posture aids performance in gymnastics.

③ MOVEMENT:
1) Muscles, attached to bones by tendons, can move bones at joints.
2) This movement is essential for good performance in sport.
3) There are different types of movement at the various joints, which are important in different sports.

② PROTECTION:
1) Bones are very tough — they protect vital organs like the brain, heart and lungs.
2) This allows you to perform well in sport without fear of serious injury.
3) E.g. the skull protects the brain, so you can head a football or take punches in a boxing match without serious injury.

④ MAKING BLOOD CELLS/PLATELETS:
1) Some bones contain bone marrow, which makes the components of blood — platelets and red and white blood cells (see p15).
2) Red blood cells are really important during exercise — they transport the oxygen that muscles need to move.
3) Athletes with more red blood cells perform better — more oxygen can be delivered to their muscles.

⑤ MINERAL STORAGE:
1) Bones store minerals like calcium and phosphorus.
2) These help with bone strength — so you're less likely to break a bone.
3) They're also needed for muscle contraction — so the body can move.

There are Different Types of Bone in the Skeleton

There are four main types of bone in the skeleton. Each type is suited to a different purpose.

LONG BONES
Long bones (e.g. the humerus in the arm) are strong and are used by muscles to assist movement.

SHORT BONES
Short bones (e.g. the tarsals in the foot) support the weight of the body — they're weight-bearing.

Short bones are also used in some smaller fine movements, e.g. moving the hand at the wrist. Long bones are used for larger gross movements, e.g. moving the leg at the hip. See p89 for more on gross and fine movements.

IRREGULAR BONES
Irregular bones (e.g. the vertebrae of the spine) are suited to protection and muscle attachment.

FLAT BONES
Flat bones (e.g. the ribs) protect internal organs. Their broad surface also allows muscle attachment.

The skeleton does more than you think in PE...

Those five functions of the skeleton are crucial in helping you perform in physical activity and sport. Try writing down an example of how each function could help performance in one sport.

Section One — Anatomy and Physiology

The Skeletal System

Time for some more skeleton-related fun — this page'll give you a hand at remembering the names of some important bones in the body, their types and what they do. I bet you can hardly wait...

Learn the Structure of the Skeleton

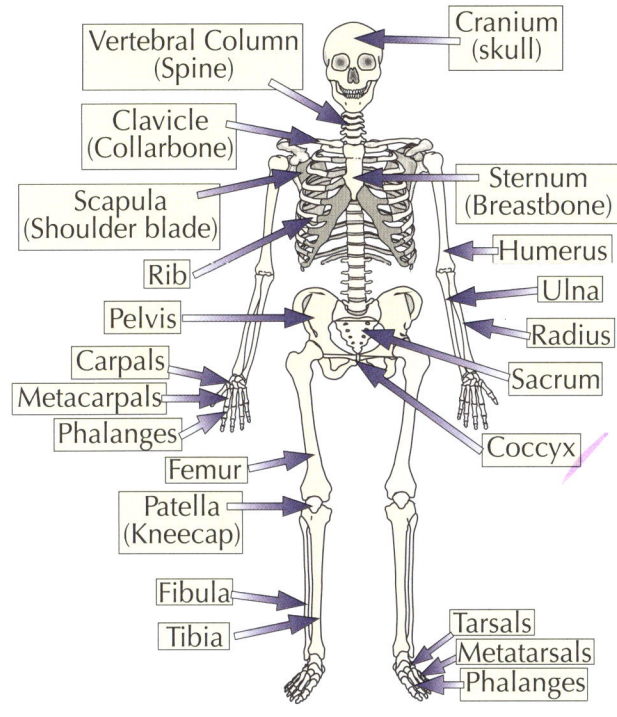

FLAT BONES

Cranium — protects the brain.

Sternum and ribs — protect the heart and lungs. The ribs also protect the kidneys.

Scapula — protects the shoulder joint and has many muscles attached to it, helping arm and shoulder movement.

Pelvis — protects the reproductive organs and the bladder. It also has many muscles attached to it, helping leg movement.

SHORT BONES

Carpals — form the wrist and give it stability, allowing movement of the hand.

Tarsals — bear the body's weight when on foot, e.g. during standing and running.

The patella is a different type of bone — it's a sesamoid bone. It protects the tendon that crosses the knee joint by stopping it rubbing against the femur.

LONG BONES

Clavicle — forms part of the shoulder joint to assist arm movement.
Humerus — used by muscles to move the whole arm, e.g. swinging a badminton racket.
Ulna and radius — used by muscles to move the lower arm, e.g. bending at the elbow.
Femur — used by muscles to move the whole leg, e.g. when running.
Fibula and tibia — used by muscles to move the lower leg, e.g. to kick a football.
Metacarpals — used by muscles to allow the hand to grip, e.g. to hold a cricket ball.
Phalanges — used by muscles to move and bend the fingers and toes.
Metatarsals — used by muscles to move the foot, e.g. when jumping.

Learn the Structure of the Vertebral Column

The vertebral column ('spine' or 'spinal column') is made up of irregular bones called vertebrae that protect the spinal cord. It can be divided into five regions:

The top two vertebrae are called the atlas and axis.

Cervical — Seven vertebrae at the top of the spine.
Thoracic — Twelve vertebrae below the cervical region.
Lumbar — Five vertebrae below the thoracic region.
Sacrum — Five vertebrae fused together below the lumbar region.
Coccyx — Four vertebrae fused together at the bottom of the spine.

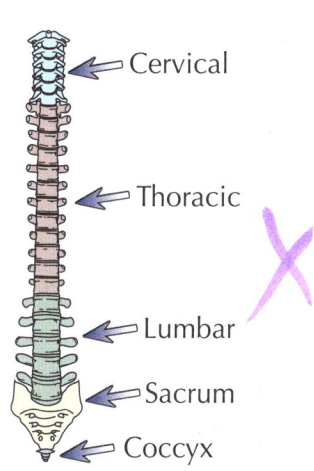

Section One — Anatomy and Physiology

The Skeletal System

Joints are really important parts of the skeleton — you need to know what they are, how they can move and what types of joints you'll find in the body. Luckily, all that is right here on this page.

There are Different Kinds of Joint Movement

1) Joints are any points where two or more bones meet. The bones that meet at a joint are called the articulating bones of the joint.

2) Here are a few examples of some of the major joints in the body, and their articulating bones:

3) There are eight joint movements that you need to know:

Hip — pelvis and femur
Shoulder — humerus and scapula
Knee — femur and tibia
Ankle — tibia, fibula and talus (one of the tarsals)
Elbow — humerus, radius and ulna

| FLEXION | EXTENSION | ADDUCTION | ABDUCTION |

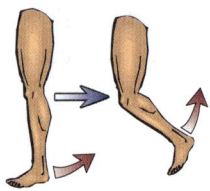 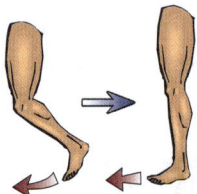  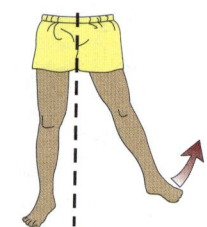

Closing a joint, e.g. the wrist movement during a basketball throw.

Opening a joint, e.g. kicking a football.

Moving towards an imaginary centre line, e.g. swinging a golf club.

Moving away from an imaginary centre line, e.g. taking back a tennis racket before swinging it.

| ROTATION | CIRCUMDUCTION | PLANTAR-FLEXION | DORSI-FLEXION |

  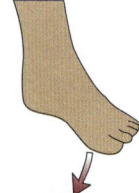 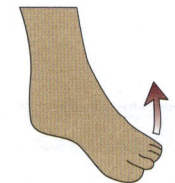

Clockwise or anticlockwise movement, e.g. the leg movement during a turnout in ballet.

Movement of a limb, hand or foot in a circular motion, e.g. to bowl a cricket ball.

Extension at the ankle, e.g. pointing the toes during gymnastics.

Flexion at the ankle, e.g. lifting the toes during gymnastics.

You might see this called 'overarm rotation'.

There are different Joint Types in the Body

You need to know about ball and socket, pivot, hinge and condyloid joints. Each type allows a certain range of movements.

type	examples	flexion and extension	adduction and abduction	rotation	circumduction
ball and socket	hip, shoulder	✓	✓	✓	✓
hinge	knee, ankle, elbow	✓	✗	✗	✗
condyloid	wrist	✓	✓	✗	✓
pivot	neck (atlas and axis)	✗	✗	✓	✗

Each joint type has a different range of movement...

Make sure you don't get adduction and abduction mixed up — ADDuction brings two bits together, like adding them. ABDuction takes them away — like being abducted by aliens.

Section One — Anatomy and Physiology

The Skeletal System

Coming up on this page — a little more on joint movements, and the different things joints are made of. As well as bones, joints have other useful bits that protect them and help them do their job well.

Sports use Lots of different Movement Types

During exercise, you'll usually use a combination of movement types, and often a combination of joints, either at the same time, or one after another. For example:

1) To do a push-up at the gym or a football throw-in, first you use flexion at the elbow to bend your arms. To straighten your arms again and complete the movements, you extend your arms at the elbow.
2) Running, kicking, basic squats and standing vertical jumps all use flexion and extension at the hip and knee. They also use plantar-flexion and dorsi-flexion at the ankle.

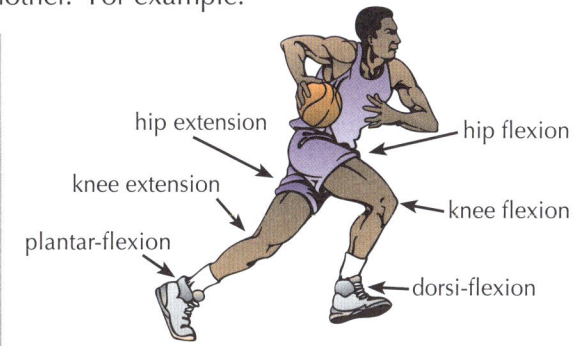

Connective Tissues Join Muscle and Bones

There are three types of connective tissue you need to know about:

LIGAMENTS — hold bones together to restrict how much joints can move. This helps maintain the stability of the skeleton and prevents dislocation of joints (see p66). They're made of tough and fibrous tissue (like very strong string).

Ligaments also protect bones and joints by absorbing shock.

TENDONS — attach muscles to bones (or to other muscles) to allow bones to move when muscles contract.

CARTILAGE — acts as a cushion between bones to prevent damage during joint movement.

Learn the Structure of a Synovial Joint

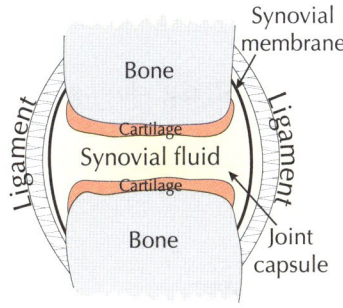

Ball and socket, hinge, condyloid and pivot joints are all synovial joints. A synovial joint is a joint that allows a wide range of movement and has a joint capsule enclosing and supporting it.

1) The bones at a synovial joint are held together by ligaments.
2) The ends of the bones are covered with cartilage and are shaped so that they fit together and can move smoothly.
3) The synovial membrane releases synovial fluid into the joint capsule to lubricate (or 'oil') the joint, allowing it to move more easily.
4) Most synovial joints also have sacs of fluid called bursae (one is a 'bursa') which reduce friction between bones and tissues in and around the joint.
5) This structure helps to prevent injury to the bones that make up your joints.

Joints joints joints — it's enough to make you hungry...

Those connective tissues are really important — they all help your performance in physical activity and sport in a different way. Keep revising what each one does so you don't get them mixed up in the exam.

Section One — Anatomy and Physiology

The Muscular System

The skeletal system can't make the body move on its own — it needs some help from the muscular system. Together, they're known as the musculo-skeletal system.

There are Different Types of Muscle

1) Like the title says, there are different types of muscle you need to know about. These are...

VOLUNTARY (SKELETAL) MUSCLES
Attached to the skeleton and are under your control. They help to move the body.

INVOLUNTARY (SMOOTH) MUSCLES
Work internal organs without effort from you, e.g. muscles in blood vessels control the amount of blood flowing to voluntary muscles.

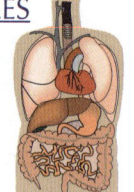

2) Cardiac muscle is a type of involuntary muscle that forms the heart.
3) It never gets tired — the heart can pump blood around your body all the time.
4) During exercise, voluntary muscles need oxygen so they can move the body. When the heart beats, it pumps blood carrying oxygen to these muscles.

Learn the Muscles at the Front of the body

You need to learn the names of some voluntary muscles, and what their main functions are. Here are the ones at the front of the body.

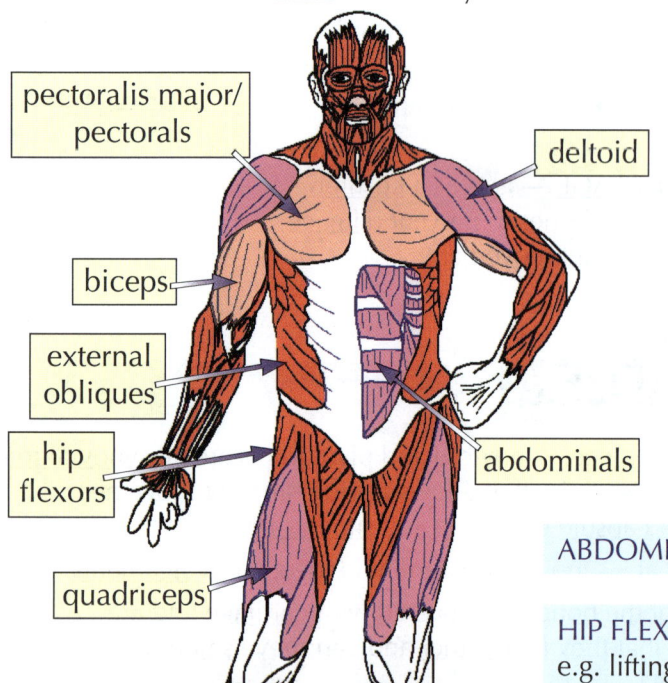

PECTORALIS MAJOR — adduction and flexion (horizontally) at the shoulder, e.g. during a forehand drive in tennis.

DELTOID — flexion, extension, abduction or circumduction at the shoulder. E.g. during front crawl in swimming.

BICEPS — flexion at the elbow, e.g. when curling weights.

EXTERNAL OBLIQUES — rotation or flexion at the waist, e.g. preparing to throw a discus.

ABDOMINALS — flexion at the waist, e.g. during a sit-up.

HIP FLEXORS — flexion of the leg at the hip, e.g. lifting the knee when sprinting.

QUADRICEPS — extension at the knee, e.g. when performing a drop kick in rugby.

TIBIALIS ANTERIOR — dorsi-flexion at the ankle, e.g. during a heel side turn in snowboarding.

My muscles don't feel like they volunteer for anything...

Don't get voluntary and involuntary muscles mixed up — voluntary muscles are ones you choose (or 'volunteer') to use. So any muscle that only works if you think about making it work is a voluntary muscle.

Section One — Anatomy and Physiology

The Muscular System

This page is all about the most important muscles and muscle groups at the <u>back</u> of the body. Just like the muscles from the last page, you need to know their <u>names</u> and their <u>roles</u> in different sport movements.

Learn the **Muscles** at the **Back** of the body

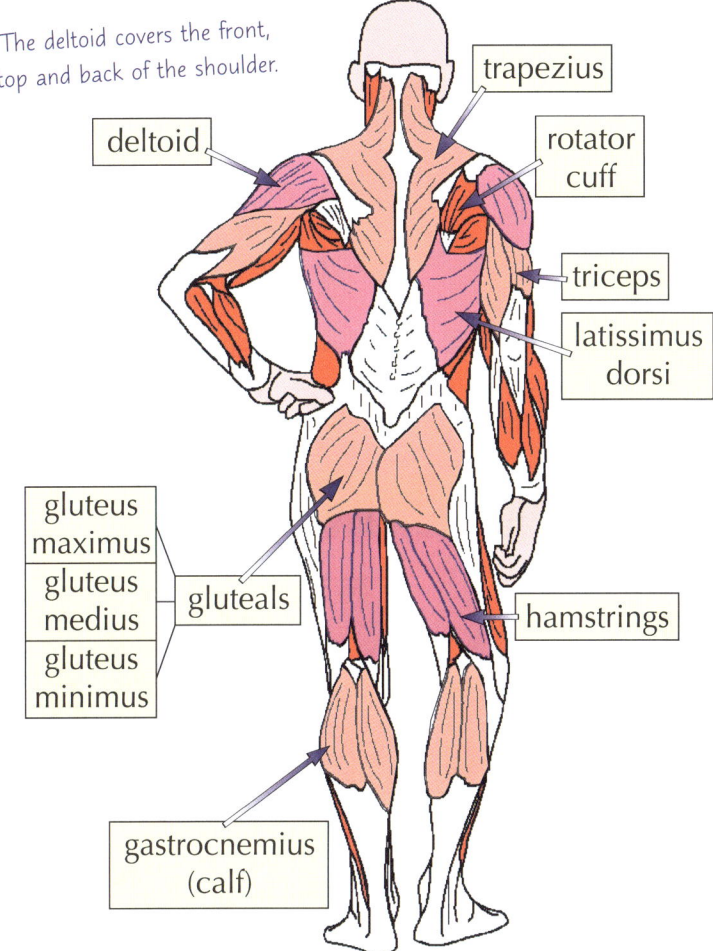

The deltoid covers the front, top and back of the shoulder.

TRAPEZIUS — <u>extension</u> at the <u>neck</u> (tilting the head back), e.g. preparing to head a football.

ROTATOR CUFFS — <u>rotation</u> and <u>abduction</u> at the <u>shoulder</u>, e.g. lifting the arms when preparing to dive. They also <u>stabilise</u> the shoulder joint during other movements.

TRICEPS — <u>extension</u> at the <u>elbow</u>, e.g. during a jump shot in netball.

LATISSIMUS DORSI — <u>extension</u>, <u>adduction</u> or <u>rotation</u> at the <u>shoulder</u>, e.g. during butterfly stroke in swimming.

GLUTEALS — <u>extension</u>, <u>rotation</u>, and <u>abduction</u> of the leg at the <u>hip</u>, e.g. pushing the body forward when running.

HAMSTRINGS — <u>flexion</u> at the <u>knee</u>, e.g. bringing the foot back before kicking a football.

GASTROCNEMIUS — <u>plantar-flexion</u> at the <u>ankle</u>, e.g. standing on the toes in ballet pointe work.

Each muscle has a specific function...

The table on the right shows the muscles and muscle groups from this page. Copy out the table, then complete it by writing down an example of an action from a physical activity or sport that uses each muscle or muscle group. Make sure your examples are different to the ones given on this page.

Muscle/muscle group	Sporting action
Trapezius	
Rotator cuffs	
Triceps	
Latissimus dorsi	
Gluteals	
Hamstrings	
Gastrocnemius	

Section One — Anatomy and Physiology

The Muscular System

Now on to more stuff about muscles — just what we were all hoping for. This page'll look at how muscles work together to produce different movement types at the joints in the body.

Antagonistic Muscles Work in Pairs

Muscles can only do one thing — pull. To make a joint move in two directions, you need two muscles that can pull in opposite directions.

1) Antagonistic muscles are pairs of muscles that work against each other.
2) One muscle contracts while the other one relaxes, and vice versa.
3) The muscle that's contracting is the agonist or prime mover.
4) The muscle that's relaxing is the antagonist.
5) Each muscle is attached to two bones by tendons.
6) Only one of the bones connected at the joint actually moves.

Here, 'contracts' means 'shortens', and 'relaxes' means 'lengthens'. But you might see 'contracts' used to mean 'creates tension' — which muscles do when they shorten and lengthen (see next page).

During this antagonistic muscle action, other muscles can help the agonist to work properly by stabilising it where it attaches to the bone that doesn't move. These muscles are known as fixators.

You need to know some Antagonistic Muscle Pairs

There are antagonistic muscle pairs at different joints in the body:

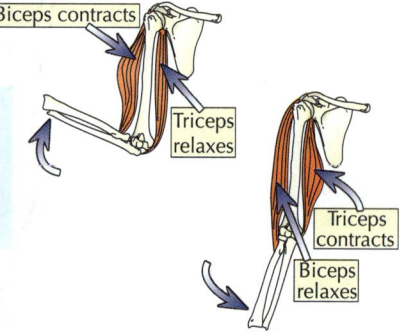

KNEE
Flexion — agonist — hamstrings
antagonist — quadriceps
Extension — agonist — quadriceps
antagonist — hamstrings

ELBOW
Flexion — agonist — biceps
antagonist — triceps
Extension — agonist — triceps
antagonist — biceps

HIP
Flexion — agonist — hip flexors
antagonist — gluteus maximus
Extension — agonist — gluteus maximus
antagonist — hip flexors

ANKLE
Plantar-flexion — agonist — gastrocnemius
antagonist — tibialis anterior
Dorsi-flexion — agonist — tibialis anterior
antagonist — gastrocnemius

SHOULDER Other muscles are used in these shoulder movements — these are just the main ones.

Flexion — agonist — front part of deltoid
antagonist — back part of deltoid
Extension — agonist — back part of deltoid
antagonist — front part of deltoid

Adduction — agonist — latissimus dorsi
antagonist — middle part of deltoid
Abduction — agonist — middle part of deltoid
antagonist — lattisimus dorsi

Rotation (turning arm outwards) — agonists — infraspinatus, teres minor
antagonist — subscapularis
Rotation (turning arm inwards) — agonist — subscapularis
antagonists — infraspinatus, teres minor

The infraspinatus, teres minor and subscapularis are muscles in the rotator cuffs at the shoulders.

Antagonists — don't let them get to you...

This page might look tricky with all these different antagonistic muscle pairs to learn, but just remember — the muscle that's the agonist in one movement will be the antagonist in the opposite movement.

Section One — Anatomy and Physiology

The Muscular System

You've reached the fourth and final page about the muscular system. It's all about how muscles contract and the different types of fibres that make up the muscles in your body.

There are Different Types of Muscle Contraction

You don't need this bit if you're doing the Edexcel or OCR course.

When a muscle contracts, it creates tension to apply force to a bone. Muscle contractions can be isometric or isotonic.

ISOMETRIC CONTRACTION
The muscle stays the same length, and so nothing moves.

Like if you pull on a rope attached to a wall.

ISOTONIC CONTRACTION
The muscle changes length and so something moves.

Like if you exercise with weights that are free to move.

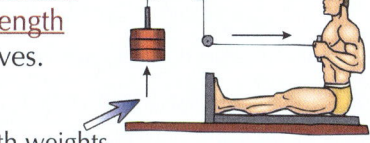

There are also two types of isotonic contraction — concentric and eccentric.

CONCENTRIC CONTRACTION
This is when a muscle contracts and shortens. This type of contraction pulls on a bone to cause a movement to happen. E.g. during the upward phase of a biceps curl, your biceps undergoes a concentric contraction to pull your forearm and lift the weight.

ECCENTRIC CONTRACTION
This is when a muscle contracts and lengthens. This helps you to control the speed of a movement. E.g. during the downward phase of a biceps curl, your biceps contracts eccentrically, creating tension so that the weight falls slowly.

Different Types of Muscle Fibre suit Different Activities

1) All muscles are made up of fibres.
2) These muscle fibres can be slow twitch (type I) or fast twitch (type IIA and type IIX).

If you're doing the AQA course, you can skip this part of the page.

SLOW TWITCH

TYPE I — Suited to low intensity aerobic work (e.g. marathon running) as they can be used for a long period of time without fatiguing.

See p21 for the definitions of aerobic and anaerobic work.

FAST TWITCH

TYPE IIA — Used in anaerobic work, but can be improved through endurance training to increase their resistance to fatigue.

TYPE IIX — Used in anaerobic work. Can generate a much greater force than other fibre types but fatigue quickly. Useful in short bursts of exercise, e.g. a 100 m sprint.

I wonder what muscle fibre type is most suited to PE revision...

There are lots of definitions on this page, so make sure you learn the ones you need for your exam. Just keep writing them down until they're lodged in your brain — then there's no way you'll forget them.

Section One — Anatomy and Physiology

Warm-Up and Worked Exam Questions

Time for some questions on the skeletal and muscular systems. There are some warm-up questions and worked exam questions to get you started, then some exam questions for you to practice on your own.

Warm-Up Questions

1) What do bones protect — vital organs, muscles or joints?
2) Name a long bone found in the leg and give an example of a sporting movement it is used in.
3) Give one function of the vertebral column.
4) Give one example of a ball and socket joint and say what types of joint movement it allows.
5) Name three types of connective tissue.
6) Describe the function of synovial fluid.
7) Which muscle is responsible for plantar-flexion at the ankle?
8) What is the name given to a pair of muscles that work against each other?
9) What type of muscle contraction happens when a muscle lengthens — concentric or eccentric?
10) What muscle fibre type would be most suited to a 10-mile run?

Worked Exam Questions

1 Protection of vital organs is one of the functions of the skeleton.

(a) Identify **three** other functions of the skeleton. *(Grade 1-3)*

Maintaining the body's shape.

Making blood cells and platelets.

Allowing movement.

You could also put "mineral storage", but you only need three functions to get the marks.

[3 marks]

(b) Explain, using **one** example, how the cranium could protect a performer when taking part in sport. *(Grade 3-5)*

During a game of hockey, if a player were to be hit on the head by the ball,

the cranium would protect the brain from a serious injury.

[2 marks]

2 Give **one** example of a sporting movement that uses abduction of the arm at the shoulder. *(Grade 3-5)*

Preparing to swing a hockey stick.

[1 mark]

You'd get the mark for any example that involves moving the arm away from an imaginary centre line on the body.

Section One — Anatomy and Physiology

Exam Questions

1 **Figure 1** shows some of the muscles in the human body.

   (a) Name the muscles labelled A-C on **Figure 1**.

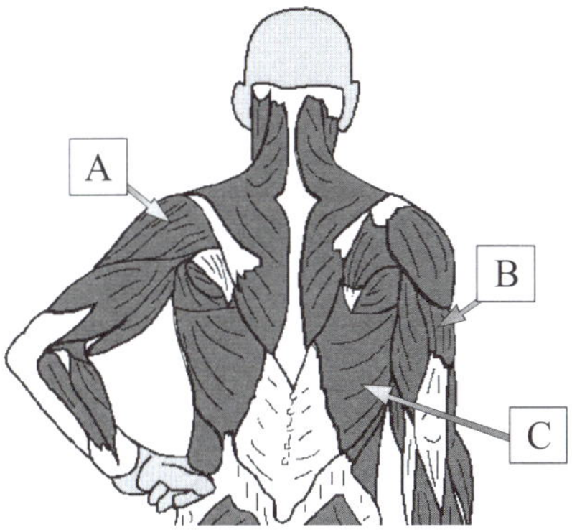

   A ....

   B ....

   C ....

   Figure 1

   [3 marks]

   (b) The hamstrings are the agonist muscle group responsible for flexion at the knee. Identify the antagonist muscle in this movement.

   ....

   [1 mark]

2 **Figure 2** shows a basketball player taking a shot at the hoop.

   Position A   Position B

   Figure 2

   Analyse the movement and muscle action at the elbow as the basketball player in **Figure 2** moves from position A to position B.

   You need to talk about what's happening in both pictures to get all the marks for this question.

   ....

   ....

   ....

   ....

   [4 marks]

Section One — Anatomy and Physiology

The Cardiovascular System

Your cardiovascular system's job is to move blood around your body. As the blood travels around, it does loads of really useful stuff to help you take part in physical activity and sport. Read on to find out more...

The Cardiovascular System has Three Main Functions

TRANSPORT OF SUBSTANCES — Transporting things around the body in the bloodstream, like oxygen, carbon dioxide and nutrients (e.g. glucose). This gives the muscles what they need to release energy to move during exercise (and takes away any waste products).

Have a look at p21 for more about how muscles use oxygen and glucose.

TEMPERATURE CONTROL — Moving more blood nearer the skin cools the body more quickly. This means you can exercise for a long time without overheating.

CLOTTING OF WOUNDS — Your blood clots to seal cuts. This stops you bleeding too much if you get a cut, and helps to prevent wounds becoming infected.

Learn How the Heart Pumps Blood Around the Body

1) The cardiovascular system is made up of three main parts — the heart, blood and blood vessels. — *Arteries, veins and capillaries are the main types of blood vessel.*
2) During any kind of physical activity, blood needs to circulate around the body to deliver oxygen and glucose to your muscles, and to take carbon dioxide away from them.
3) The cardiovascular system has a double-circulatory system — this just means there are two circuits:

PULMONARY CIRCUIT

- Deoxygenated blood enters the right ventricle through the tricuspid valve.
- The right ventricle contracts, pushing the blood through the right semi-lunar valve into the pulmonary artery, which carries the blood to the lungs to be oxygenated.
- Oxygenated blood from the lungs enters the left atrium through the pulmonary veins.

Pressure in the heart causes the valves to open. They close to stop blood flowing the wrong way.

The word for more than one atrium is 'atria'.

SYSTEMIC CIRCUIT

- Oxygenated blood enters the left ventricle through the bicuspid valve.
- The left ventricle contracts, pushing the blood through the left semi-lunar valve into the aorta (an artery), which carries the oxygenated blood to the rest of the body — including the muscles.
- When the muscles have used the oxygen in the blood, it becomes deoxygenated. It then enters the right atrium through the vena cava vein.

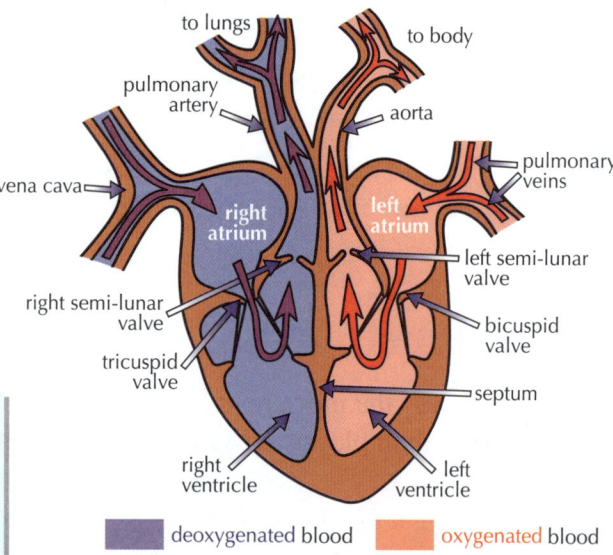

'Diastole' is when the heart fills with blood.
'Systole' is when it pumps the blood out.

Section One — Anatomy and Physiology

The Cardiovascular System

Your cardiovascular system has different types of blood vessels that carry blood around your body. This page'll tell you all about them, as well as all the weird and wonderful stuff your blood is made of.

Arteries, Veins and Capillaries Carry Blood

1) Blood vessels transport blood — they have a hollow centre called the lumen so blood can flow through.
2) Different types of blood vessel are suited to different roles:

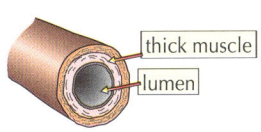

ARTERIES — carry blood away from the heart. All arteries carry oxygenated blood except for the pulmonary arteries. Their thick, muscular walls allow them to carry blood flowing at high pressure.

Blood pressure is how strongly the blood presses against the walls of blood vessels.

The (smooth) muscle in the walls of arteries and veins allows them to widen and narrow to control blood flow (see p23).

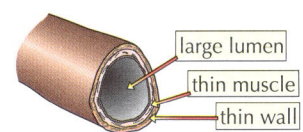

VEINS — carry blood towards the heart. They have valves to stop blood flowing the wrong way. All veins carry deoxygenated blood, except for the pulmonary veins. They carry blood at low pressure, so they have thinner walls and less muscle than arteries.

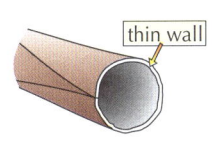

CAPILLARIES — carry blood through the body to exchange gases and nutrients with the body's tissues. They have very thin walls so substances can easily pass through. They're also very narrow, which means lots of them can fit into the body's tissues — giving them a large surface area to let gas exchange happen more easily. It also means that blood can only flow through them slowly — giving more time for gas exchange.

3) There are also two other small types of blood vessel — arterioles (which branch off arteries) and venules (which meet to form veins).
4) Oxygenated blood flows through arteries into arterioles, then into capillaries.
5) After gases have been exchanged between the capillaries and the body tissues, blood is transported from the capillaries into venules, where it flows back into the veins.

Your Blood is made up of Cells, Platelets and Plasma

Lots of different things make up the blood in your body. Each bit has its own job, which is really important in helping your body to take part in physical activity.

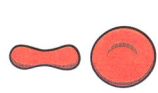

RED BLOOD CELLS — Carry oxygen and transport it around the body to be used to release energy needed by muscles during physical activity. They also carry carbon dioxide to the lungs. Haemoglobin (a protein in red blood cells) stores the oxygen and carbon dioxide.

Oxyhaemoglobin is formed by oxygen and haemoglobin combining.

PLATELETS — Help blood to clot at wounds so they don't become infected and so you don't lose too much blood.

WHITE BLOOD CELLS — Fight against disease so you stay healthy and perform well.

PLASMA — carries everything in the bloodstream. That includes blood cells, digested food (e.g. glucose) and waste (e.g. carbon dioxide).

Each type of blood vessel has a different job...

If you're struggling to remember whether veins and arteries carry blood to or from the heart, just remember — arteries carry blood away from the heart, so veins must carry blood towards it.

Section One — Anatomy and Physiology

The Respiratory System

You'll probably recognise most of this stuff from biology — but there's no harm in a quick recap.

Learn the Structure of the Respiratory System

The respiratory system is everything you use to breathe.
It's found in the chest cavity — the area inside the chest.

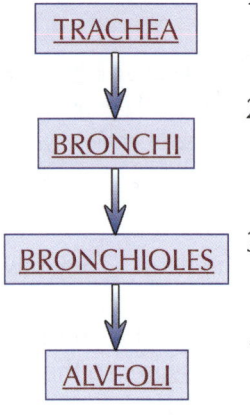

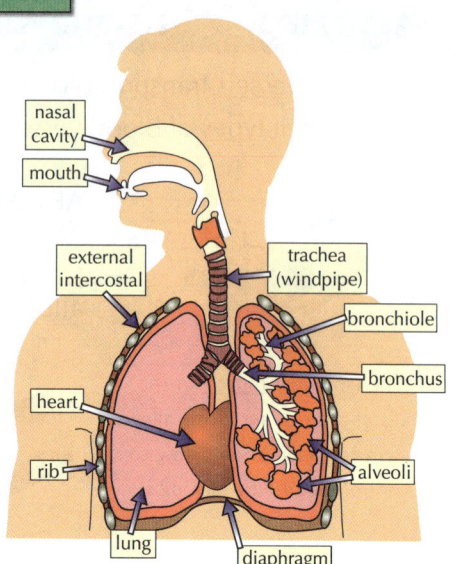

1) Air passes through the nose or mouth and then on to the trachea.
2) The trachea splits into two tubes called bronchi (each one is a 'bronchus') — one going to each lung.
3) The bronchi split into progressively smaller tubes called bronchioles.
4) The bronchioles finally end at small bags called alveoli (each one is an 'alveolus') where gases are exchanged (see below).

The diaphragm and external intercostal muscles help the air to move in and out:

1) When you breathe in, the diaphragm and external intercostals contract to move the ribcage upwards and expand the chest cavity. This decreases the air pressure in the lungs, drawing air in.
2) When you breathe out, the diaphragm and the external intercostals relax, moving the ribcage down and shrinking the chest cavity. Air pressure in the lungs increases, forcing air out of the lungs the same way it came in.

Oxygen and Carbon Dioxide are Exchanged in the Alveoli

1) The cardiovascular and respiratory systems have to work together to get oxygen to the muscles, and carbon dioxide away from them. They do this by exchanging gases between the alveoli and capillaries surrounding them.

The cardiovascular and respiratory systems together make up the cardio-respiratory system.

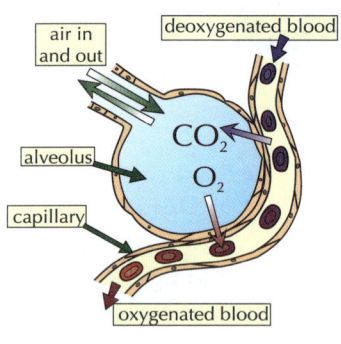

1) Oxygenated blood delivers oxygen and collects carbon dioxide as it circulates around the body. Deoxygenated blood returns to the heart and is then pumped to the lungs.
2) In the lungs, carbon dioxide moves from the blood in the capillaries into the alveoli so it can be breathed out.
3) Oxygen from the air you breathe into the lungs moves across from the alveoli to the red blood cells in the capillaries.
4) The oxygenated blood returns to the heart and is pumped to the rest of the body. The red blood cells carry the oxygen around the body and deliver it where it's needed, e.g. the muscles.

2) Alveoli are surrounded by lots of capillaries, giving them a large blood supply to exchange gases with.
3) They also have a large surface area and moist, thin walls — so gases can easily pass through them.
4) This exchange of gases happens through a process called diffusion. This means the gases move down a concentration gradient — from a place of higher concentration to a place of lower concentration:

IN ALVEOLUS		IN CAPILLARY
High concentration of O_2	DIFFUSION OF O_2 →	Low concentration of O_2
Low concentration of CO_2	← DIFFUSION OF CO_2	High concentration of CO_2

O_2 = oxygen
CO_2 = carbon dioxide

Section One — Anatomy and Physiology

The Respiratory System

You might have noticed that you take bigger breaths when you exercise. That's just 'cos the air we breathe in contains the stuff we need more of for exercise, and the air we breathe out contains the stuff we don't want.

Air is made up of Different Gases

You only need to know this bit for the Edexcel course.

1) You need to know the composition of the air we inhale (breathe in) and exhale (breathe out). This just means the different gases it's made up of.

	% of inhaled air	% of exhaled air
Oxygen	21%	16%
Carbon dioxide	0.04%	4%
Nitrogen (as well as argon and other gases)	79%	79%

These percentages are just approximate values — both inhaled and exhaled air also contain small amounts of water vapour (exhaled air has slightly more).

2) Exhaled air contains less oxygen than inhaled air. This is because some of the oxygen in inhaled air is used up by the body to release energy through aerobic respiration.

3) Exhaled air also contains more carbon dioxide than inhaled air. This is because carbon dioxide is produced when energy is released through aerobic respiration. The body needs to get rid of this carbon dioxide, so we breathe it out.

Tidal Volume Increases during Exercise

1) The amount of air you breathe in or out during one breath is known as your tidal volume.
2) After a normal breath in, you can still breathe in more air — this extra volume of air is your inspiratory reserve volume (IRV).
3) You can also breathe out more air after a normal breath out — the extra air you can breathe out is your expiratory reserve volume (ERV).
4) During exercise, your tidal volume increases. This means your IRV and ERV decrease — you're breathing in and out more air than normal, so you can't breathe in or out as much extra air.
5) Your tidal volume increases for a couple of reasons:

> 1) To bring in more oxygen. This helps to release extra energy in the muscles (during aerobic activity) and remove lactic acid from them (produced during anaerobic activity).
> 2) To breathe out the extra carbon dioxide produced during aerobic activity.

Have a look at p21 for more about aerobic and anaerobic activity.

Vital Capacity — the Most Air you can Breathe In

1) Your tidal volume is only a fraction of your vital capacity:

> **VITAL CAPACITY** — the most air you could possibly breathe in after breathing out the largest volume of air you can.

Don't panic if you see this definition with "in" and "out" swapped around — it makes no difference.

2) The larger your vital capacity, the more oxygen you can take in and absorb into your bloodstream in each breath — and the more oxygen you can supply to your muscles.
3) You can increase your vital capacity through exercise — see page 25.
4) Your vital capacity isn't the total volume of air in your lungs (your lung capacity). After you've breathed out as much as you can, there's still some air left in the lungs. This is called the residual volume.

 ## Learn about the respiratory system — then take a breather...

It's easy to get tidal volume and vital capacity mixed up — so make sure you keep revising their definitions by scribbling them down until you can remember them without looking at this page.

Section One — Anatomy and Physiology

Spirometers

A snazzy machine called a spirometer can tell you all sorts about the lungs, and what they're doing during exercise. You only need this page if you're doing the AQA course — if you're not, skip to the next page.

A Spirometer Trace shows Lung Air Volumes

You can measure the volume of air moving in and out of someone's lungs by getting them to breathe into a machine called a spirometer. A spirometer produces a graph called a spirometer trace.

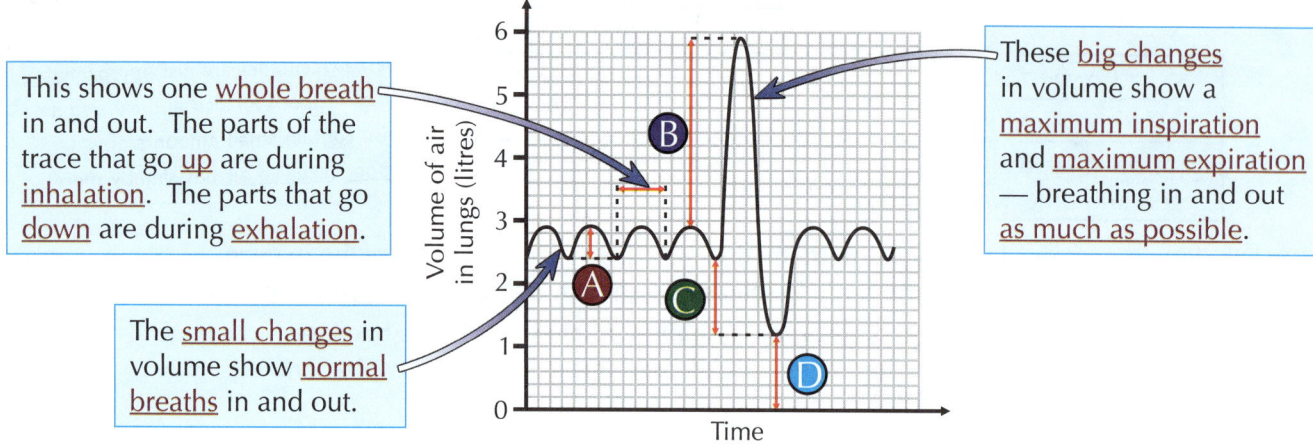

This shows one whole breath in and out. The parts of the trace that go up are during inhalation. The parts that go down are during exhalation.

These big changes in volume show a maximum inspiration and maximum expiration — breathing in and out as much as possible.

The small changes in volume show normal breaths in and out.

You need to be able to read some lung volumes from a spirometer trace:

A The difference in volume between a 'peak' and a 'dip' shows the tidal volume. When you're not exercising, an average tidal volume is about 500 ml.

B The difference in volume here is the inspiratory reserve volume. It's usually about 3 litres when you're not exercising.

C This difference in volume gives the expiratory reserve volume. This is usually about 1.2 litres when you're at rest.

D This shows the residual volume. It's normally around 1.2 litres — both at rest and during exercise.

You can Analyse a Spirometer Trace

A spirometer trace can show you whether the person breathing into it was resting or exercising.

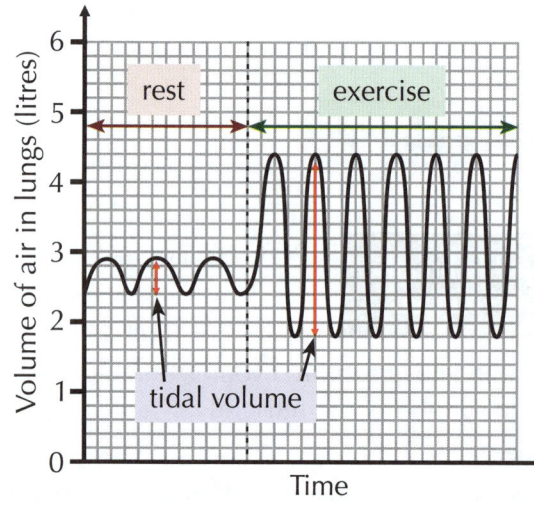

1) When you exercise, your tidal volume increases — you take deeper breaths in and out.
So during the 'exercise' part of the spirometer trace, the 'peaks' are higher and the 'dips' are lower than during the 'rest' part.

2) Your breathing rate also increases when you exercise — you take more breaths per minute than when you're resting. This is shown on the spirometer trace by the 'peaks' being closer together during exercise.

Have a look at p22 for more about the effects of exercise on your breathing.

 **A spirometer trace changes when exercise starts...**
You might need to draw a spirometer trace on a set of axes in your exam. But don't panic if you do — just remember that the 'peaks' of the trace get taller and closer together during exercise.

Section One — Anatomy and Physiology

Warm-Up and Worked Exam Questions

Before you try the cardiovascular and respiratory system exam questions on the next page, warm up with these quick questions and make sure you can follow the answers to the exam questions below.

Warm-Up Questions

1) Which circuit of the cardiovascular system contains the lungs — pulmonary or systemic?
2) Which type of blood vessel carries blood away from the heart?
3) Which type of blood cell carries oxygen around the body — red or white?
4) Which component of the respiratory system does air pass through next after the nose or mouth?
5) Which contains more carbon dioxide — inhaled or exhaled air?
6) Explain the difference between tidal volume and vital capacity.

Worked Exam Questions

1 State the **three** main functions of the cardiovascular system.

   Transporting substances such as oxygen, carbon dioxide and nutrients.

   Controlling body temperature.

   Clotting blood at wounds.

   [3 marks]

2 Describe the action of the diaphragm when inhaling and exhaling.

   During inhalation, the diaphragm contracts to expand the chest cavity and draw air into the lungs. During exhalation, it relaxes to shrink the chest cavity, forcing air back out of the lungs.

   [2 marks]

3 **Figure 1** shows part of a spirometer trace when the subject was at rest.

   Complete the spirometer trace in **Figure 1** to show the trace during exercise.

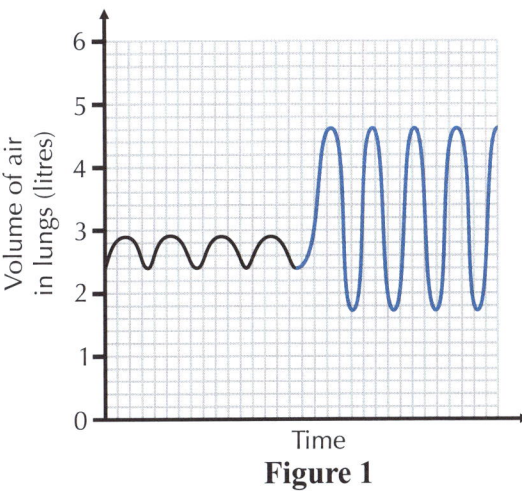

Remember, the difference between a 'peak' and a 'dip' is tidal volume, which increases during exercise — so this distance increases. Breathing rate also increases — so the distance between the 'peaks' gets shorter.

Figure 1

[1 mark]

Section One — Anatomy and Physiology

Exam Questions

1 Which one of the following is the component of the respiratory system where oxygen and carbon dioxide are exchanged?

- A Bronchi ☐
- B Trachea ☐
- C Bronchioles ☐
- D Alveoli ☑

[1 mark]

2 Explain how the cardiovascular system controls temperature and how this aids performance in physical activity and sport.

....

....

[2 marks]

3 Explain **one** way that the structure of arteries makes them suited to their function.

thick walls can carry blood ~~under~~ high pressure.

[2 marks]

4 Explain how the thin walls of alveoli assist them in their function.

- semi-permiable membrane
- allows oxygen to diffuse from high conc to low conc
- has high surface area to allow for higher rate of gaseous exchange.

[3 marks]

5 Assess the importance of the number of red blood cells to an endurance athlete.

....

....

....

....

[3 marks]

Section One — Anatomy and Physiology

Aerobic and Anaerobic Exercise

Your body can release energy in different ways — it all depends on how hard and how long you're exercising. And different sources of fuel can be used to release energy in the muscles. Fantastic stuff.

Aerobic Activity — With Oxygen

1) All the living cells in your body need energy. Normally the body uses oxygen to release energy from glucose (a sugar found in food). This is called aerobic respiration.

$$\text{Glucose + Oxygen} \rightarrow \text{Carbon dioxide + Water + Energy}$$

Carbon dioxide and water are by-products of aerobic respiration.

2) If your body's keeping up with the oxygen demand of its cells, it means there's enough oxygen available for aerobic respiration.

3) Activities where your body can keep up with oxygen demand are called aerobic activities.

> AEROBIC ACTIVITY: 'with oxygen'. If the exercise you're doing isn't too fast and you're exercising at a steady rate, your heart and lungs can supply your muscles with all the oxygen they need.

4) You breathe out the carbon dioxide through your lungs, while the water is lost as sweat, urine, or in the air you breathe out.

5) As long as your muscles are supplied with enough oxygen, you can do aerobic exercise — so if you're exercising for long periods, you'll be producing your energy aerobically.

6) Aerobic respiration is how marathon runners get their energy — it's the most efficient way to get it.

Anaerobic Activity — Without Oxygen

1) During vigorous exercise, your body can't supply all the oxygen needed. When this happens, your muscles release energy without using oxygen in a different process called anaerobic respiration.

$$\text{Glucose} \rightarrow \text{Lactic acid + Energy}$$

Lactic acid is a by-product of anaerobic respiration.

2) Activities where your body has to do this are called anaerobic activities.

> ANAEROBIC ACTIVITY: 'without oxygen'. If you exercise in short, intense bursts, your heart and lungs can't supply your muscles with oxygen as fast as your cells use it.

3) The lack of oxygen during anaerobic respiration means it can only provide energy for short periods of time — so you can't exercise at high intensity for very long.

4) During the first few seconds of exercise (at any intensity), your muscles get energy anaerobically in a different way — using the 'ATP-PC' system. This just means they use an energy source called creatine phosphate, which is already stored in the muscles.

You only need to know about the ATP-PC system for the Eduqas course.

5) Creatine phosphate runs out very quickly. Once it's gone, your muscles will need to use aerobic or anaerobic respiration to release energy.

6) Sprinters get their energy anaerobically — they have to run quickly for short durations.

Carbohydrates and Fats are used as Fuel

1) Your body needs a source of fuel so that respiration can provide energy.
2) Carbohydrates (from foods such as pasta) and fats stored in the body can both be used as fuel.

> CARBOHYDRATES — the body's main source of fuel. They're used during aerobic activities and for high intensity anaerobic activities.

> FATS — used as fuel for aerobic activity at low intensity. Fats provide more energy than carbohydrates, but they can't be used as fuel for higher intensity activities.

Section One — Anatomy and Physiology

Short-Term Effects of Exercise

Exercise has loads of different short-term effects on the body — some that help you to exercise, and others that are just a bit nasty. This page'll look at the effects on your muscles and your breathing.

There are Short-Term Effects on the Muscular System

There are loads of different effects on your muscles during exercise, and straight after it.

1) When you exercise, your muscles release extra energy for movement. Producing this energy also generates heat, which can make you feel hot and sweaty.
2) Also, during anaerobic activity, your muscles produce lactic acid. If you use your muscles anaerobically for too long, the lactic acid starts to build up. This leads to a rise in the lactate levels in the body — lactate accumulation.
3) Lactic acid build-up makes your muscles painful and causes muscle fatigue (tiredness).
4) If your muscles are fatigued, they need oxygen to remove the lactic acid and recover. The amount of oxygen you need is the oxygen debt, or 'EPOC' — excess post-exercise oxygen consumption.
5) To repay oxygen debt, you'll need to slow down or stop the activity you're doing for a while, which can have a negative impact on your performance.
6) During a training session where you do anaerobic activity, you'll need to have periods of rest or low intensity exercise before you can work anaerobically again.

Working your muscles really hard during a workout can also affect your body a day or two after exercise.

1) You might feel tired because your muscles used up lots of energy during your workout.
2) You could also feel sick and light-headed.
3) Some people also get 'delayed onset of muscle soreness' (DOMS), or muscle cramp.

There are Short-Term Effects on the Respiratory System

1) During exercise, muscles such as the pectorals and the sternocleidomastoid (in the neck) expand your lungs more to let in extra air. Muscles in your abdomen also work to pull your ribcage down and shrink the chest cavity quicker, so you breathe out faster.
2) These changes help to increase your depth of breathing and rate of breathing (the number of breaths per minute), which leads to an increase in your minute ventilation (or 'minute volume') — the volume of air you breathe in or out each minute.

Increasing your depth of breathing increases your tidal volume (see p17).

3) This means more oxygen is taken in and transferred to the blood, which helps to meet the increased demand for oxygen in the muscles during physical activity.
4) It also helps you to breathe out the extra carbon dioxide produced during aerobic respiration.
5) These changes allow you to do aerobic activity for long periods of time.
6) If you've been doing anaerobic activity, your breathing rate and depth will remain higher than normal until you've taken in enough oxygen to 'pay off' your oxygen debt.

> These changes to your respiratory system will all be more extreme if you exercise really intensely. So you'll breathe deeper and quicker when you're exercising hard than when you're doing light exercise.

Brain fatigue — a short-term effect of PE revision...

It's not enough just knowing that you breathe faster and deeper during exercise — you need to know why, too. So remember, you need to get extra oxygen into the lungs, and extra carbon dioxide out of them.

Section One — Anatomy and Physiology

Short-Term Effects of Exercise

Your cardiovascular system works extra hard during exercise to make sure your muscles get what they need to work properly. This includes using your blood vessels to send your blood where it's needed the most.

There are Short-Term Effects on the Cardiovascular System

1) Your heart rate is the number of times your heart beats per minute. An adult's resting heart rate (their heart rate when they aren't exercising) is usually about 60-80 bpm (beats per minute).
2) Your stroke volume is the amount of blood each ventricle pumps with each contraction (or heartbeat).
3) During exercise, your heart rate and stroke volume both increase.
4) This leads to an increase in your cardiac output — the volume of blood pumped by a ventricle per minute.

> cardiac output (Q) = heart rate × stroke volume

5) It also increases the pressure of your blood as your heart beats — your systolic blood pressure. Diastolic blood pressure is your blood's pressure when your heart is relaxed. It doesn't change much during exercise.
6) An increase in cardiac output increases the blood and oxygen supply to your muscles — so they can release the energy they need for physical activity. It also removes more carbon dioxide from the muscles and takes it to the lungs to be breathed out.
7) Your heart rate, stroke volume and cardiac output will remain higher than normal after exercise until any oxygen debt is paid off.

> The harder you're exercising, the higher your heart rate, stroke volume and cardiac output will be. So if you're only doing very light exercise, they'll be lower than if you were doing really strenuous exercise.

Your Blood Vessels Change when you Exercise

When you exercise, blood is redistributed around the body to increase the supply of oxygen to your muscles — this is known as 'vascular shunting'.

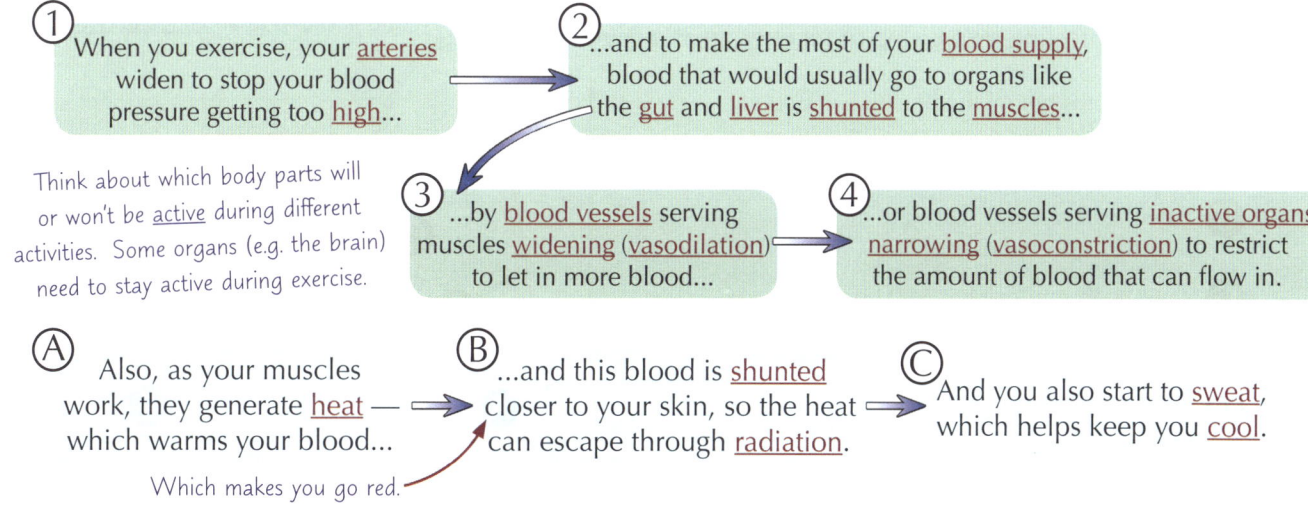

① When you exercise, your arteries widen to stop your blood pressure getting too high...

② ...and to make the most of your blood supply, blood that would usually go to organs like the gut and liver is shunted to the muscles...

③ ...by blood vessels serving muscles widening (vasodilation) to let in more blood...

④ ...or blood vessels serving inactive organs narrowing (vasoconstriction) to restrict the amount of blood that can flow in.

Think about which body parts will or won't be active during different activities. Some organs (e.g. the brain) need to stay active during exercise.

Ⓐ Also, as your muscles work, they generate heat — which warms your blood...

Ⓑ ...and this blood is shunted closer to your skin, so the heat can escape through radiation.

Which makes you go red.

Ⓒ And you also start to sweat, which helps keep you cool.

The amount of blood that's redistributed depends on how intensely you're exercising. So during light exercise, only a small amount of blood is shunted towards your working muscles. But if you're exercising really hard, a lot more blood is shunted.

Give your brain a quick exercise — learn this page...

Remember, vascular shunting happens during exercise because your muscles need blood more than some of your organs do. And this couldn't happen without vasodilation and vasoconstriction of blood vessels.

Section One — Anatomy and Physiology

Short-Term Effects of Exercise

This page'll show you how the cardiovascular and respiratory systems team up to help you exercise. It'll also give you some handy tips on how to interpret exercise data that you might see in the exam.

The Cardiovascular and Respiratory Systems Work Together

1) During exercise (and immediately after), more oxygen is delivered to the muscles than normal. Extra carbon dioxide is also taken away from them and breathed out.
2) The cardiovascular and respiratory systems work together to make this happen. When you exercise:

MORE O_2 DELIVERED

1) Breathing rate and depth increase, so more oxygen is delivered to the alveoli in the lungs.
2) Cardiac output also increases — so blood passes through the lungs at a faster rate, and picks up the extra oxygen from the alveoli. It's then delivered to the muscles.

MORE CO_2 REMOVED

1) Increased cardiac output means that the blood can transport carbon dioxide from the muscles to the lungs more quickly.
2) Here it moves back into the alveoli, and the higher breathing rate and depth allow it to be quickly breathed out.

3) These changes create a high concentration gradient — after you breathe in, there's a lot more oxygen in the alveoli than the capillaries, and a lot more carbon dioxide in the capillaries than the alveoli.
4) This causes diffusion of the gases to happen much quicker during exercise.
5) These processes help you to release enough energy to exercise aerobically and to recover from oxygen debt after anaerobic activity (see p22).

For more on diffusion, have a look at page 16.

Short-Term Effects can be shown Graphically

1) In your exam, you might get a graph or table showing someone's heart rate, stroke volume or cardiac output during a workout.
2) These things all increase when you exercise, and gradually go back to normal once you stop exercising.
3) You can use these facts to interpret data and work out whether a person was resting, exercising or recovering at a specific time.

Your heart rate might go up slightly just before you start exercising — this is known as an anticipatory rise.

A This point is before the person has started exercising. Their heart rate is at its lowest point — it's their resting heart rate.

B Their heart rate has started to increase — they've started to exercise.

C Their heart rate reaches 130 bpm and stays the same for five minutes — they exercise at the same intensity for that time.

D This part of the graph is when the workout is at its highest intensity. The person's heart rate is at its highest point on the graph.

E Their heart rate is decreasing — exercise has stopped, or they're completing a cool down. Their heart rate stays fairly high for a while to help with recovery.

F They've returned to their resting heart rate of 70 beats per minute.

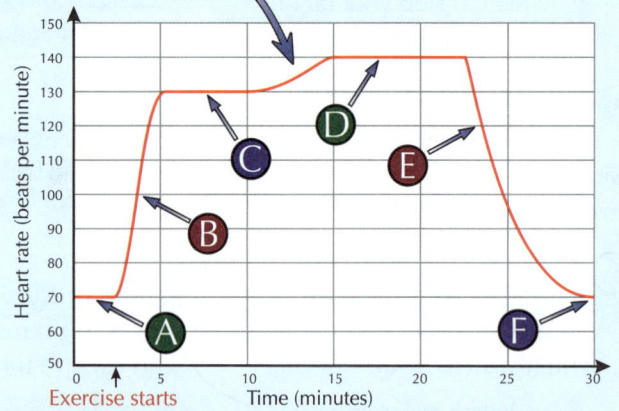

Graphs and tables — this doesn't sound like PE...

EXAM TIP If you get given a question about heart rate, stroke volume or cardiac output data in your exam, just remember that they all go up during exercise, and back down afterwards. Then you'll be able to use that fact to work out what was going on when the values were recorded.

Section One — Anatomy and Physiology

Long-Term Effects of Exercise

Exercising regularly eventually leads to loads of adaptations in the body's systems. These benefit your health and different components of fitness (see pages 37-40), which will help improve your performance.

Exercise Improves the Musculo-Skeletal System

See p72-73 for more about the long-term benefits of exercise.

MUSCLE HYPERTROPHY

1) Doing regular exercise (especially resistance training) will make your muscles thicker and your muscle girth larger (see p83) — which can change your body shape.
2) This thickening of muscles is called hypertrophy. It happens to all muscles when they're exercised, including your heart.
3) The thicker a muscle is, the more strongly it can contract — so this increases your strength.
4) Hypertrophy also improves your muscular endurance — so you can use your muscles for longer.

Stronger muscles and bones can help improve your posture.

Anaerobic training improves your muscles' ability to work without oxygen.

INCREASED BONE DENSITY

1) The denser your bones, the stronger they are.
2) Exercise usually puts stress or forces through bones, and will cause the body to strengthen those bones.
3) The stronger your bones, the less likely they are to break or fracture.

STRONGER LIGAMENTS & TENDONS

Having stronger ligaments and tendons can make you more flexible and less likely to injure yourself, e.g. dislocation (see p66).

Exercise Improves the Cardio-Respiratory System

BIGGER/STRONGER HEART

1) Your heart is just a muscle — when you exercise, it adapts and gets bigger and stronger. *This is called 'cardiac hypertrophy'.*
2) A bigger, stronger heart will contract more strongly and pump more blood with each beat — so your resting stroke volume and maximum cardiac output will increase.
3) A larger stroke volume means your heart has to beat less often to pump the same amount of blood around your body. This means your resting heart rate decreases. *This is called 'bradycardia'.*

LARGER LUNG CAPACITY

1) Your diaphragm and external intercostal muscles (the muscles between the ribs) get stronger — so they can make your chest cavity larger. The number of alveoli in your lungs also increases.
2) This increases your maximum tidal volume and minute ventilation during exercise. Your vital capacity and lung capacity increase — you can breathe in more air.
3) The larger your lung capacity, the more oxygen you can get into your lungs and into your bloodstream per breath — so you can take in the same amount of oxygen with a lower breathing rate.

LOWER BLOOD PRESSURE

With regular exercise, your veins and arteries get bigger and their muscular walls become more elastic — so your blood pressure falls.

MORE CAPILLARIES IN THE MUSCLES

This increases the blood supply to the muscles, so they receive more oxygen.

MORE RED BLOOD CELLS

So the blood can carry more oxygen.

The better the blood and oxygen supply to your muscles, the better your cardiovascular fitness is. This means you can exercise more intensely and for longer, as well as recover more quickly after exercise.

Training that involves aerobic activity works best to improve the cardio-respiratory system.

Breaking news — exercise is good for you...

To get all these effects, you need to rest after exercise to recover and let your body adapt to any changes.

Section One — Anatomy and Physiology

Warm-Up and Worked Exam Questions

That's respiration and the effects of exercise all done. These warm-up questions will make sure you've got the basics, then you can look at the exam answers below and try some exam questions for yourself.

Warm-Up Questions

1) Which type of respiration uses oxygen — aerobic or anaerobic?
2) When is the ATP-PC energy system used?
3) What is 'oxygen debt'?
4) What effect does exercise have on your breathing rate?
5) What happens to your stroke volume when you exercise?
6) How could you calculate your cardiac output?
7) Give one example of a long-term effect of exercise on the musculo-skeletal system.
8) What is 'cardiac hypertrophy'?

Worked Exam Questions

1 State **one** short-term effect of exercise on the cardiovascular system. *(Grade 1-3)*

Increased heart rate.

There are lots of possible answers here. For example, you might have said increased blood pressure or cardiac output.

[1 mark]

2 One long-term effect of exercise can be an increase in muscle girth. *(Grade 5-7)*

Explain, using **one** example, how this could benefit performance in physical activity and sport.

An increase in muscle girth would lead to an increase in strength, which would benefit, for example, a rugby player during a tackle as it would help them to pull an opponent to the ground.

[3 marks]

3 Hitesh has been training for a marathon for six months. During this time, he has noticed a decrease in his resting heart rate. *(Grade 7-9)*

Explain how Hitesh's marathon training will have led to a decrease in his resting heart rate.

Think about the effects on the heart during a marathon training session, and the effect this would have in the long term.

Running is an aerobic activity which causes the heart to work harder, which leads to muscle hypertrophy of the heart in the long term. This increases resting stroke volume and therefore decreases resting heart rate, as the heart can deliver the same amount of blood to the rest of the body with fewer beats.

[4 marks]

Section One — Anatomy and Physiology

Exam Questions

1 The body uses respiration to release energy.

(a) Describe the conditions under which anaerobic respiration occurs.

without oxygen, short intense bursts of exercise

[1 mark]

(b) Identify the by-product of anaerobic respiration and explain how it may affect performance.

Lactic acid - makes muscles painful/causes muscle fatigue and causes DOMS (delayed onset muscle soreness)

[2 marks]

2 Exercise affects the body in many ways, both immediately and in the long term.

(a) State **one** long-term effect of regular exercise on the respiratory system.

....

[1 mark]

(b) Explain why breathing rate and heart rate may remain high after exercise has stopped.

....

....

[2 marks]

3 **Figure 1** shows the heart rate of a performer during two 40-minute workouts on a cross trainer.

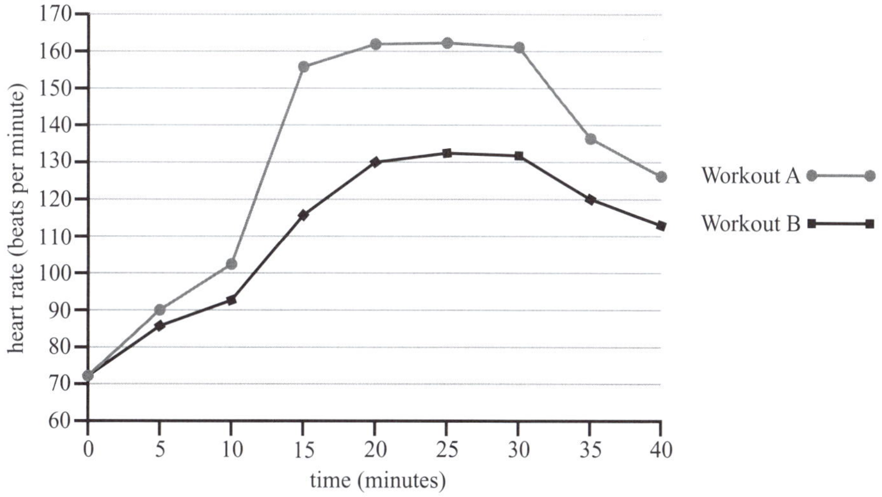

Figure 1

Analyse the heart rate data in **Figure 1** to explain what it suggests about the difference in intensity between the two workouts.

....

....

....

[2 marks]

Section One — Anatomy and Physiology

Exam Questions

4   Blood can be redistributed around the body to meet the demands of physical activity. *(Grade 5-7)*

   (a) Identify **two** areas of the body that would experience an increase in blood flow when swimming.

   1 upper arms

   2 legs

   [2 marks]

   (b) Explain your choices.

   - you use upper arms to pull yourself through the water.
   - Using legs to push yourself through the water.

   [3 marks]

5   Evaluate the importance of aerobic and anaerobic respiration during a 50-mile cycling race.

   These extended writing questions can look pretty tricky, but don't panic — you can pick up a few marks just by describing aerobic and anaerobic respiration.

   [9 marks]

Section One — Anatomy and Physiology

Revision Questions for Section One

Well, that's Anatomy and Physiology all wrapped up — time to see how much you know about the body.
- Try these questions and tick off each one when you get it right.
- When you've done all the questions for a topic and are completely happy with it, tick off the topic.

The Musculo-Skeletal System (p4-11)
1) Name the five main functions of the skeleton.
2) State the four main types of bone in the body.
3) Name the five regions of the vertebral column.
4) Which two bones meet to make the hip joint?
5) Which joint movement involves pointing the toes upwards?
6) Give an example of a condyloid joint.
7) What is the function of:
   a) Cartilage?
   b) Ligaments?
   c) Tendons?
8) What is the function of the synovial membrane within a joint?
9) Which type of muscle is involved in moving the skeleton — voluntary, involuntary, or cardiac?
10) Which two muscles make up the antagonistic muscle pair operating at the elbow joint?
11) What is the difference between an isometric and an isotonic muscle contraction?
12) Why would type IIA and IIX muscle fibres not be suitable for use in a marathon?

The Cardio-Respiratory System (p14-18)
13) What are the three main functions of the cardiovascular system?
14) Which vein does deoxygenated blood pass through to enter the heart?
15) The pulmonary artery carries oxygenated blood to the rest of the body. TRUE or FALSE?
16) Name the three main types of blood vessel found in the body.
17) What is the function of plasma?
18) Explain how oxygen and carbon dioxide are exchanged between the alveoli and capillaries.
19) Give the compositions of inhaled and exhaled air.
20) Describe what is meant by a) tidal volume, and b) vital capacity.

Aerobic and Anaerobic Exercise (p21)
21) Describe aerobic and anaerobic respiration.
22) What is the main fuel source used in both aerobic and anaerobic activity?

The Short-Term and Long-Term Effects of Exercise (p22-25)
23) Why do muscles become fatigued during anaerobic activity, and how do they recover?
24) Explain why your depth and rate of breathing increase during exercise.
25) Why do heart rate, stroke volume and cardiac output remain higher after exercise?
26) Explain what vasodilation and vasoconstriction are and why they happen.
27) What is muscle hypertrophy and why does it happen?
28) How does regular exercise benefit the bones, ligaments and tendons?
29) Explain why regular exercise leads to increased oxygen supply to the muscles.

Section One — Anatomy and Physiology

Section Two — Movement Analysis

Lever Systems

When the muscular and skeletal systems work together, they create lever systems that help us to move.

Lever Systems Help the Body to Move

A lever is a solid bar that moves about a fixed point when force is applied to it.
When a muscle pulls on a bone to move a body part about a joint, it uses the body part as a lever.
This lever makes up part of a lever system that has four different components:

1) The lever arm — the bone or body part being moved about a point.
   On a diagram of a lever system, it's shown as a straight line.
2) The fulcrum — the joint where the lever arm pivots. It's shown as a triangle.
3) The effort — the force applied by the muscles to the lever arm. It's shown by an arrow pointing in the direction of the force. The perpendicular distance between the fulcrum and the action of the effort is the 'effort arm'.
4) The load — the resistance against the pull of the muscles on the lever arm. E.g. the weight of the body, or body part, or something being lifted. A square or an arrow is used to represent the load. The perpendicular distance between the fulcrum and the action of the load is the 'weight arm' (or 'resistance arm').

'Perpendicular' means 'at 90 degrees to'.

Levers can be First, Second or Third Class

First Class Levers

1st Class — The load and effort are at opposite ends of the lever. The fulcrum is in the middle.

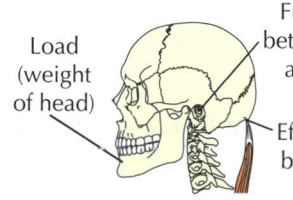

First class levers are used in neck extension (e.g. when heading a football) and in elbow extension.

Second Class Levers

2nd Class — The fulcrum and effort are at opposite ends of the lever. The load is in the middle.

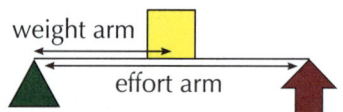
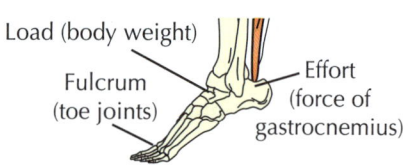

Second class levers are used in plantar-flexion and dorsi-flexion at the ankle while standing. E.g. when you stand on your toes to jump.

Third Class Levers

3rd Class — The fulcrum and load are at opposite ends of the lever. The effort is in the middle.

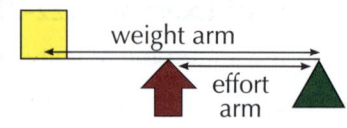
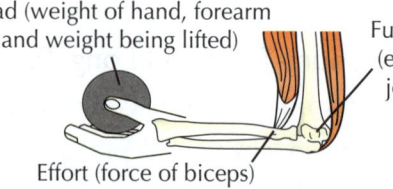

Third class levers are used in elbow flexion (e.g. lifting a weight) and in flexion and extension at the shoulder, hip and knee.

Moving joints — you'd better lever little space...

You can tell the class of a lever by its middle component. So to remember which class is which, use '1, 2, 3, F, L, E'. The letters tell you the middle component of each lever — for 1st class levers it's the fulcrum, for 2nd class levers it's the load, and for 3rd class levers it's the effort.

Lever Systems

Levers help the body use its muscles effectively. Different levers have different benefits — some help to move heavier loads, while others increase the speed a load can be moved at, or the range of movement.

Some Levers have a **Mechanical Advantage**

1) A lever in the body with a mechanical advantage can move a large load with a small effort from the muscles. However, it can only move the load short distances at low speeds.

> **If the effort arm is longer than the weight arm, the lever has a mechanical advantage.**

2) You can calculate the mechanical advantage of a lever using this formula:

> **Mechanical advantage = effort arm ÷ weight arm**

3) Second class levers always have a mechanical advantage — the fulcrum and the effort are at opposite ends of the lever, so the effort arm is always longer than the weight arm.

4) For example, the second class lever used at the ankle when you stand on your toes has a mechanical advantage. There is only a small effort from your gastrocnemius, but it moves a large load (your whole body weight).

5) First class levers can have a mechanical advantage if the fulcrum is closer to the load than it is to the effort — this makes the effort arm longer than the weight arm.

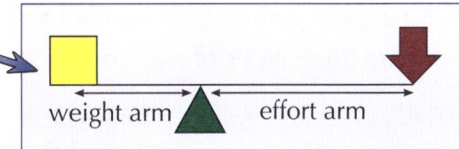

Some Levers have a **Mechanical Disadvantage**

1) A lever with a mechanical disadvantage requires a large effort from the muscles to move a small load — but it can move the load quickly through a large range of movement.

2) It might sound like a bad thing for a lever to have a mechanical disadvantage, but it's not. It just means a lever is better at moving large distances quickly than it is at moving heavy loads.

3) Third class levers always have a mechanical disadvantage — the effort is between the load and fulcrum, so the effort arm is always shorter than the weight arm.

4) For example, the third class lever used during elbow flexion has a mechanical disadvantage. Your biceps only has to shorten slightly to move your hand and forearm a large distance very quickly.

5) First class levers can also have a mechanical disadvantage if the fulcrum is closer to the effort than it is to the load — this makes the effort arm shorter than the weight arm.

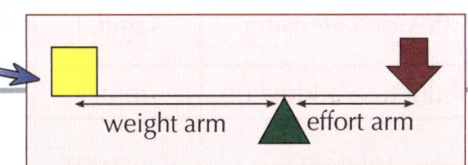

Mechanical disadvantage — not really a disadvantage...

'Mechanical disadvantage' is a bit of a confusing name — it makes it sound like third class levers are really useless. So don't forget, levers only have a mechanical disadvantage because they're not very good at moving heavy loads — but they're great at moving quickly and through a large range of movement.

Planes and Axes of Movement

It might seem strange that there's a page about planes and axes in a PE book — but it'll all make sense soon. Basically, you can describe a body movement using the plane it moves in and the axis it moves around.

Movements Happen In Planes

1) A plane of movement is an imaginary flat surface which runs through the body.
2) Planes are used to describe the direction of a movement.
3) When you move a body part (or your whole body), it moves in a plane.
4) There are three planes of movement you need to know:

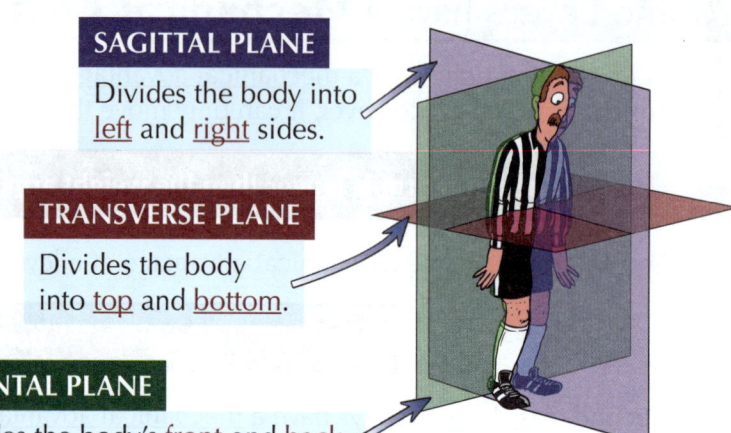

SAGITTAL PLANE Divides the body into left and right sides.

TRANSVERSE PLANE Divides the body into top and bottom.

FRONTAL PLANE Divides the body's front and back.

Movements Happen Around Axes

1) An axis of movement (two or more are called 'axes') is an imaginary line which runs through the body.
2) When a body part (or your whole body) moves, it moves around (or 'about') an axis.
3) There are three types of axis you need to know:

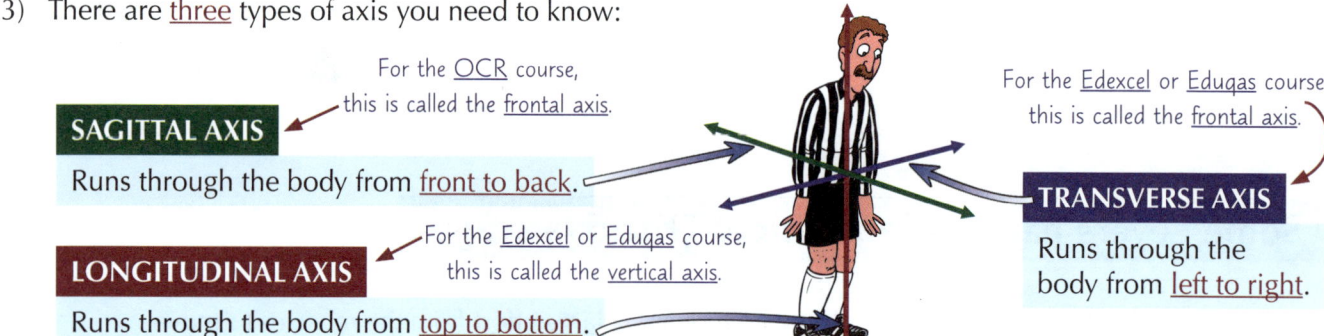

For the OCR course, this is called the frontal axis.

SAGITTAL AXIS Runs through the body from front to back.

For the Edexcel or Eduqas course, this is called the vertical axis.

LONGITUDINAL AXIS Runs through the body from top to bottom.

For the Edexcel or Eduqas course, this is called the frontal axis.

TRANSVERSE AXIS Runs through the body from left to right.

Movements use Different Planes and Axes

Every body movement uses both a plane and an axis.
Learn the plane and axis pairs for these movement types and sporting examples.

Have a look at page 6 for more examples of the movement types.

MOVEMENT TYPE	PLANE	AXIS	SPORT MOVEMENTS
flexion/extension	sagittal	transverse	tucked and piked somersaults, running, forward roll
abduction/adduction	frontal	sagittal	cartwheel
rotation	transverse	longitudinal	full twist jump (trampolining), discus throw rotation, ice skating spin

These plane and axis pairs are always the same, e.g. movements that happen in the transverse plane always happen around the longitudinal/vertical axis.

There are lots of new terms here to get your head around...

It's easier to work out the plane and axis being used if you remember that the combinations are always the same — so make sure you learn the pairs, and that you know the right axis names for your course, too.

Section Two — Movement Analysis

Warm-Up and Worked Exam Questions

Movement analysis can be quite a tricky topic — luckily, there are some questions here so you can check it's all sunk in properly.

Warm-Up Questions

1) What provides the effort in the body's lever systems?
2) Give an example of a second class lever in the body.
3) Draw a diagram of a first class lever with a mechanical advantage.
4) Why do third class levers have a mechanical disadvantage?
5) Describe the transverse plane.
6) Which axis of movement does rotation at the shoulder happen around?

Worked Exam Questions

1   **Figure 1** shows a diagram of a lever system. *(Grade 1-3)*

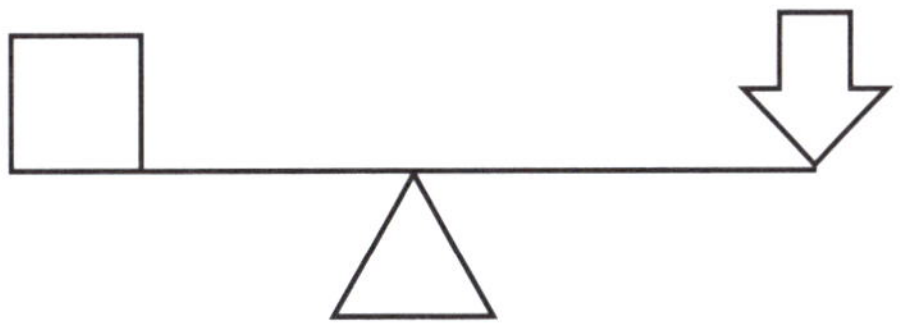

Figure 1

Complete the following statements about the components of the lever system in **Figure 1**.

The square is used to represent the ......**load**...... of the lever system. The arrow represents the ......**effort**...... and the triangle represents the ......**fulcrum**.......

[3 marks]

2   Identify the movement plane that divides the body into left and right sides. *(Grade 1-3)*

The sagittal plane.

[1 mark]

3   When kicking a football, a lever system operates to move the knee joint from flexion to extension. *(Grade 5-7)*
Identify the load, fulcrum and effort in this lever system.

> To identify the effort in a lever system, you need to know which muscles are responsible for which joint movements — see pages 8-9.

The load is the weight of the lower leg below the knee, the fulcrum is the knee joint and the effort is the force of the quadriceps.

[3 marks]

Section Two — Movement Analysis

Exam Questions

1 State the plane and axis used during the following movements. *(Grade 3-5)*

(i) Cartwheel

....

....

[2 marks]

(ii) Forward roll

....

....

[2 marks]

(iii) Ice skating spin

....

....

[2 marks]

2 A gymnast uses the body's lever systems to stand on their toes.

(a) Classify the lever operating at the ankle as the gymnast stands on their toes. *(Grade 5-7)*

....

[1 mark]

(b) Analyse how the lever operating at the ankle assists the gymnast when standing on their toes. *(Grade 7-9)*

Think about the benefits of the lever class you gave in part (a), and how they would help someone to stand on their toes.

....

....

....

....

....

....

[3 marks]

Section Two — Movement Analysis

Revision Questions for Section Two

Well, Section Two was short and sweet... Try these revision questions to make sure you took it all in.
- Try these questions and tick off each one when you get it right.
- When you've done all the questions for a topic and are completely happy with it, tick off the topic.

Lever Systems (p30-31) ☐

1) Name the four components of a lever system.
2) What is the effort arm of a lever? What is the weight arm?
3) State the class of each of the levers below.
   a)   b)   c)
4) Give two examples of first class levers in the body.
5) Which class of lever is used in the foot when jumping?
6) Which lever class is used during elbow flexion?
7) Explain what is meant if a lever system in the body has a:
   a) mechanical advantage
   b) mechanical disadvantage
8) How do you calculate the mechanical advantage of a lever?
9) Which class of lever always has a:
   a) mechanical advantage?
   b) mechanical disadvantage?
10) When does a first class lever have a mechanical advantage?

Planes and Axes of Movement (p32) ☐

11) What is a plane of movement?
12) Which plane of movement divides:
    a) the top and bottom of the body?
    b) the left and right sides of the body?
    c) the front and back of the body?
13) What is an axis of movement?
14) Which axis runs through the body from:
    a) top to bottom?
    b) front to back?
    c) left to right?
15) Which plane and axis are used during both tucked and piked somersaults?
16) Which plane and axis are used during a cartwheel?
17) Which plane and axis are used during a full twist jump in trampolining?

Section Two — Movement Analysis

Section Three — Physical Training

Health and Fitness

First up in section three, four important words: health, fitness, exercise and how they affect performance.

Fitness is just One Part of being Healthy

1) Being healthy is more than just having a healthy body.
   Here's the definition used by the World Health Organisation (WHO):

   > Health is a state of complete physical, mental and social well-being and not merely the absence of disease or infirmity.

2) Fitness is one part of good health — here's the definition:

   > Fitness is the ability to meet the demands of the environment.

   So, being fit means you're physically able to do whatever you want or need to do, without getting tired quickly.

3) Fitness helps with physical health, but you can have a high level of fitness without necessarily being physically healthy — e.g. some athletes overtrain and end up getting injured.

4) Mental and social well-being is also part of being healthy —
   if you're always unhappy, then you're not healthy.

Exercise Keeps You Fit and Healthy

It doesn't have to be a competitive sport.

> Exercise is a form of physical activity done to maintain or improve health and/or fitness.

1) By exercising, you can improve components of fitness (see p37-40) and general physical health.
2) As well as keeping you physically fit, exercise also helps with emotional and social well-being:
   - Exercise is a good stress relief and is enjoyable.
   - Exercise can be a social activity — e.g. joining a yoga class can help you make new friends or socialise with current friends.

See p73 for more about how exercise helps emotional and social well-being.

You need to be Fit and Healthy to Perform Well

1) Your level of health and fitness will affect your performance.

   > Performance is how well a task is completed.

2) Your performance won't be as good if you're unfit — e.g. in the second half of a football match you'll get tired and be less effective.
3) Being unhealthy will also affect performance — if you have the flu, playing sport is going to be tricky...

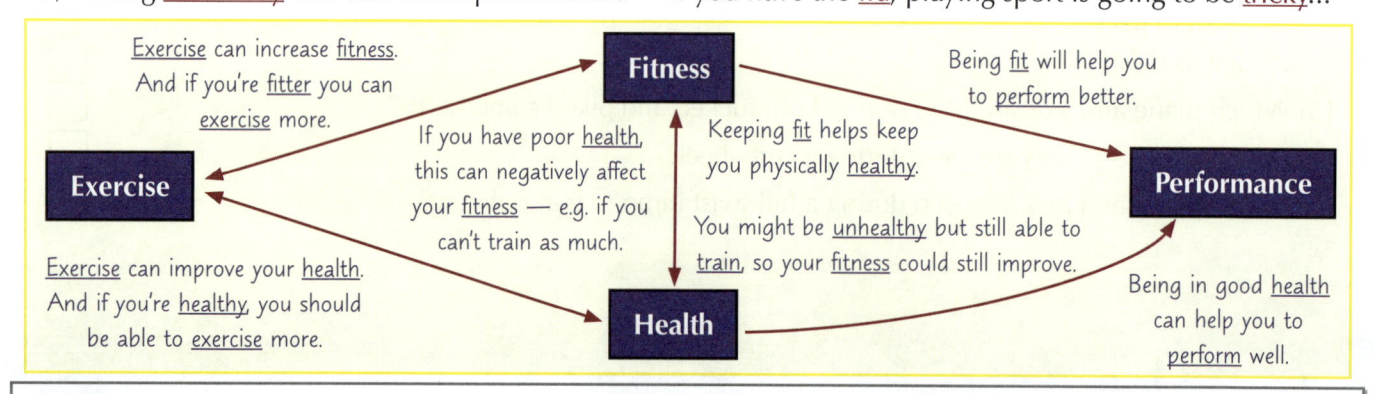

Exercise can increase fitness. And if you're fitter you can exercise more.

Exercise can improve your health. And if you're healthy, you should be able to exercise more.

If you have poor health, this can negatively affect your fitness — e.g. if you can't train as much.

Keeping fit helps keep you physically healthy.

You might be unhealthy but still able to train, so your fitness could still improve.

Being fit will help you to perform better.

Being in good health can help you to perform well.

Exercise → **Fitness** → **Performance** ← **Health**

REVISION TASK — Feeling fit and healthy ready for this section...

Make sure you understand how health, fitness, exercise and performance are related to each other. Test you've got it by drawing out the diagram in the yellow box from memory.

Components of Fitness

Fitness can be split up into different components. Six of these components are needed to cope with the physical demands of an activity or sport. Here are the first three, so hop to it and get learning...

Cardiovascular Endurance — Getting Oxygen to the Muscles

1) Your heart and lungs work together to keep your muscles supplied with oxygen. The harder you work your muscles, the more oxygen they need.

This might also be called cardiovascular fitness, aerobic endurance, aerobic power or stamina.

> **CARDIOVASCULAR ENDURANCE** is the ability of the heart and lungs to supply oxygen to the muscles, so that the whole body can be exercised for a long time.

2) So if you have a high level of cardiovascular endurance, your body is able to supply the oxygen your muscles need to do moderately intense whole-body exercise for a long time.
3) Most sports require good cardiovascular endurance. For example, a squash player needs to be able to keep up a fast pace all game. If a tennis player finds they are getting tired and losing points late on in a match, they will want to work on their cardiovascular endurance.
4) A high level of cardiovascular endurance is particularly important for endurance sports like long-distance running, or cycling.

Strength — the Force a Muscle can Exert

You might see 'muscular strength' instead of 'strength' — don't panic though, it's the same thing.

1) Strength is just how strong your muscles are.

> **STRENGTH** is the amount of force that a muscle or muscle group can apply against a resistance.

2) It's very important in sports where you need to lift, push or pull things using a lot of force, like weightlifting and judo.
3) Sports that require you to hold your own body weight also need a lot of strength — like the parallel bars and rings in gymnastics.
4) Strength can be broken down into different types:

- Maximal strength is the most amount of force a muscle group can create in a single movement.
- Static strength is when the muscles don't move, but still apply a force — e.g. when holding a handstand.
- Explosive strength uses a muscle's strength in a short, fast burst — it's similar to power (see p40).
- Dynamic strength means using your strength to move things repeatedly. It's like muscular endurance...

Muscular Endurance — How Long 'til You get Tired

1) When you work your muscles they can get tired and start to feel heavy and weak (fatigued).

> **MUSCULAR ENDURANCE** is the ability to repeatedly use muscles over a long time, without getting tired.

2) Muscular endurance is really important in any physical activity where you're using the same muscles over and over again — e.g. in racquet sports like tennis where you have to repeatedly swing your arm.
3) It's also important towards the end of any long-distance race — rowers and cyclists need muscular endurance for a strong sprint finish.

EXAM TIP — The things I have to endure...
Make sure you're specific about how components of fitness are used in different activities — e.g. instead of just saying 'strength helps in gymnastics' say 'strength helps the gymnast hold their body weight on the parallel bars'. This shows the examiner you really know your stuff.

Section Three — Physical Training

Components of Fitness

Three more components of fitness on this page: flexibility, body composition and speed. Learn what they are — then make sure you learn what sports and activities each one's important in as well. Right, here we go...

Flexibility — Range of Movement

1) Flexibility is to do with how far your joints move. This depends on the type of joint and the 'stretchiness' of the muscles around it.

FLEXIBILITY is the amount of movement possible at a joint.

2) It's often forgotten about, but flexibility is dead useful for any physical activity. Here's why...

- **FEWER INJURIES:**
  If you're flexible, you're less likely to pull or strain a muscle or stretch too far and injure yourself.

- **BETTER PERFORMANCE:**
  You can't do some activities without being flexible — e.g. doing the splits in gymnastics.
  Flexibility makes you more efficient in other sports so you use less energy — e.g. swimmers with better flexibility can move their arms further around their shoulders. This makes their strokes longer and smoother.

- **BETTER POSTURE:**
  Bad posture can impair breathing and damage your spine.
  More flexibility means a better posture and fewer aches and pains.

Body Composition — % of Fat, Muscle and Bone

BODY COMPOSITION is the percentage of body weight made up by fat, muscle and bone.

1) If you're healthy, your body will normally be made up of between 15% and 25% body fat.
2) Having too much body fat can put strain on your muscles and joints during physical activity.
3) Different activities and sports demand different body compositions, depending on whether you need to be heavy, light, strong, fast, etc.
   - Rock climbers have to be light and strong, so have a high muscle percentage, and a low body fat percentage.
   - In rugby or American football, heavy players have an advantage as they are harder to knock over, so will have a higher body fat percentage than many other sports players.

Many physical activities become harder to do, and the increased strain on your body means you have a higher risk of injuring yourself.

Speed — How Quickly

1) Speed is a measure of how quickly you can do something.
2) This might be a measure of how quickly you cover a distance. It could also be how quickly you can carry out a movement, e.g. how quickly you can throw a punch.

SPEED is the rate at which someone is able to move, or to cover a distance in a given amount of time.

3) To work out speed, you just divide the distance covered by the time taken to do it.
4) Speed is important in lots of activities, from the obvious like a 100 m sprint, to the less obvious (like the speed a hockey player can swing their arm to whack a ball across the pitch).

Body composition — muscle, bone and flab...

Body composition is a little tricky — it's not always obvious how it impacts on performance. It's usually about balancing the strength gains that come from having more muscle with the impact of weighing more.

Section Three — Physical Training

Components of Fitness

Now it's time to look at five components of fitness that require skill. Just like the more physical ones, you need to be able to judge their importance for different activities. First up — agility, balance and coordination.

Agility — Control Over Your Body's Movement

1) Agility is important in any activity where you've got to run about, changing direction all the time, like football or hockey.
2) Jumping and intercepting a pass in netball or basketball involves a high level of agility too.

> **AGILITY** is the ability to change body position or direction quickly and with control.

Balance — More Than Not Wobbling

Having a good sense of balance means you don't wobble or fall over easily. Here's a slightly fancier definition.

> **BALANCE** is the ability to keep the body's centre of mass over a base of support.

1) You can think of the mass of any object as being concentrated at just one point. This point is called the centre of mass (or centre of gravity).
2) Everything has a centre of mass — and that includes us.
3) As you change body position, the location of your centre of mass will change too.
4) Whatever activity you're doing, you need to have your centre of mass over whatever is supporting you (your base of support) to balance. If you don't, you'll fall over.

This is true whether you're moving (dynamic balance)...

...changing orientation and shape (like in dance and gymnastics)...

...or just staying still (stationary or static balance).

Base of support: Geoff

Base of support: arms

Base of support: legs

5) Balance is crucial for nearly every physical activity. Any sport that involves changing direction quickly — like football or basketball — requires good balance.
6) An action that is performed with balance is more efficient — e.g. a cyclist might work on improving their balance to increase the speed they can go round corners.

Coordination — Using Body Parts Together

> **COORDINATION** is the ability to use two or more parts of the body together, efficiently and accurately.

1) Hand-eye coordination is important in sports that require precision. E.g. being able to hit a ball in tennis, or shoot a bull's-eye in archery.
2) Limb coordination allows you to be able to walk, run, dance, kick, swim...
3) Coordinated movements are smooth and efficient. E.g. a runner with well coordinated arms and legs will be able to run faster than someone who is less coordinated.
4) Limb coordination is really important in sports like gymnastics or platform diving, where your performance is judged on your coordination.

Agility, Balance and Coordination — as easy as ABC...

Agility, balance and coordination all go together really. You can't be agile if you're not balanced and coordinated. Make sure you know the definitions of all three and what sporting actions they help with.

Section Three — Physical Training

Components of Fitness

You're nearly there now, just two more components to go. Reaction time is about how quickly you can react to something. Power is being able to do strength actions with speed — it's like explosive strength (see p37).

Reaction Time — The Time It Takes You to React

REACTION TIME is the time taken to move in response to a stimulus.

1) In many sports and activities, you need to have fast reactions.
2) The stimulus you respond to could be, e.g. a starter gun, a pass in football, or a serve in tennis.
3) You need fast reactions to be able to hit a ball or dodge a punch.
   It doesn't matter how fast you can move, if you don't react in time you'll miss or get hit.
4) Having fast reactions can effectively give you a head start.

Getting away quickly at the start of a sprint can mean the difference between winning and losing.

Having faster reactions in team sports can help you get away from your opponents, so you can get into better playing positions.

Power Means Speed and Strength Together

POWER is a combination of speed and strength.   **power = strength × speed**

Most sports need power for some things. It's important for throwing, hitting, sprinting and jumping — e.g. in the long jump, both the sprint run-up and the take-off from the board require power. Here are some more examples:

SPORT	YOU NEED POWER TO...
Football	...shoot
Golf	...drive
Table tennis	...smash
Tennis	...serve and smash
Cricket	...bowl fast and bat

Coordination and balance also help make the most of power — an uncoordinated or off-balance action will not be as powerful.

Some Components are More Important than Others

1) To be good at any physical activity, you're going to need to have a high level of a number of different components of fitness.
2) For a particular activity, there will always be some components of fitness which are more important than others — e.g. in weightlifting, your strength is more important than your reaction time.
3) To compare the importance of different components, think about the kinds of actions the performer does — e.g. a batsman in cricket has to react to the bowler (reaction time), hit the ball (coordination and power), and then run (speed and cardiovascular endurance).

REVISION TASK

I have the power...
Congratulations, you've made it. No more components of fitness to learn. Now, list all the components of fitness, and give an example of a sport that each one is important for.

Section Three — Physical Training

Fitness Testing

So, you know what the components of fitness are — now you need to know how to measure them... First up, why we carry out fitness testing and three different ways to test cardiovascular endurance.

Fitness Testing Helps Identify Strengths and Weaknesses

Fitness testing gives you data that you can analyse to help improve your fitness.

1) Fitness tests are designed to measure specific components of fitness. It's important you choose the right one for the specific component you're interested in — otherwise the test is meaningless.
2) You can use fitness testing to measure your level of fitness before starting a training programme. The data will show your strengths and weaknesses, so you can plan a personal exercise programme (see p50) that focuses on what you need to improve. Some of the tests are quite demanding, so you need to make sure you are fit enough to manage them.
3) The data from fitness tests can be compared with national averages (see p46).
4) You can carry out fitness tests throughout a training programme to monitor your progress and see whether or not the training you're doing is working. This can help to motivate you by showing you where you're improving, and can help you to set yourself new goals.

Tests need to be carried out using the same procedure each time so comparisons with previous tests are meaningful.

These Three Tests are for Cardiovascular Endurance...

HARVARD STEP TEST

Equipment needed: stopwatch and 45 cm step.

1) Do 30 step-ups a minute (that's a step every two seconds) for 5 minutes.
2) Then take three pulse readings: the first one minute after you finish the test, the second two minutes after and the third three minutes after.
3) Put these numbers into a clever formula to work out your score — the higher your score, the better your cardiovascular endurance.
4) There are different versions of this test — check the procedures match before you compare results from different tests.

COOPER 12-MINUTE RUN AND SWIM TESTS

I've only got room to describe the run test here — the swim test's the same, just wetter...

Equipment needed: stopwatch and a 400 m track.

1) Run round a track as many times as you can in 12 minutes (or walk if you get too tired to run).
2) The distance you run/walk is recorded in metres. The further it is, the better your cardiovascular endurance.

MULTI-STAGE FITNESS TEST (MSFT)

You might know this one as the 'bleep test'. Make sure to use its proper name in the exam though.

Equipment needed: tape measure, cones, multi-stage fitness test recording and some speakers to play it through.

1) A recording of a series of timed bleeps is played. You have to run 'shuttles' between two lines, 20 metres apart, starting on the first bleep.
2) Your foot must be on or over the next line when the next bleep sounds.
3) The time between the bleeps gets shorter as you go through the difficulty levels, so you have to run faster.
4) If you miss a bleep, you are allowed two further bleeps to catch up. If you miss three bleeps in a row, the level and number of shuttles completed are noted as your final score.
5) The higher the level and number of shuttles completed, the better your cardiovascular endurance.

The Harvard staircase test — a step too far...

These tests are all for cardiovascular endurance, but some are more useful to an athlete than others. E.g. the Cooper swim test is a more useful test of a swimmer's cardiovascular endurance than the Harvard Step Test.

Section Three — Physical Training

Fitness Testing

All the fitness tests on this page focus on your muscles. The one rep max and the grip dynamometer both test strength. The sit-up bleep test and one-minute sit-up and press-up tests all measure your muscular endurance.

These Tests are for **Muscular Strength**...

GRIP DYNAMOMETER TEST — STRENGTH

Equipment needed: a dynamometer.

1) A dynamometer is a device used to measure grip strength — the strength in the hand and forearm.
2) You grip as hard as you can for about five seconds and record your reading in kilograms.
3) Usually, you do this three times and take your best score — the higher the score, the stronger your grip.

The one rep max is a good example of a maximal test (see p46) as it finds the actual maximum weight you can safely lift.

ONE REP MAX — MAXIMAL STRENGTH

Equipment needed: gym weight equipment.

1) The aim here is to find the heaviest weight you can lift safely using a particular muscle group. The heavier this weight, the stronger the muscle group.
2) Start with a weight you know you can lift. Once you successfully lift it, rest for a few minutes before trying something heavier.
3) Increase the weight you attempt in small steps until you reach a weight with which you can't complete a single lift. The last weight you managed to successfully lift is your one rep max.

These Tests are for **Muscular Endurance**...

ONE-MINUTE SIT-UP AND ONE-MINUTE PRESS-UP TESTS — MUSCULAR ENDURANCE

Equipment needed: stopwatch and a non-slip surface.

1) You just do as many sit-ups or press-ups as you can in a minute.
2) Your result is a number of sit-ups or press-ups per minute — the higher the number, the better your endurance.
3) Sit-ups test your abdominal muscles' endurance, press-ups test the endurance of your upper body.

'Sit-ups' are sometimes called 'abdominal curls' — so sometimes these tests might have 'abdominal curl' in the title...

SIT-UP BLEEP TEST — MUSCULAR ENDURANCE

Equipment needed: a metronome (or another way of measuring rate) and a non-slip surface.

1) This is like the one-minute sit-up test, but you have to stick to a set pace of 25 sit-ups a minute.
2) The test is finished either when you fail to do a full sit-up in time twice in a row, or if you manage to keep going for four minutes.
3) You count how many sit-ups you complete. The more you do the better your abdominal muscular endurance.

You need a good grip of these tests, so sit up and pay attention...

To remember which component of fitness is measured by which test, think about the action you're doing. If you're generating lots of force at once, it's testing strength, but if you're repeating a strength action, it's testing muscular endurance. Repeat it over and over to yourself, and test your own brainular endurance...

Section Three — Physical Training

Fitness Testing

To help you remember the names of these fitness tests, try to think about the action involved — for speed you sprint, for agility you run and for power you jump (either vertically or horizontally). Handy that...

Test your **Speed** and **Agility** by **Sprinting** and **Running**...

ILLINOIS AGILITY RUN TEST — AGILITY

Equipment needed: stopwatch, cones and a tape measure.

1) Set out a course using cones like this.
2) Start lying face down at the start cone. When a start whistle blows, run around the course as fast as you can.
3) The course is set up so you have to constantly change direction. The shorter the time (in seconds) it takes you to complete the course, the more agile you are.

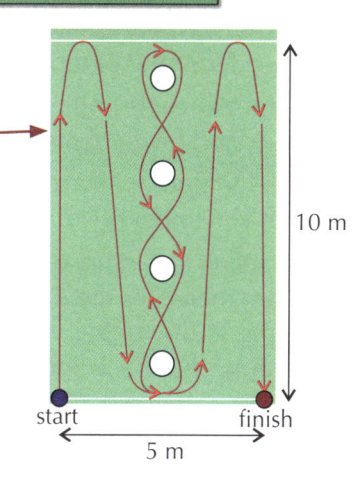

10 m
5 m
start   finish

30 m SPRINT TEST — SPEED

Equipment needed: stopwatch, tape measure and cones.

1) Run the 30 m as fast as you can and record your time in seconds. The shorter the time (in seconds), the quicker you are.
2) The sprint test can be done over different distances, e.g. 50 m is often used.

You can **Test** your **Power** by **Jumping**...

STANDING JUMP TEST

Equipment needed: long jump pit and a tape measure.

1) Place your feet over the edge of the sand pit. Then jump as far forward as possible without a run-up (you can still swing your arms to help). You have to land on both feet.
2) The distance you jump is measured in centimetres — the further you jump the more powerful your leg muscles are.

VERTICAL JUMP TEST

Equipment needed: chalk, tape measure and a wall.

1) Put chalk on your fingertips and stand side-on to a wall.
2) Raise the arm that's nearest the wall and mark the highest point you can reach.
3) Still standing side-on to the wall, jump and mark the wall as high up as you can.
4) Measure between the marks in centimetres. The larger the distance, the more powerful your leg muscles are.

I wonder what the Illinois agility run test measures...

There's nothing too tricky on this page — just learn which test measures which component of fitness. It's worth thinking about how the two different types of jump test are better suited for different performers — e.g. the standing jump is good for long jumpers and the vertical jump is better suited to basketball players.

Section Three — Physical Training

Fitness Testing

This page has four more tests for you to learn. They're for flexibility, coordination, balance and reaction time.

These tests are for Flexibility and Coordination...

SIT AND REACH TEST — FLEXIBILITY

Equipment needed: ruler or tape measure and a box.
1) This test measures flexibility in the back and lower hamstrings.
2) You sit on the floor with your legs straight out in front of you and a box flat against your feet.
3) You then reach as far forward as you can and an assistant measures the distance reached in centimetres — the further you can reach, the more flexible your back and hamstrings are.
4) The distance reached can be measured in different ways — usually it's how many centimetres past your toes that you manage to reach.

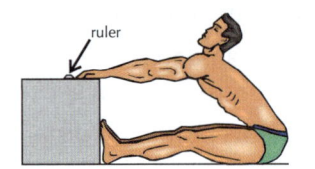

ALTERNATE HAND THROW TEST — COORDINATION

Equipment needed: stopwatch, a ball and a wall.
1) This tests hand-eye coordination.
2) Start by standing 2 m away from a wall.
3) Throw a ball underarm from your right hand against the wall and catch it in your left hand — then throw it underarm from your left hand against the wall and catch it in your right hand. You repeat this for 30 seconds and count the number of catches.
4) The more successful catches you make, the better your coordination.
5) This is sometimes called the 'wall toss' or 'wall throw' test.

These tests are for Balance and Reaction Time

THE STANDING STORK TEST — BALANCE

Equipment needed: stopwatch.
1) Stand on your best leg with your other foot touching your knee and your hands on your hips.
2) Raise your heel so you're standing on your toes and time how long you can hold the position for in seconds. Wobbling is allowed, but the test finishes if your heel touches the ground, or your other foot or hands move.
3) You usually take the best of three times in seconds — the longer your time, the better your balance.

RULER DROP TEST — REACTION TIME

Equipment needed: ruler.
1) Get a friend to hold a ruler vertically between your thumb and first finger. The 0 cm mark on the ruler should be in line with the top of your thumb.
2) Your friend drops the ruler — you have to try and catch it as soon as you see it drop.
3) Read off the distance the ruler fell before you managed to catch it.
4) The slower your reactions, the longer it takes you to catch the ruler, so the further up the ruler you'll catch it. This means the smaller the distance recorded, the quicker your reaction time.

REVISION TASK

Here's another test for you...
Write down the tests for agility, speed, power, flexibility, coordination, balance and reaction time.

Section Three — Physical Training

Fitness Testing

There are two tests for body composition you need to know. Remember, body composition is the percentage of your body weight made up of fat, muscle and bone. If you're not doing the Eduqas course, skip this page.

With the Right Equipment, you can Test Body Composition...

SKINFOLD TEST

Equipment needed: skinfold calipers.

1) The person carrying out the test pinches your skin and underlying fat at different points on your body. They use skinfold calipers to measure the pinched 'fold' in millimetres. Two or three readings are taken at each point, and the average recorded. These average measurements are added together to give a total measurement. This can be put into an equation to estimate your body fat percentage.
2) To get a good estimate the test has to be carried out by someone who's properly trained.
3) The percentage of your total body fat stored under the skin depends on factors like age and gender. You can use different equations to take this into account and make your estimate more accurate.

BODY DENSITY TEST

This is also called 'hydrostatic weighing'.

Equipment needed: scales and specialist underwater weighing equipment.

1) You weigh yourself on land and underwater.
2) Then you use the two measurements and some clever maths to work out your body density and percentage body fat.

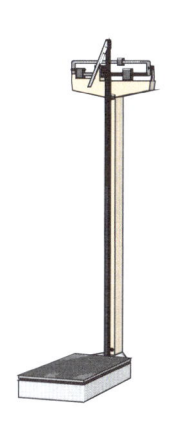

Other Measuring Tools can also be used to Monitor Fitness...

As well as the tests of specific components of fitness, there are other ways of measuring fitness and health:

- Monitoring blood pressure. Blood pressure is recorded as two numbers, e.g. 120/80 mmHg. If both these numbers start to decrease, this indicates that your blood pressure is getting lower. This can mean that your fitness and cardiovascular endurance are improving.

- Measuring heart rate (see pages 119 and 121). As you get fitter, and your cardiovascular system improves, your resting heart rate should start to decrease.

- Keeping track of the amount of calories you take in, and how many you use up exercising (see p83).

- Completing health questionnaires (e.g. a PARQ — see p63).

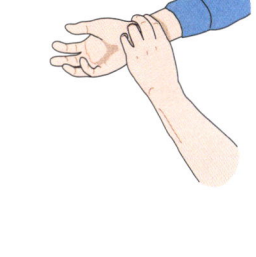

There sure are a lot of ways to measure fitness...

Don't get confused by the fact that one of the body composition tests involves weighing and the other involves measuring skin folds — both tests are used to estimate your body fat percentage.

Section Three — Physical Training

Fitness Testing

You need to understand that these fitness tests are not perfect. But they still give you lots of useful data.

These Fitness Tests have their Limitations

When using any of the fitness tests, you need to consider their limitations:

1) Many of the tests do not test specific sporting actions or the movements involved in an activity.
2) Fitness tests may not tell you how an athlete will actually perform under pressure in a competition.
3) Maximal tests require working at maximum effort — e.g. the one rep max test. The results of these tests will not be accurate if the performer is not motivated to work as hard as they possibly can.
4) Submaximal tests may be used with a formula to predict the maximum performance — the actual maximum is unknown. These formulas can't take into account the differences between individuals, so results can be inaccurate.
5) For some of the tests, you might get better scores just by getting more practice at taking the test, without the relevant component of fitness improving.

> Procedures must be followed correctly to make sure the tests are valid and reliable:
> - If a test is valid, this means it tests the component of fitness that it's supposed to test.
> - If a test is reliable, it will give the same results if it's repeated under the same conditions. So if you see an improvement in the score, it must be because the athlete is doing better at the test.

All these Tests give you Data about your Fitness levels

These numbers are quantitative data (see p117).

Fitness testing gives you a number — e.g. a score, a distance, a time, etc. This is data that you can analyse to assess your fitness levels and make decisions.

1) You can compare your data over time to see how your training is going — e.g. if each week you're recording a bigger distance on the vertical jump test, you know you're increasing your leg power. There's an example of comparing data over time on page 119 — go and have a peek if you like...
2) You can also compare your own performance in a fitness test with average ratings. This can tell you how you rank compared to other people in your age group or gender.
3) Each type of fitness test will have a table that you can compare your results with.

These can be called normative data tables.

The table below shows average ratings for 16 to 19 year-olds taking the grip dynamometer test. Let's say you want to find the rating for an 18-year-old girl who scored 26 kg:

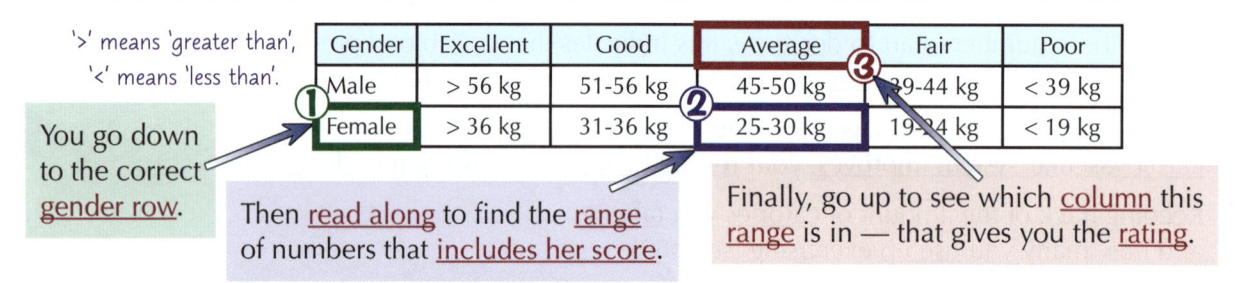

'>' means 'greater than', '<' means 'less than'.

Gender	Excellent	Good	Average	Fair	Poor
Male	> 56 kg	51-56 kg	45-50 kg	39-44 kg	< 39 kg
Female	> 36 kg	31-36 kg	25-30 kg	19-24 kg	< 19 kg

① You go down to the correct gender row.
② Then read along to find the range of numbers that includes her score.
③ Finally, go up to see which column this range is in — that gives you the rating.

So, an 18-year-old girl who scored 26 kg on the grip dynamometer test has average grip strength for her gender.

I have a new revision workout for you — number crunches...

Analysing data might not be your favourite way to spend time, but it's key to making sense of the results of all the different fitness tests. So, you should really take your time and make sure this stuff has sunk in.

Section Three — Physical Training

Warm-Up and Worked Exam Questions

Now you've learned everything there is to know about components of fitness and fitness testing, you need to check that it's all sunk in. Luckily, there are three whole pages of questions here for you to do just that...

Warm-Up Questions

1) What is meant by 'exercise'?
2) Which one of the following needs static strength — a gymnast holding a hand stand, a sprinter leaving the starting blocks or someone doing a set of press-ups?
3) How can a high level of flexibility help to prevent injury?
4) Define 'body composition'.
5) Is agility more important for a 100 m sprinter, or a football player?
6) Give one example of when a gymnast would need good balance.
7) What is meant by 'reaction time'?
8) What is power a combination of?
9) List three tests for cardiovascular endurance.
10) Name two tests for power.
11) What does the skinfold test measure?
12) Give three limitations of fitness testing.

Worked Exam Questions

1 Define **speed**. Give **one** example of when this component of fitness would be needed in a physical activity. *(Grade 1-3)*

> Speed is the rate at which someone can move or cover a distance.
>
> It's needed in hockey to outrun an opponent to the ball.

There are lots of other examples you could give here for a sporting action that speed helps with — but you only need one to get the mark.

[2 marks]

2 Christine trains regularly. She has achieved a high level of fitness with her training programme.

(a) Define the term **health**. *(Grade 1-3)*

> Health is a state of complete physical, emotional and social well-being.

[1 mark]

(b) Explain why Christine might not be classed as healthy, despite her high level of fitness. *(Grade 5-7)*

> Christine could have a high level of physical fitness, but still be unhappy or suffering from high stress levels. To be classified as healthy, Christine would need to have a good state of emotional and social well-being, as well as being physically fit and healthy.

There are lots of different answers you could give here. As long as you link your explanation back to the definition of health, you'll get both marks.

[2 marks]

Section Three — Physical Training

Exam Questions

1 Which one of the following components of fitness is **least** important when throwing a shot-put? *(Grade 1-3)*

- A Power ☐
- B Muscular Strength ☐
- C Coordination ☐
- D Cardiovascular Endurance ☑

[1 mark]

2 Table 1 shows ratings for the grip dynamometer test for people aged 16-19 years old. *(Grade 1-3)*

Gender	Excellent	Good	Average	Fair	Poor
Male	>56 kg	51-56 kg	45-50 kg	39-44 kg	<39 kg
Female	>36 kg	31-36 kg	25-30 kg	19-24 kg	<19 kg

Table 1

Gabrielle is 17. She took the grip dynamometer test and scored 33 kg.

Select the correct rating for Gabrielle.

- A Good ☑
- B Average ☐
- C Fair ☐
- D Poor ☐

[1 mark]

3 Explain, using **one** example, how good muscular endurance could impact performance in a physical activity. *(Grade 1-3)*

....
....

[2 marks]

4 Haruki is planning a training programme to improve his flexibility, reaction time and muscular endurance. *(Grade 3-5)*

Identify and describe how to carry out **two** fitness tests that he should use before planning a training programme.

1 ....
....
....

2 ....
....
....

[6 marks]

Section Three — Physical Training

Exam Questions

5 Eric is planning a training programme.

(a) Describe **two** ways that Eric can use fitness testing to help him plan and carry out his training programme. *(Grade 3-5)*

1 ....

....

2 ....

....

[2 marks]

Eric is training to compete in a triathlon.

(b) Explain why the Cooper 12-minute run test might be more useful to him than the 30 m sprint test. *(Grade 5-7)*

....

....

....

[3 marks]

After six weeks of training, Eric finds that the distance he manages to run on the Cooper 12-minute run test has not increased.

(c) What does this tell Eric about the effectiveness of his training programme? *(Grade 3-5)*

....

[1 mark]

6 Discuss the importance of power and cardiovascular endurance for a long jumper.

Think about the sporting actions a long jumper has to do, and whether those actions require either of these components of fitness.

....

....

....

....

....

....

....

....

[6 marks]

Section Three — Physical Training

Principles of Training

Training isn't about running for as long as possible, or lifting the heaviest weights you can. There's much more to it than that — you need to know how training is matched to different people.

Train to Improve Your Health, Fitness or Performance

1) To improve your health, fitness or performance, you'll need a Personal Exercise Programme (PEP).
2) A PEP is a training programme designed to improve whatever you want it to improve — it could be your general health and fitness, or a particular component of fitness that will improve your performance in a sport or activity.
3) Different training methods involve different types of exercise and are designed to improve different components of fitness.
4) So you need to choose the right training method. Some key factors to consider will be:

You will probably have completed a PEP as part of your course...

What area of your sport or activity you want to improve. You'll need to think about which components of fitness are involved, and which parts of the body too.

For example, you might want to improve your spike in volleyball.

What level of fitness you are currently at — you can use fitness testing to find this out. Some methods of training may be too demanding if you are unfit. With any training method, if you're really unfit you'll want to start easy and build up the intensity slowly.

What facilities and equipment you have access to. Some training methods involve lots of specialist equipment and some will also need lots of indoor space.

SPORT — The Five Principles of Training

To get the most out of your training, you need to follow these five principles:

S — SPECIFICITY — matching training to the activity and components of fitness to be developed.

Make sure you're training using the muscles and actions you want to improve — e.g. a cyclist would be better off improving their muscular endurance on an exercise bike than a treadmill. You should also match the intensity of your training to the activity you're training for (see p52) and to the individual needs of the performer.

P — PROGRESSION — gradually increasing the level of training.

This needs to be a gradual process to allow your body time to adapt. If you try to do too much too quickly, you can end up getting injured.

AQA and Edexcel combine these and call it 'progressive overload'.

O — OVERLOAD — the only way to get fitter is to work your body harder than it normally would.

To overload, you can increase the frequency, intensity, or time spent training (see next page).

R — REVERSIBILITY — any fitness improvement or body adaptation caused by training will gradually reverse and be lost when you stop training.

Unfortunately, it takes longer to gain fitness than to lose fitness.

T — TEDIUM — there needs to be variety in your training, otherwise it can become boring.

If you always train in exactly the same way, it'll become boring and you'll lose motivation. Variation in training helps to keep it fresh and interesting.

The principle of keeping training varied is called 'variance' if you're doing the Eduqas course.

Section Three — Physical Training

Principles of Training

The best training programmes aren't just thrown together — they have to be carefully planned. Part of this planning is leaving enough time for rest and recovery, so your body has time to adapt to the training.

Training Programmes can be Planned using FITT

Frequency, Intensity and Time are all part of making sure you overload while you're training.

F = FREQUENCY of training — how often you should exercise.

You can overload by increasing how often you exercise, e.g. gradually increasing the number of training sessions. You need to make sure you leave enough time between sessions to recover though (see below).

I = INTENSITY of training — how hard you should exercise.

You can overload by gradually increasing the intensity of your exercise — e.g. lifting heavier weights. How intensely you train depends on the type of fitness you want to improve (see next page) and your level of fitness — someone who hasn't trained for a while should start at a low intensity and gradually increase.

T = TIME spent training — how long you should exercise for.

You can overload by gradually increasing the time you spend on a certain exercise or by increasing the overall time spent exercising — e.g. making training sessions five minutes longer each week.

T = TYPE of training — what exercises and methods of training you should use.

You need to match the type of exercise and method of training to what it is you're training for — e.g. if you want to improve cardiovascular endurance, you need to do exercise that uses lots of muscles, like running or cycling, and you should select an appropriate method of training, e.g. continuous training (see p55). Varying types of exercise also helps stop training becoming boring and reduces stress on tissues and joints.

All training programmes need to be constantly monitored to make sure that the activities are still producing overload. As you get fitter your PEP will need to change to keep improving your fitness.

Your Body Adapts During Rest and Recovery

1) Training makes your body change to cope with the increased exercise. This means you get fitter.
2) These adaptations take place during rest and recovery, so it's vital you allow enough time between training sessions for the body to adapt.
3) It's also important that you allow enough recovery time between workouts to avoid overtraining. Overtraining is when you don't rest enough — it can cause injury by not giving your body enough time to recover from the last training session and repair any damage.
4) When you're training, you need to balance your recovery time with the effects of reversibility.
5) If you rest for too long, you'll lose most of the benefits of having done the training in the first place. If you don't rest enough, you could injure yourself through overtraining.
6) If you get injured, not only have you got to wait for your injury to heal, but thanks to reversibility your fitness will start to decrease while you do. It doesn't seem fair really...

Someone's been really creative with these acronyms...

Want to be fit? Use FITT — Frequency, Intensity, Time and Type. And remember that recovery time is part of training too, because your body needs time to adapt and repair itself if you want to avoid overtraining.

Section Three — Physical Training

Training Target Zones

To improve aerobic or anaerobic fitness, you need to be training at the right intensity. To work this out, you have to do calculations based on your heart rate. If you're doing the OCR course you can skip this page.

Heart Rate — Heartbeats per Minute

See pages 23-24 for more on how exercise affects your heart rate.

1) Your heart rate is the number of times your heart beats per minute (bpm).
2) When you exercise, your heart rate increases to increase the blood and oxygen supply to your muscles. The harder you work, the more your heart rate will increase.
3) You can find your theoretical maximum heart rate (MHR) by doing: ➡ MHR = 220 − Age
4) And you can use this value to work out how hard you should work to improve your fitness.

Get your Heart Rate in the Target Zone

Aerobic activity is 'with oxygen' and anaerobic activity is 'without oxygen' — see page 21 for more.

1) To improve your aerobic or anaerobic fitness, you have to exercise at the right intensity.
2) You can do this by making sure that your heart rate is in a target zone — there are different target zones for aerobic and anaerobic training:

> **AEROBIC TARGET ZONE** — 60%-80% of maximum heart rate.
>
> **ANAEROBIC TARGET ZONE** — 80%-90% of maximum heart rate.

3) The boundaries of the training zones are called training thresholds. If you're a beginner, you should train nearer the lower threshold. Serious athletes train close to the upper threshold.

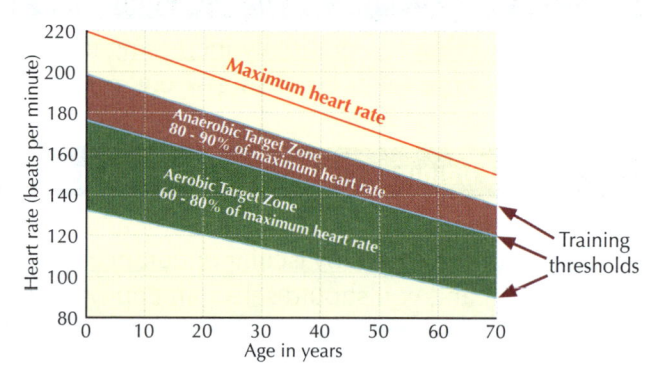

Calculating Target Zones — Example

For the anaerobic thresholds, you'd use 0.8 and 0.9.

Let's say you want to work out the aerobic target zone for a 20-year-old:
1) First, you calculate their maximum heart rate by subtracting their age from 220 — that's 220 − 20 = 200.
2) Next you find the thresholds. Because you're calculating the aerobic target zone, the lower threshold is 60% of the maximum heart rate — that's 200 × 0.6 = 120. The upper threshold is 80% of the maximum heart rate — so 200 × 0.8 = 160.
3) So the target zone for aerobic training is between 120 and 160 beats per minute.

Your Training Intensity Should Suit Your Activity

1) If you want to be good at an aerobic activity, like long-distance running, then you should do a lot of aerobic activity as part of your training. It improves your cardiovascular system.
2) Anaerobic training helps your muscles put up with lactic acid. They also get better at getting rid of it. For anaerobic activity like sprinting, you need to do anaerobic training.
3) In many team sports, like lacrosse, you need to be able to move about continuously (aerobic), as well as needing to have spurts of fast movement (anaerobic). You should have a mix of aerobic and anaerobic activities in your training for these.

REVISION TASK — **Get in the zone...**
Make sure you know the percentages that are used to calculate the thresholds of these target zones. Get some practice by working out your own aerobic and anaerobic target zones...

Section Three — Physical Training

Warm-Up and Worked Exam Questions

The principles of training can be really tricky, and so can the training target zones. This means you're going to need plenty of practice with this stuff before your exam, which is what the next two pages are for...

Warm-Up Questions

1) What is a PEP and what is it designed to do?
2) What is overload?
3) Explain why training programmes should be constantly monitored.
4) Why is it important to allow time for rest and recovery between exercise sessions?
5) What type of activity should a rugby player do in training — aerobic, anaerobic or both?

Worked Exam Questions

1 Give **three** methods of achieving overload in training.

1 *You can increase the frequency that you train.*
2 *You can increase the intensity of training.*
3 *You can increase the amount of time each training session lasts.*

You can also achieve overload by varying the type of training you do.

[3 marks]

2 In order to improve cardiovascular endurance, training should be done in the aerobic training zone.

Explain how to calculate the thresholds of this training zone.

First calculate 220 - age to find the theoretical maximum heart rate.
The lower threshold of the aerobic training zone is 60% of maximum heart rate.
The upper threshold is 80% of maximum heart rate.

[3 marks]

3 Tedium is a principle of training.

Remember, if you're doing the Eduqas course, this principle of training is called 'variance', not 'tedium'.

Explain why tedium is an important consideration when planning a training programme.

Doing exactly the same type of training repeatedly can become boring. This could lead to a performer losing focus and motivation. Therefore, a training programme should include variation, to keep the training interesting.

[3 marks]

Section Three — Physical Training

Exam Questions

1 Lisa has been unable to train for four weeks due to a groin strain.

(a) State what is likely to have happened to her fitness levels. *[Grade 1-3]*

....
[1 mark]

(b) Explain why athletes need to balance the effects of reversibility with the need for rest and recovery. *[Grade 3-5]*

....
....
[2 marks]

2 Fatima is training for a weightlifting competition. *[Grade 3-5]*

State whether Fatima should spend more of her time training aerobically or anaerobically. Justify your answer.

....
....
....
[2 marks]

3 Lucy is planning a training programme to prepare herself for taking part in a marathon. *[Grade 3-5]*

(a) Define the principle of **specificity**.

....
....
[1 mark]

(b) Give **one** example of how Lucy could apply specificity to her training.

....
....
....
[1 mark]

Section Three — Physical Training

Training Methods

Next up, training methods. You have to match the type of training with what you are training for. This means training the right components of fitness, and training at the right intensity — e.g. aerobic, anaerobic or both.

Continuous Training Means No Resting

1) Continuous training involves exercising at a steady, constant rate — doing aerobic activities like running or cycling for at least 20 minutes with no breaks. This is also known as steady-state training.
2) It improves cardiovascular endurance and muscular endurance, and is great for body composition as well.
3) It usually means exercising so that your heart rate is in your aerobic training zone (see p52). This means it's good training for aerobic activities like long-distance running.
4) Overload is achieved by increasing the duration, distance, speed or frequency.

ADVANTAGES:
- It's easy to do — going for a run doesn't require specialist equipment.
- Not resting helps prepare for sports where you have to play for long periods of time without a break.

DISADVANTAGES:
- It only involves aerobic activity so doesn't improve anaerobic fitness.
- It can become boring doing one exercise at a constant rate.

Fartlek Training is all about Changes of Speed

1) Fartlek training is a type of continuous training, but it involves changes in the intensity of the exercise over different intervals — e.g. by changing the speed or the terrain (type or steepness of the ground).

   For example, part of a fartlek run could be to sprint for 10 seconds, then jog for 20 seconds (repeated for 4 minutes), followed by running uphill for 2 minutes.

2) It's great for cardiovascular endurance and muscular endurance and also helps to improve speed.
3) You can include a mix of aerobic and anaerobic activity, so it's good training for sports that need different paces, like hockey and rugby.
4) Overload is achieved by increasing the times or speeds of each bit, or the terrain difficulty (e.g. running uphill).

ADVANTAGE:
- It's very adaptable, so you can easily tailor training to suit different sports and different levels of fitness.

DISADVANTAGE:
- Frequent changes to intensity can mean that training lacks structure — this makes it easy to skip the hard bits and tough to monitor progress.

Fartlek means 'speed play' in Swedish — in case you're wondering...

Fartlek training can be easily adapted to suit people of varying degrees of fitness. For example, it can be made really intense, with lots of difficult sections, or a bit easier, with plenty of slow-paced sections.

Section Three — Physical Training

Training Methods

Interval training improves your cardiovascular and anaerobic fitness. Weight training works on your muscles.

Interval Training uses Fixed Patterns of Exercise

1) Interval training uses fixed patterns of periods of high-intensity exercise and either low-intensity exercise or rest. It has a strict structure. For high-intensity interval training (HIIT) you use maximum effort for the high-intensity bits, and an active, low-intensity rest period.

2) By combining high- and low-intensity work, interval training allows you to improve both cardiovascular endurance and anaerobic fitness. The high-intensity periods can also improve speed.

3) It's great training for sports where you have to move continuously (aerobic), then have sudden spurts of fast movement (anaerobic) — like rugby or water polo.

4) To overload you have to increase the proportion of time spent on the high-intensity exercise, or the intensity — e.g. run faster.

ADVANTAGE:
- It's easily adapted to improve aerobic or anaerobic fitness by changing the intensity and length of work and recovery periods.

DISADVANTAGE:
- Interval training is exhausting. This can make it difficult to carry on pushing yourself.

Resistance/Weight Training works on your Muscles

Resistance or weight training means using your muscles against a resistance. You can use weights, elastic ropes or your own body weight (like in a pull-up) as the resistance.

Improving your strength also helps to improve your power.

1) Resistance/weight training can be used to develop both muscular endurance and strength.
2) It's anaerobic training, so is good for improving performance in anaerobic activities like sprinting.
3) Increasing strength/power means you can hit or kick something harder (hockey, football), throw further (javelin, discus), sprint faster, out-muscle opposition (judo), etc.
4) There are two different ways to train — either by holding a position or by moving:

You can train by increasing the tension in a muscle, without changing the muscle's length (so there's no movement).

Example: THE WALL SIT
Sit with your back to the wall and your knees bent at 90° and hold it.

You overload by staying in the position for longer, or holding weights while you're in the position.

You can train by contracting your muscles to create movement. Each completed movement is called a 'rep' (repetition), and a group of reps is called a 'set'.

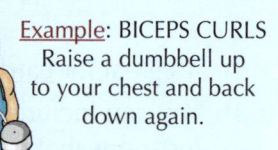

Example: BICEPS CURLS
Raise a dumbbell up to your chest and back down again.

- To increase muscular endurance, you use low weight (below 70% of your one rep max) but a high number of reps. To overload, gradually increase the number of reps.
- To increase strength you use high weight (above 70% of your one rep max) but a low number of reps. To overload, gradually increase the weight — but decrease the reps to avoid injury.

For how to calculate your one rep max, see p42.

DISADVANTAGES:
- It puts muscles under high stress levels, so can leave them very sore afterwards.
- If your weightlifting technique is poor, it can be dangerous. Also, some lifts require an assistant called a spotter.

ADVANTAGES:
- It's easily adapted to suit different sports — you can focus on the relevant muscles.
- Many of the exercises (press-ups, sit-ups, etc.) require little or no equipment.

Section Three — Physical Training

Training Methods

Plyometrics helps make you more powerful, but you need to be quite fit to use it. Circuit training allows you to train lots of different components of fitness and skills all at once, but requires lots of equipment and time.

Plyometric Training Improves Power

Loads of sports require explosive strength and power (see p40), e.g. for fast starts in sprinting, or sports where you need to jump high, like basketball or volleyball. You can train muscular power using plyometrics.

1) When muscles 'contract' to give movement, they either shorten or lengthen.
2) If a muscle lengthens just before it shortens, it can help to generate power. When a muscle gets stretched and lengthens, extra energy is stored in the muscle (like storing energy in an elastic band by stretching it). This extra energy means the muscle can generate a greater force when it shortens.
3) The extra energy doesn't last very long though. So, the quicker your muscles can move between the lengthening and shortening phases, the more powerful the movement will be.
4) Plyometric training improves the speed you can switch between the two phases, so it improves your power. It's anaerobic exercise and often involves jumping.

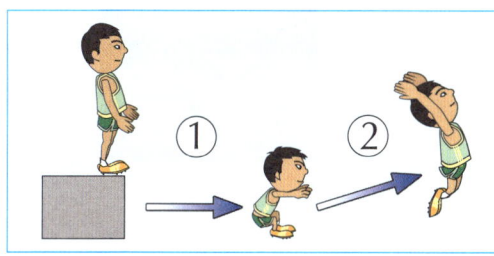

> Depth jumps are a form of plyometric training. They improve the power of your quadriceps and increase how high you can jump.
> You drop off a box then quickly jump into the air. The first stage lengthens your quadriceps as you land and squat, the second stage shortens them as you jump.

ADVANTAGE:
- It's the only form of training that directly improves your power.

DISADVANTAGE:
- It's very demanding on the muscles used — you need to be very fit to do it, otherwise you'll get injured.

Circuit Training Uses Loads of Different Exercises

Each circuit has between 6 and 10 'stations' in it. At each station you do a specific exercise for a set amount of time before moving on to the next station.

1) A circuit's stations can work on aerobic or anaerobic fitness — e.g. star jumps for cardiovascular endurance, tricep dips for strength, shuttle runs for speed, etc.
2) You're allowed a short rest between stations. An active rest, e.g. jogging instead of stopping exercising, will improve cardiovascular endurance.
3) Overload is achieved by doing more repetitions at each station, completing the circuit more quickly, resting less between stations, or by repeating the circuit.

ADVANTAGES:
- Because you design the circuit, you can match circuit training to an individual and any component of fitness — e.g. you can improve muscular endurance, strength, cardiovascular endurance... anything you want really.
- Also, the variety keeps the training interesting.

DISADVANTAGE:
- It takes a long time to set up and requires loads of equipment and space.

EXAM TIP

Plyometric training — a whole lot of jumping...

In the exam, you might be asked to weigh up the suitability of various training methods for a given performer. To do this, you need to think about the actions the performer has to do in their sport, and then match them with a training method — e.g. 'a basketball player could use plyometric training to improve how high they can jump, which would help them to win more rebounds.'

Section Three — Physical Training

Training Methods

High-altitude training improves cardiovascular endurance for a short time, and stretching improves flexibility. You only need to know about high-altitude training for the AQA course.

High-Altitude Training Improves Cardiovascular Endurance

1) At high altitude the air pressure is lower. This means you take in less oxygen with each breath.
2) Your body adapts to this by creating more red blood cells, so enough oxygen can still be supplied to the muscles and organs.

   Land at high altitude is a long way above sea level.

3) Some athletes take advantage of this by training at high altitude to increase their red blood cell count. This gives them an advantage when they compete at a lower altitude.
4) More red blood cells means a better oxygen supply to the muscles, so it increases a performer's cardiovascular endurance and muscular endurance. This means it suits endurance athletes.
5) Training at high altitude makes it harder to reach the same intensity levels as you could training at a low altitude, so it's not well suited for anaerobic training.
6) The effects of altitude training only last for a few weeks. Once the athlete returns to a lower altitude, the body doesn't need to create extra red blood cells any more.

ADVANTAGE:
- It improves cardiovascular and muscular endurance, which helps endurance athletes perform better.

DISADVANTAGES:
- The effects only last for a short time.
- It can be very expensive to transport athletes to mountainous regions.
- While at high altitude, you can get altitude sickness. This could mean you lose valuable training time recovering.

Stretching can be used to Improve Flexibility

1) Static stretching is done by gradually stretching a muscle and then holding the position.
2) You hold the stretch at the point where you feel mild discomfort — stretching shouldn't hurt.
3) It's best to do static stretching after a workout, when the muscles are warm. To improve flexibility, you should hold the stretches for 30 seconds.
4) To avoid injury you should always stretch gradually. This avoids overstretching the muscle.
5) Static stretching can either be active or passive:

   In an ACTIVE static stretch, you use your own muscles to hold the stretch position.   Stretched muscle

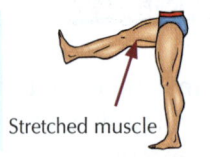

   In a PASSIVE static stretch, you use someone else or a piece of equipment to help you hold the stretch.   Stretched muscle

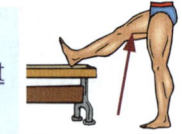

6) Dynamic stretching means moving a joint through its range of motion. This should be done during a warm-up as it helps to loosen up muscles, which helps to prevent injury.   Stretched muscle

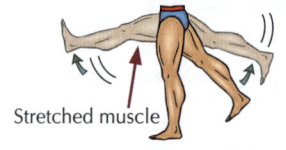

Altitude training — it's not going to help your fear of heights...
A lot of the time, altitude training isn't an option for amateur athletes — most people don't live near any mountains, and they might not have the money to travel to them like professional athletes do.

Section Three — Physical Training

Training Methods

Right, last page of training methods... If you're not doing the AQA course you can skip the last part.

Fitness Classes make Training More Social and More Fun

As well as all those training methods, there's a host of activities and classes that help improve fitness. Classes can also make training a more social experience.

YOGA AND PILATES

Both yoga and Pilates use a series of exercises and stretches that help increase strength, flexibility and balance. Yoga exercises the whole body, while Pilates focuses more on the core torso muscles, e.g. the abdominals. Both help to prevent injury as well as making you fitter.

SPINNING®

This is a high-intensity workout using exercise bikes which can be set to different levels of resistance by participants. It's good for improving both your cardiovascular endurance and anaerobic fitness.

AEROBICS

This involves doing aerobic exercises to music. It's good for improving cardiovascular endurance, strength and flexibility.

BODYPUMP™

This is a choreographed workout that combines weight training and aerobics. It's good for improving strength, muscular endurance and cardiovascular endurance.

Using any of the training methods covered on the last five pages over an extended period of time has long-term effects on the body systems. By improving components of fitness, you can improve the performance of the musculo-skeletal and cardio-respiratory systems — see page 25 for the details. These changes have a positive effect on both your health and performance in physical activity and sport.

Training needs to be Planned Around when you Compete

Most sportspeople don't compete all year round, so they change their training programmes depending on whether it's before, during or after the competition season:

1) Pre-season (preparation) — a performer makes sure they're ready for the competitive season. The focus is on general fitness and developing the specific components of fitness and skills they need to compete.

2) Competition / playing season (peak) — the performer should be at the peak of their fitness and ability. The focus is on maintaining their current level of fitness, and continuing to develop specific skills to improve their performance. Too much training should be avoided so the performer doesn't become fatigued.

3) Post-season (transition) — once the competition season is over, the performer needs to rest and relax to allow their body to recover. Light aerobic training is done to maintain general fitness.

REVISION TASK

So many fitness classes to learn — my head is spinning...

This stuff is really important, and getting it right in the exam could be worth big marks. So, look back over the last five pages and, for each training method, write down two types of performer who would benefit from using it. For each one, add a sentence explaining why.

Section Three — Physical Training

Warm-up and Worked Exam Questions

So, that wraps up methods of training. Now, have a go at these questions to make sure you've got it.
If there's anything you struggle with — go back and read it again, and again, and again, until it sinks in...

Warm-Up Questions

1) What is fartlek training?
2) Describe the difference between a 'rep' and a 'set' in weight training.
3) Name two anaerobic training methods.
4) Give one disadvantage of circuit training.
5) What type of athlete would benefit from altitude training? Why?
6) Describe the difference between active and passive stretching.
7) Which components of fitness can Bodypump™ be used to improve?
8) Competition season is one of the training seasons for competitive athletes. Name the other two.

Worked Exam Questions

1 Sharon wants to improve her muscular endurance using fartlek training. *(Grade 1-3)*

   (a) Give **one** advantage of fartlek training.

   It is easily adapted to suit an individual's training needs.
   Make sure you know the advantages and the disadvantages of all the training methods. *[1 mark]*

   (b) Name **two** other types of training that would improve her muscular endurance.

   1 Continuous training

   2 Weight training
   You could also put circuit training
   or high-altitude training here. *[2 marks]*

2 Complete the following table about two training methods, the component of fitness *(Grade 3-5)* each one improves and one long-term adaptation to the body each method can cause.

Training method	Component of fitness improved	Long-term training adaptation to body systems
Weight	Strength	Muscular hypertrophy
Continuous	Cardiovascular Endurance	Increased number of red blood cells.

You could also put muscular endurance, or body composition here.   This final column draws on knowledge from page 25.   *[4 marks]*

Section Three — Physical Training

Exam Questions

1 Which of the following training methods is **most** suitable for increasing cardiovascular endurance?

- A Plyometric training ☐
- B Weight training ☐
- C Fartlek training ☐
- D Static stretching ☐

[1 mark]

2 Which of the following training methods is **most** suitable for increasing power?

- A Plyometric training ☐
- B Altitude training ☐
- C Fartlek training ☐
- D Continuous training ☐

[1 mark]

3 Complete the following statement about resistance training.

Resistance training can be used to improve strength, muscular endurance and ....

To improve strength, a .... weight is used, with a .... number of reps.

[3 marks]

4 George is training for the school cross-country team.

(a) Identify a suitable training method for George. Justify your choice.

....

....

[2 marks]

(b) Give **one** advantage and **one** disadvantage of this type of training.

Advantage

....

Disadvantage

....

[2 marks]

Section Three — Physical Training

Exam Questions

5 **Figure 1** shows the heart rate of an athlete during a period of their training.

Grade 5-7

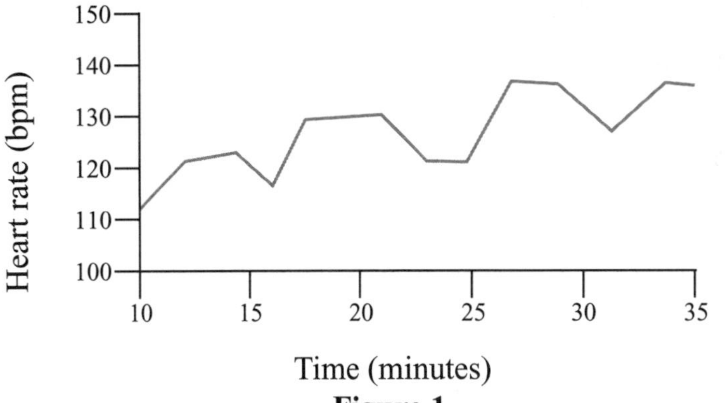

Figure 1

Analyse the graph and state **one** method of training the athlete could be using. Justify your answer.

....

....

[2 marks]

6 Evaluate the use of interval training and continuous training by a basketball player.

Don't be put off by these longer questions — just start off by explaining what the two types of training are. Then apply these to a basketball player's performance, and evaluate how suitable they are.

....

....

....

....

....

....

....

....

....

....

....

....

....

Don't forget to write a conclusion at the end.

[9 marks]

Section Three — Physical Training

Preventing Injuries

With any physical activity there's always a risk of injury. You need to know how to make it as safe as possible.

PARQ — Physical Activity Readiness Questionnaire

1) PARQs are made up of 'yes or no' questions, designed to assess whether it's safe for you to increase your physical activity.
2) It's a good idea to fill one in before you start a training programme.
3) If you answer yes to any of the questions, you need to visit your doctor to make sure it's safe first. This could also lead to changes in the programme to make sure it's safe for you to participate.

PARQ — Yes No
- Have you ever been diagnosed with a heart problem?
- Are you currently being prescribed any medication?
- Do you have any problems with your joints?

Before you Exercise do these Three Things...

CHECK EQUIPMENT/FACILITIES
- Use the right equipment — and check it's not damaged and is in good condition.
- Check for possible dangers in the area you're going to be exercising in — e.g. glass hidden in the grass on a football pitch, slippery patches caused by bad weather on a running track, loose or slippery tiles around a swimming pool.

STRUCTURE TRAINING CORRECTLY
- Apply the Principles of Training (see p50-51).
- This means planning your training correctly — you need to allow time for rest and recovery, otherwise you can get overuse injuries.
- Also, make sure the intensity of exercise matches your level of fitness.

WARM UP

A warm-up gets your body ready for exercise by gradually increasing your work rate. It should involve:

1) Raising your pulse — light exercise increases your heart rate and gets blood flowing to the muscles.
   - This raises your body temperature and warms up muscles, ligaments and tendons so they can move more freely and are less likely to get injured. Warmer muscles can also contract more quickly.
   - It also helps to ease your body into exercising by gradually increasing the exercise intensity, and it increases the oxygen supply to the muscles.

2) Stretching and mobility exercises — this increases flexibility at your joints. It should focus on the muscles and movements you will use in the activity — e.g. shoulder circles before playing tennis.
   - This helps increase the range of movement of your muscles and joints, which will help you perform better and avoid injury. It's best to use dynamic stretches (see p58).

3) Practice actions — e.g. practice shots in netball, throwing and catching in rounders, etc.
   - This prepares the muscles that will be used in the activity, so they perform better.
   - It also helps with your mental preparation, as it focuses you on the activity and gets you "in the zone".

You could also use mental preparation techniques so you're calm, confident and focused (see page 96).

A warm-up makes your muscles warmer...
Warming up is especially important for more intense, anaerobic activities, where it's easy to get an injury. Make sure you know what a warm-up involves, and how it can be tailored to different sports.

Section Three — Physical Training

Preventing Injuries

It's in your best interests to learn these six ways of preventing injury during activity — they'll stop you hurting yourself and help you pass your exams. So, hop to it and get learning...

During Exercise do these Six Things...

USE THE CORRECT CLOTHING/EQUIPMENT

- Make sure you're not wearing anything that could get caught (e.g. jewellery, watches).
- Wear suitable footwear — e.g. wearing studded football boots or spiked running shoes can make you less likely to slip and injure yourself.
- Use protective clothing/equipment where appropriate — e.g. gumshields, cycling helmets.

MAINTAIN HYDRATION

- Drink plenty of water to replace the water lost while exercising. This stops you becoming dehydrated (see p80).

USE THE CORRECT TECHNIQUE

- Make sure that you use the correct technique — e.g. lifting weights properly, or stretching in the right way.
- Also, make sure that you use the right technique for moving and carrying equipment.

COMPETE AT THE APPROPRIATE LEVEL

- You should exercise with people at a similar level to yourself, so you don't overdo it — e.g. join a running club who run at a similar pace to yourself.
- You need to compete in the right age range too — e.g. a 10-year-old shouldn't play rugby with adults.

USE TAPING AND BRACING

- You can use special tape or an elastic brace to support joints.
- This restricts the range of movement at a joint, which helps to prevent sprains (see p66).
- It's particularly important that this is done for joints that have been recently injured, to help avoid another injury.

PLAY BY THE RULES

- Know and follow the rules. Some rules are there to help stop injuries — e.g. giving yellow cards for bad tackles in football.
- Use officials (e.g. a referee) to ensure there's fair play and the rules are followed.

All this talk of injuries is making my brain hurt...

When you're learning these ways of preventing injury, try to think of how these can be applied to specific activities — for example, think about the different types of equipment needed to play different sports.

Section Three — Physical Training

Preventing Injuries

What you do after exercise is just as important as how you prepare for exercise. As well as preventing injuries, the techniques on this page help your body to recover quickly after exercise.

What you do After you Exercise is Important too...

LEAVE ENOUGH RECOVERY TIME
- You need to leave enough time for your body to repair and rebuild after exercise. If you don't you could end up overtraining (see p51).

EAT AND REHYDRATE
- Exercising will have used up a lot of the energy stored in your body. You need to replenish this energy, e.g. by eating carbohydrates (see p79).
- You'll also need to drink plenty of water to rehydrate (see p80).

ICE BATHS/MASSAGE
- Some athletes will take ice baths or get sports massages following exercise. These may help to prevent delayed onset of muscle soreness (DOMS).

COOL DOWN
A cool-down gets your body back to normal after exercise by gradually decreasing the intensity of work to control your return to resting levels. It should involve:

1) Gentle exercise like jogging to keep the heart and lungs working harder than normal. You should gradually reduce the intensity of this exercise so that your heart rate, breathing rate and body temperature decrease gradually.
   - This means you can continue taking in more oxygen to help get rid of the lactic acid and other waste products in your muscles (repaying the oxygen debt — see p22). It also helps you to remove the extra carbon dioxide in your blood.
   - It keeps the blood flowing back from the muscles, so stops blood pooling in the legs and arms — blood pooling can cause dizziness and even fainting.

2) Stretching the muscles that have been used in the activity to speed up recovery and improve flexibility.
   - Stretching while the muscles are warm helps to improve flexibility — in particular using static or PNF stretches. PNF stretches involve contracting the muscle you are stretching to increase mobility gains.
   - It may also help to prevent delayed onset of muscle soreness (DOMS).

After you exercise, make sure you cool down...

A cool-down is really important, especially after intense exercise — it helps the body to remove lactic acid from the muscles and repay the oxygen debt built up during anaerobic activity. This helps to speed up your recovery. Make sure you learn all the different ways to prevent injury after you've finished exercising.

Section Three — Physical Training

Injuries and Treatment

You only need to read these next two pages about injuries if you're doing the Edexcel course.

Soft Tissues can get Stretched, Ripped and Torn

Soft tissues are skin, muscles, tendons and ligaments. Basically, all the bits of you that aren't bone...

Damage to the Skin is Common in Sport

1) Grazes, blisters and chafing are all types of abrasion. They can break the skin and cause bleeding.
2) Cuts also damage the skin and cause bleeding. A deep cut will damage the tissue beneath the skin as well. Deep cuts like this will require medical attention.
3) Injuries to the skin can occur in most physical activities, although they're especially common in full-contact sports like rugby or boxing.

Strains are Tears in Muscles or Tendons

1) Strained (pulled) muscles and tendons are tears in the tissue. They're often caused by sudden overstretching.
2) Pulled hamstrings and calf muscles are common injuries in sports like football and cricket, where you use sudden bursts of speed.

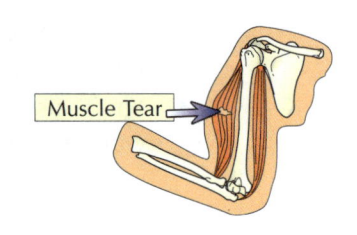

Sprains are Damage to Ligaments

1) Sprains are joint injuries where the ligament has been stretched or torn, usually because of violent twisting.
2) These types of injuries are common in sports where players have to change direction quickly, like football and basketball.

See page 7 for more about tendons and ligaments.

Some Injuries are Caused by Continuous Stress...

Continuous stress on part of the body over a long period of time can cause all sorts of problems:

1) Tennis players can develop tennis elbow — painful inflammation of tendons in the elbow due to overuse of certain arm muscles.
2) Golfers get a similar injury called, wait for it... golfer's elbow.
3) You're more at risk of this type of injury if you train too hard or don't rest enough between training sessions.
4) As these are injuries to tendons, they are also types of soft-tissue injury.

...others by Sudden Stress

1) Cartilage can be damaged by sudden movements.
2) E.g. the cartilage of the knee can be torn by a violent impact or twisting motion.
3) Joints can get dislocated as well.
4) The bone is pulled out of its normal position — again, it's twisting that usually does it.
5) This can damage the ligaments, muscles and tendons around the joint too.

This type of injury is common in sports like football and rugby.

See page 7 for more about cartilage.

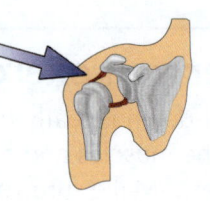

Dislocated shoulder
Humerus pulled out of joint.

Section Three — Physical Training

Injuries and Treatment

You can treat injuries using the RICE method — Rest, Ice, Compression and Elevation.

Broken Bones are Called Fractures

1) A fracture is a break in a bone. It's usually accompanied by bruising and swelling.
2) This is because a fracture also damages the blood vessels in or around the bone.
3) It'll also cause a lot of pain because of the damaged nerves inside the bone.
4) There are four types of fracture you need to know:

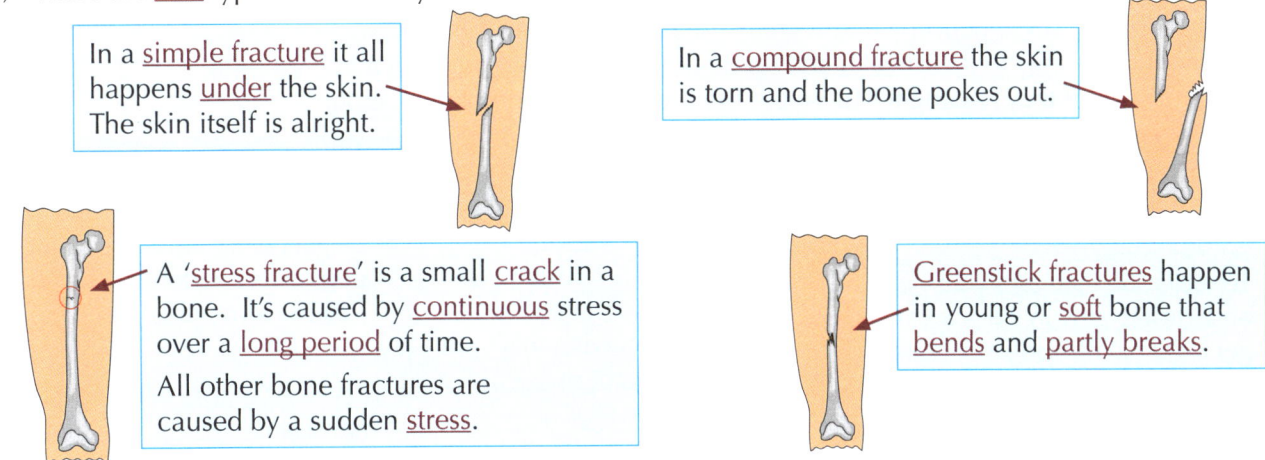

In a simple fracture it all happens under the skin. The skin itself is alright.

In a compound fracture the skin is torn and the bone pokes out.

A 'stress fracture' is a small crack in a bone. It's caused by continuous stress over a long period of time.
All other bone fractures are caused by a sudden stress.

Greenstick fractures happen in young or soft bone that bends and partly breaks.

Concussion is Caused by a Blow to the Head

1) A concussion is a mild brain injury caused by a nasty blow to the head.
2) The symptoms of concussion are: disorientation, memory loss and possibly loss of consciousness.
3) If someone with concussion is unconscious, check they've not injured their neck or spine, then place them in the recovery position (with the head tilted so the airway won't be blocked by the tongue or by vomit) and get an ambulance. If they're conscious, keep them under observation for at least 48 hours.

Use the RICE Method to Treat Injuries

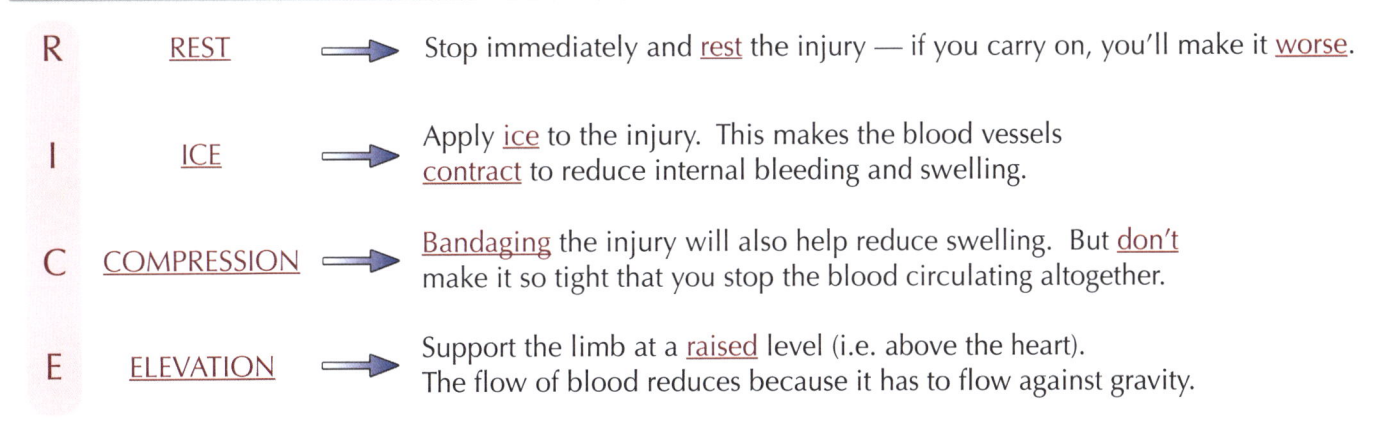

R	REST	→	Stop immediately and rest the injury — if you carry on, you'll make it worse.
I	ICE	→	Apply ice to the injury. This makes the blood vessels contract to reduce internal bleeding and swelling.
C	COMPRESSION	→	Bandaging the injury will also help reduce swelling. But don't make it so tight that you stop the blood circulating altogether.
E	ELEVATION	→	Support the limb at a raised level (i.e. above the heart). The flow of blood reduces because it has to flow against gravity.

The RICE method is a good treatment for joint and muscle injuries like sprains or strains. It reduces pain, swelling and bruising. But, if there's an injury to the neck or spine, it's best not to move the person.

RICE — Rest, Ice, Compression, Elevation...

RICE is a really handy way of remembering how to treat injuries. But it's not so easy with the different types of fracture — you'll just have to keep scribbling down the names and descriptions of each one.

Section Three — Physical Training

Performance-Enhancing Drugs

Some people cheat by taking drugs. Drugs can help them perform better, but they can also cause serious health problems. You need to know the positive and negative effects of these drugs on the performer...

Performance-Enhancing Drugs can Improve Performance

1) Some performers use drugs to improve their performance and be more successful in their sport, which can lead to wealth and fame. Some performers also claim they use drugs to level the playing field — if other competitors use drugs, you're at a disadvantage unless you use them too.
2) The use of these drugs in sport is usually banned, and they can have nasty side effects.
3) Unfortunately, some performers still break the rules by taking them anyway — even with the risks to their health and reputation and to the reputation and credibility of their sport if they're caught. These are the drugs you need to know about:

See p112 for more about punishments for using drugs.

ANABOLIC STEROIDS (AGENTS)
- Mimic the male sex hormone testosterone.
- Testosterone increases your bone and muscle growth (so you can get bigger and stronger). It can also make you more aggressive.

But...
- They can cause high blood pressure, heart disease and infertility, and can increase the risk of developing cancer.
- Women may grow facial and body hair, and their voice may deepen.

DIURETICS
- Increase the amount you urinate, causing weight loss — which may be important if you're competing in a certain weight division.
- Can mask traces of other drugs in the body.

But...
- They can cause cramp, dehydration, loss of salts, muscle weakness and heart damage.

NARCOTIC ANALGESICS
- Kill pain — so injuries and fatigue, e.g. from overtraining, don't affect performance and training so much.

But...
- They're addictive, with unpleasant withdrawal symptoms.
- Feeling less pain can make an athlete train too hard, causing overtraining.
- They can lead to constipation and low blood pressure.

PEPTIDE HORMONES
- Cause the production of other hormones — similar to anabolic steroids.
- EPO (Erythropoietin) is a peptide hormone that causes the body to produce more red blood cells.
- GH (Growth Hormones) are peptide hormones that make the body build more muscle.

But...
- They can cause strokes and heart problems. GH can also cause abnormal growth and diabetes.

STIMULANTS
- Affect the central nervous system (the bits of your brain and spine that control your reactions).
- They can increase mental and physical alertness.

But...
- They can lead to high blood pressure, heart and liver problems, and strokes.
- They're addictive.

BETA BLOCKERS
- Reduce heart rate, muscle tension, blood pressure and the effect of adrenaline. This steadies shaking hands, which improves fine motor skills, and has a calming, relaxing effect.

But...
- They can cause nausea, weakness, low blood pressure, cramp and heart failure.
- They're banned in some sports and if allowed must be prescribed by a medical professional.

Blood Doping is Banned

You can improve your performance by increasing the number of red blood cells in your bloodstream to increase the oxygen supply to your muscles. Blood doping is a form of cheating that increases a performer's number of red blood cells unfairly. It can be done in one of two ways:

1) Before a competition a performer can be injected with red blood cells. Possible side effects of injecting red blood cells include allergic reactions, kidney damage, blood thickening, blocked blood vessels (embolism) and increased risk of heart attack. If the blood is from someone else there's also the risk of catching viruses like HIV.
2) Performers can also take EPO to increase their red blood cell count (see peptide hormones above).

Section Three — Physical Training

Warm-up and Worked Exam Questions

Coming up — two pages of questions about injuries and performance-enhancing drugs. Look over the aptly named warm-up and worked exam questions before you try the exam questions for yourself.

Warm-Up Questions

1) Why is a PARQ carried out?
2) Why might a performer include practice actions in their warm-up?
3) Give an example of something that can be done after a training session to help prevent injury.
4) Name a joint injury caused by overuse.
5) List four types of fracture.
6) Why is ice used to treat injuries?
7) Give one negative side effect of beta blockers.

Worked Exam Questions

1 Complete the table below about performance-enhancing drugs to identify **one** effect on performance and **one** negative side effect of each drug. *(Grade 1-3)*

Name of Drug	Drug's effect on performance	Negative side effect
Stimulants	increase alertness	high blood pressure
narcotic analgesics	kill pain so athlete can train for longer/harder	constipation
EPO	more red blood cells — can exercise for longer	heart problems
Diuretics	weight loss caused by frequent urination	dehydration

[4 marks]

2 Many sports performers suffer from injuries during their careers.

(a) Explain the difference between a sprain and a strain. *(Grade 1-3)*

A sprain is a joint injury where a ligament is stretched or torn, whereas a strain is a tear in a muscle or tendon.

[2 marks]

(b) Describe how to treat a strain. *(Grade 3-5)*

Rest the injury, apply ice to it, then apply compression using a bandage and elevate the injured body part so that it is higher than the heart.

Don't just say RICE — say what you would actually do.

[4 marks]

Exam Questions

1 James regularly takes part in training sessions with a running club. At the beginning of each training session, he jogs lightly for ten minutes to warm up. *(Grade 3-5)*

Explain how this warm-up could help James to avoid injury during a training session.

....

....

....

[2 marks]

2 Mrs Costanza is a PE teacher. She has started an after school hockey club. She always makes sure that students warm up before playing, and cool down afterwards.

(a) State **three** more actions she can take to reduce the risk of injury to students during hockey club. *(Grade 3-5)*

1 ....

2 ....

3 ....

[3 marks]

(b) Explain how **two** of the actions listed above can reduce the risk of injury for hockey players. *(Grade 5-7)*

1 ....

....

2 ....

....

[4 marks]

3 Explain what is meant by the term 'blood doping' and what effect it can have on performance. *(Grade 5-7)*

....

....

....

[3 marks]

Section Three — Physical Training

Revision Questions for Section Three

Phew, Physical Training was a long section — now, time to see how much of it sank in.
- Try these questions and tick off each one when you get it right.
- When you've done all the questions for a topic and are completely happy with it, tick off the topic.

Health and Fitness (p36) ☐
1) Write a definition of fitness.
2) Write a definition of performance.
3) Give two ways that exercise can help to keep you healthy.

Components of Fitness (p37-40) ☐
4) What is cardiovascular endurance?
5) Give an example of a sport where muscular endurance is important.
6) Define flexibility. Give one benefit of increased flexibility for an athlete.
7) Describe coordination. How does having good coordination help a sprinter?
8) What is power? Give an example of when power would be needed in golf.

Fitness Testing (p41-46) ☐
9) Describe the Harvard step test. Which component of fitness does it measure?
10) Outline a fitness test that measures: a) speed, b) power, c) muscular endurance, d) agility.
11) Which component of fitness does the sit and reach test measure? What units are the results in?
12) What is meant by a reliable fitness test?

Training Principles and Methods (p50-59) ☐
13) Name five important principles of training.
14) What are the four principles of FITT?
15) Describe how to calculate your anaerobic target zone.
16) Describe the interval training method. Give an advantage and a disadvantage.
17) Which component of fitness does plyometric training improve?
18) How is overload achieved in circuit training?
19) Describe common differences in pre-season and playing-season training programmes.

Injuries and Treatment (p63-67) ☐
20) What does PARQ stand for? Should it be used before or after a training programme?
21) Outline two benefits of warming up and two benefits of cooling down.
22) Name the soft tissue damaged in: a) an abrasion, b) a sprain, c) a strain.
23) Give three symptoms of a concussion.
24) What does RICE stand for? Give two types of injury that can be treated with the RICE method.

Performance-Enhancing Drugs (p68) ☐
25) Describe the positive and negative effects of: a) beta blockers, b) diuretics, c) stimulants.
26) Which performance-enhancing drugs mimic the male sex hormone testosterone?

Health, Fitness and Well-being

Regular physical activity helps you to be healthy by improving your physical, emotional and social health and well-being. First up, the obvious one — exercise helps keep you physically healthy...

If your Body Works Well, you are Physically Healthy

See p25 for more about how exercise benefits your body systems.

1) Physical health and well-being is an important part of being healthy and happy.
2) Taking part in sport or other physical activities has loads of physical benefits.

PHYSICAL HEALTH AND WELL-BEING:
1) Your body's organs, e.g. the heart, and systems, e.g. the cardiovascular system, are working well.
2) You're not suffering from any illnesses, diseases or injuries.
3) You're strong and fit enough to easily do everyday activities.

1) By exercising you can improve components of fitness (see p37-40), which benefits your physical health:
- Aerobic exercise improves your cardiovascular endurance — your heart, blood vessels and lungs work more efficiently, so you can exercise more intensely and for longer. Your blood pressure also decreases.
- Exercise can benefit your musculo-skeletal system — muscles and bones get stronger, and joints more flexible.
- Exercise can improve body composition — you can attain a healthy weight, which reduces strain on your body.

2) These positive effects on the body reduce the risk of obesity and other long-term health problems (see below). Stronger muscles and more flexible joints can make injury less likely and improve your posture. Avoiding injury also means you can continue training.

3) Physical activity makes you stronger and fitter — so everyday tasks like climbing stairs and lifting shopping are easier. This can help your emotional well-being too (see next page). It's not all good though — overtraining (see p51) can have a negative effect on your health.

Exercise Reduces Risks to Long-Term Health

Regular physical activity can help reduce the risks of you getting certain diseases. For example:

1) Regular aerobic exercise helps prevent high blood pressure by keeping your heart strong and arteries elastic, and helping to remove cholesterol from artery walls.
2) This means blood can flow easily round the body, which reduces the risk of coronary heart disease (CHD), strokes and damage to your arteries.

Exercise increases levels of high density lipoprotein (HDL). HDL helps to remove cholesterol from the arteries.

Type-2 diabetes is a disease that gives you a high blood sugar level. Your blood sugar level is controlled by a hormone called insulin. If you have diabetes, this means you don't have enough insulin or your body's cells aren't reacting to insulin properly (they're insulin-resistant).
Regular exercise helps you avoid diabetes in two ways:
1) Regular exercise helps you maintain a healthy weight. This makes you far less likely to get diabetes.
2) Regular exercise helps improve how sensitive to insulin your cells are. This means you are less likely to become insulin-resistant.

Middle-aged and older adults have a far higher risk of diabetes, so exercise is a great way for them to lower that risk.

Regular exercise helps prevent obesity. Exercise uses up energy, meaning that your body doesn't store it as fat (see p83).

Weight-bearing exercise can help to prevent osteoporosis — a disease where your bones become fragile. As you get older, the risk of osteoporosis increases. Weight-bearing exercise, where your legs and feet support your whole body weight (like aerobics or running), helps to strengthen your bones by increasing bone density.

Section Four — Health, Fitness and Well-being

Health, Fitness and Well-being

As well as making you physically healthy, exercise is great for your emotional and social health. You need to be able to give examples of how and why exercise can help you emotionally and socially.

Emotional Health is about how you Feel

1) Being healthy is more than just having a body that works well — you also have to take into account how you feel. Your emotional health and well-being is based on how you feel about yourself and how you respond to different situations.
2) Taking part in physical activity and sport can have emotional benefits:

EMOTIONAL HEALTH AND WELL-BEING:
1) You feel content and confident in yourself.
2) You are able to manage your emotions and cope with challenges.
3) You don't have too much stress or anxiety.
4) You're not suffering from any mental illnesses.

1) Physical activity can increase your self-esteem (your opinion of yourself) and confidence and generally make you feel better about yourself, e.g. if you feel you've achieved something. Seeing improvements in your physical health, e.g. losing weight or gaining strength, can improve your self-image.
2) Competing against others (or yourself) can improve your ability to deal with pressure and manage emotions, e.g. by giving you a controlled way to channel your aggression. It's also a great way for young children to learn these skills.
3) Doing physical activity can help relieve stress and tension by taking your mind off whatever's worrying you and by making you feel happier. This helps prevent stress-related illnesses.

4) When you do physical activity, the level of endorphins in your brain increases. Endorphins help you to feel good, which can reduce your risk of mental illnesses like depression. Exercise also increases the level of serotonin in your brain. This may help reduce the risk of mental illness, as low levels of serotonin are connected with depression.

Social Health is about how you Relate to Society

1) Your social health and well-being is about how you interact with others and form relationships.
2) There can be plenty of social benefits from doing physical activity and sport:

SOCIAL HEALTH AND WELL-BEING:
1) You have friends.
2) You believe you have some worth in society.
3) You have food, clothing and shelter.

1) Doing physical activity can help you make friends with people of different ages and backgrounds. For example, some elderly folk may have fewer opportunities to socialise, so sport can be a great way to make new friends. It's also a great way of socialising with your current friends.
2) By taking part in team activities like football, you have to practise teamwork — how to cooperate and work with other people. These skills are useful in all walks of life and can help you to be successful, which will increase your sense of worth. Being part of a team can help you to feel more involved in society as a whole.

3) For many people, physical activity probably won't put a roof over their heads. But the skills you learn through exercise and sport can help you succeed at work as well as at the gym or on the playing field. Being physically fit can also help if your job involves manual labour or being on your feet all day.

How about a little revision to get the endorphins flowing...

These benefits are less obvious than those on the last page — especially the social health ones. But take your time and jot them down again and again until you've got them all stored away and memorised.

Section Four — Health, Fitness and Well-being

Lifestyle Choices

Lifestyle choices — like how you eat and drink, whether or not you smoke and how much sleep you get — will all have a knock-on effect on your fitness and your health. So, choose wisely and read this whole page.

Key Lifestyle Choices — Think DRAW

There are four areas of lifestyle choices that you need to know — Diet, Recreational drugs, Activity level and your Work/rest/sleep balance. The first letters spell DRAW, which is handy for remembering them.

1) Diet

Pages 79-81 cover diet in more depth...

1) A balanced diet helps support a healthy lifestyle. Your body needs the right nutrients to work well — and these nutrients provide energy so you can exercise and improve your health.
2) A diet that's too high in some fats, sugar or salt can have negative effects on your health and can increase the risk of obesity. Too much salt can also increase blood pressure. This increases the risk of strokes and heart disease.
3) Not eating enough is also dangerous and can lead to malnutrition — this is where the body does not have enough nutrients to maintain good health.

2) Recreational Drugs — Alcohol and Nicotine

ALCOHOL

1) Alcohol affects your coordination, speech and judgement. Your reaction time gets slower.
2) Drinking large amounts often causes an increase in blood pressure, so increases your risk of stroke and heart disease.
3) Eventually, heavy drinking will damage your liver, heart, muscles, brain and the digestive and immune systems.

SMOKING

1) The chemicals in cigarette smoke cause damage to cells in the lungs and small hairs in your windpipe called cilia.
2) This increases the risk of getting infections, which can lead to bronchitis (inflammation of the major airways) or pneumonia (inflammation deep in the lungs).
3) The damage to alveoli causes them to lose their shape, so they work less efficiently. This is called emphysema.
4) The damage to your lungs can also cause lung cancer.
5) Tobacco also contains the addictive drug nicotine, which raises your heart rate and blood pressure.

Any damage to the lungs makes breathing more difficult, so affects fitness and performance.

3) Activity Level

To be healthy, you need to be active. See p72-73 for all the positive effects of physical activity and how it can reduce health risks. There's more about the impact of an inactive lifestyle on the next page.

To improve health and fitness, you can design a personal exercise programme (PEP — see p50). Your PEP should be tailored to your individual needs and monitored so you get the benefits you want.

4) Work/Rest/Sleep Balance

1) You need to make time to rest and relax after work to help relieve any stress or anxiety you're feeling.
2) If you're feeling stressed, your blood pressure increases. If this continues over a long period of time, it increases the risk of heart disease and strokes.
3) Stress and anxiety also affects your emotional well-being. They can cause insomnia (trouble sleeping) and depression.
4) Sleep is vital for your body as it allows it to rest and recover after a day's work.
5) Lack of sleep affects your ability to concentrate. It also makes you uncoordinated and your muscles become fatigued quicker. In the long term it can lead to anxiety and depression.

Section Four — Health, Fitness and Well-being

Sedentary Lifestyle

You've read all about the benefits of exercise, now you need to learn about the risks of a sedentary lifestyle.

A Sedentary Lifestyle has Many Long-term Health Risks

Basically, if you have a sedentary lifestyle, it means you don't exercise enough:

A sedentary lifestyle is one where there is little, irregular or no physical activity.

1) If you aren't active enough, you don't use up all the energy you get from food. Any excess energy is stored as fat, which increases your risk of becoming overweight, overfat or even obese.

| Being OVERWEIGHT means weighing more than is normal. | Being OVERFAT means having more body fat than you should. | Being OBESE means having a lot more body fat than you should. |

2) Being overfat (or obese) puts more strain on your cardiovascular system and decreases cardiovascular endurance. Increased body fat can also lead to high cholesterol and fatty deposits in the arteries, making it harder for the heart to pump blood. This increases blood pressure and the risk of strokes and coronary heart disease.

If you're inactive but skinny, you're still at risk of health problems.

3) You are also more likely to develop type-2 diabetes if you are obese (see p72), and are more at risk of getting certain cancers.

4) Being overweight decreases flexibility, speed and agility, so affects your performance too.

5) A sedentary lifestyle also affects the musculo-skeletal system. By not exercising enough, the body loses muscle tone, joints get stiffer and bones become weaker — increasing the risk of osteoporosis. Being overweight puts strain on your back and joints. This can lead to bad posture and joint damage.

6) A sedentary lifestyle and obesity can cause lethargy (always feeling tired) and poor sleep, and lead to emotional health problems like low confidence and self-esteem, poor body image and depression. These problems can affect social health if it becomes hard to go out and socialise with others.

Data About Health Issues can be Plotted as a Graph

You can analyse data on health issues to understand how things are changing over time. This allows you to spot trends and make predictions about the future.

Here's an example of the kind of graph you could get in your exam:

- You can either describe what's happening over time (see 1), or at certain points in time (see 2 and 3).

- Be specific — give the exact dates for the part of the graph you're describing — e.g. 'in 2010', 'from 1993 to 2009'.

- Make sure you say enough to get all the marks.

- If you're asked to describe or predict a trend from the graph, you need to look at the graph as a whole to see whether it is going up or going down in the long term. Then you need to predict whether this is likely to continue. E.g. in the graph above, there's a general upward trend in obesity rates for men and women. This trend looks like it will continue for men, but rates for women have started decreasing.

Percentage of obese adults (16+) in England from 1993 to 2013

1) From 1993 to 2009, women had a higher obesity rate than men.
2) In 2009 obesity rates for men and women were lower than they were in 2008.
3) In 2010, men had a higher obesity rate than women for the first time.

Source: Health Survey for England 2014. Health and Social Care Information Centre.

Section Four — Health, Fitness and Well-being

Warm-Up and Worked Exam Questions

There's a lot of stuff to know squeezed onto those four pages, so there's three pages of questions here to check that it's all sunk in. If there are questions here you struggle with, go back and read that page again.

Warm-Up Questions

1) What long-term effect can regular exercise have on blood pressure?
2) Explain how exercise can lead to an increase in someone's self-esteem.
3) What is meant by social well-being?
4) What effect can alcohol have on blood pressure?
5) Which chemical in tobacco is addictive?
6) Give one way that being overweight could affect performance.

Worked Exam Questions

1 Khalid has just started a new job and is finding that he is feeling more stressed than he used to. A friend suggests that doing regular exercise may help.

(a) Explain how regular exercise could help Khalid. *(Grade 3-5)*

Exercise could help take Khalid's mind off the things he is worried about which could help to reduce his stress levels.

Remember that you need to link your answer back to the fact that Khalid is feeling stressed. *[2 marks]*

(b) State **two** ways exercise could help Khalid's social well-being. *(Grade 1-3)*

1 *It could give him an opportunity to meet new people and make new friends.*

2 *If he joins a team he will have the opportunity to practise teamwork and cooperation with others.*

[2 marks]

2 Assess the impact of lack of sleep on performance in gymnastics. *(Grade 5-7)*

Lack of sleep will negatively affect a gymnast's performance because it can reduce coordination and concentration. This would affect a gymnast's ability to move their limbs in a controlled way or focus on their routine. This could mean that they would struggle to carry out complex gymnastics moves skilfully, such as a dismount from the uneven bars.

[3 marks]

Section Four — Health, Fitness and Well-being

Exam Questions

1 Which of the following describes the effect of nicotine on the body?

    A It raises heart rate and blood pressure ☐
    B It damages cilia, leading to a higher risk of infection ☐
    C It damages alveoli, causing emphysema ☐
    D It increases the risk of pneumonia ☐

[1 mark]

2 Which of the following is an emotional benefit of exercise?

    A Regular exercise makes you stronger and more flexible ☐
    B Regular exercise helps you maintain a healthy weight ☐
    C Regular exercise improves your cardiovascular system ☐
    D Regular exercise can help to increase self-esteem ☐

[1 mark]

3 Complete the following statement about the effect of exercise on the brain.

Exercise increases the level of endorphins and .... in your brain, which may make you feel happier and help to reduce the risk of depression.

[1 mark]

4 Explain **one** way that regular exercise helps to prevent type-2 diabetes.

....
....
....
....

[2 marks]

Section Four — Health, Fitness and Well-being

Exam Questions

5   **Figure 1** shows the proportion of smokers in Great Britain from 1974 to 2012.

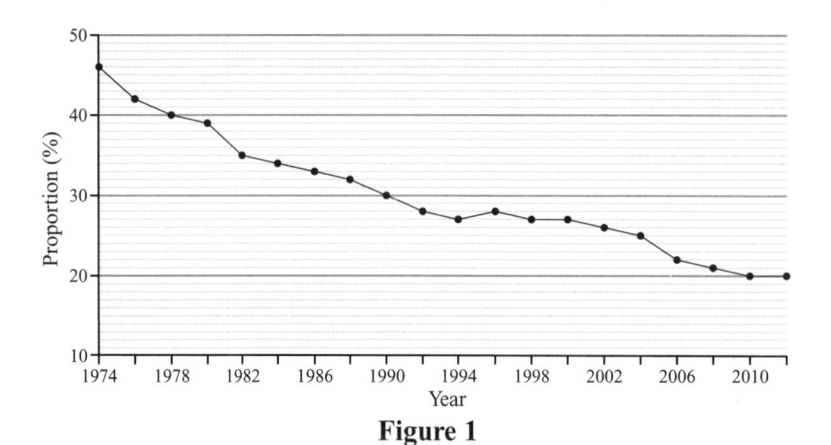

Figure 1

(a) State the proportion of people who smoked in 2002.

....
[1 mark]

(b) Analyse **Figure 1** and state the trend shown.

....
[1 mark]

6   A sedentary lifestyle can lead to a wide range of health problems.

(a) Define a **sedentary lifestyle**.

....
[1 mark]

(b) State two possible long-term effects of a sedentary lifestyle on the musculo-skeletal system.

1 ....

2 ....
[2 marks]

(c) Explain how exercise can help to prevent the long-term effects described in (b).

1 ....

....

2 ....

....
[4 marks]

Diet and Nutrition

A big part of being healthy is having a balanced diet. This means getting the right amount of nutrients to support your lifestyle. How much the 'right amount' is depends on lots of personal factors...

You Should Eat a Balanced Diet to be Healthy

1) Eating a balanced diet is an important part of being healthy and helps you perform well in sport.
2) What makes up a balanced diet is slightly different for everyone — e.g. if you exercise loads, you need more high-energy foods than someone who doesn't. You need the right energy balance (see p83).

> **A balanced diet contains the best ratio of nutrients to match your lifestyle.**

3) The 'best ratio' means the right amount of each nutrient in relation to the other nutrients. There isn't one type of 'superfood' that has everything your body needs — you need a mix of foods.
4) A balanced diet supports your lifestyle by providing the nutrients your body needs for energy, growth and hydration. It helps prevent health problems and injury, and to speed up recovery following exercise.

You Need More of Some Nutrients Than Others

There are two main groups of nutrients your body needs:

Macronutrients — nutrients your body needs in large amounts.

Micronutrients — nutrients your body still needs, but in smaller amounts.

On top of these, you also need plenty of water and fibre in your diet (see next page).
The best way to get all of these nutrients is to eat a varied diet with plenty of fruit and vegetables.

Carbohydrates, Fats and Proteins Give You Energy

Carbohydrates, fats and proteins are macronutrients — they make up a lot of your food.
They provide you with energy and help you grow and repair.

CARBOHYDRATES

1) For most people, carbohydrates are the main source of energy for the body. Carbohydrates are vital for providing energy for your muscles during physical activity.
2) You can get simple ones like sugar, and complex ones, e.g. starch from pasta or rice.
3) Whenever you eat carbohydrates, some will get used by the body straight away.
4) The rest gets stored in the liver and muscles, ready for when it's needed (or turned into fat).

FATS

1) Fats are made from molecules called fatty acids.
2) They provide energy for low-intensity exercise. They also help to keep the body warm and protect organs, which helps to prevent injury.
3) Some vitamins can only be absorbed by the body using fats.
4) Fats are a source of the 'essential fatty acids' omega-3 and omega-6.

This pie chart shows the rough amounts of each macronutrient an average person should eat.

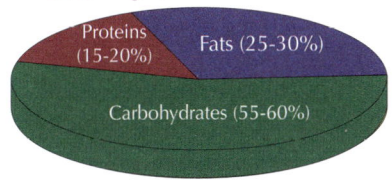

Proteins (15-20%)
Fats (25-30%)
Carbohydrates (55-60%)

PROTEINS

1) Proteins help the body grow and repair itself. They're vital for building and repairing muscles after exercise.
2) They're made from molecules called amino acids — your body can make new proteins from the amino acids you get from food.
3) Meat, fish, eggs and beans are all rich in protein.

A balanced diet is a key part of being healthy...

Make sure that you understand how carbohydrates, fats and proteins help you to do physical activity.

Section Four — Health, Fitness and Well-being

Diet and Nutrition

Vitamins and minerals are micronutrients. They're just as important as macronutrients in a balanced diet.

You need Small Amounts of Vitamins and Minerals

VITAMINS

1) Vitamins help your bones, teeth, skin and other tissues to grow. They're also needed for many of the body's chemical reactions, e.g. some are used in the processes that release energy from food.
2) Fat-soluble vitamins can be stored in the body. Here are a couple of examples:
   - Vitamin A — needed for your growth and vision. It can be found in meat, fish and eggs.
   - Vitamin D — needed for strong bones so helps to prevent injury and osteoporosis. It can be made by the skin in sunshine, but it's also found in milk, fish, liver and eggs.
3) Water-soluble vitamins can't be stored, so you need to eat them regularly. For example:
   - Vitamin C — good for your skin and helps to hold your body tissues together. It's also really important for your immune system, so helps you to stay healthy so you can train and perform well. It's found in fruit and veg — especially in lemons, oranges and other citrus fruit.

MINERALS

1) Needed for healthy bones and teeth, and to build other tissues.
2) Minerals help in various chemical reactions in the body:
   - Calcium — needed for strong bones and teeth, but also for muscle contraction. Lots in green vegetables, milk and cheese.
   - Iron — used in making red blood cells, which carry oxygen round the body, e.g. to the muscles. There's tons in beans and green vegetables.

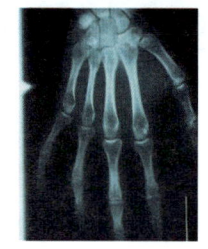

Water and Fibre are Just as Important

WATER

1) Water is needed in loads of chemical reactions in the body. It's also used in sweat to help you cool down when your body temperature rises, e.g. through exercise. As well as sweating, you also lose water through your breath, urine and faeces.
2) If you don't drink enough to replace the water you've used or lost, you become dehydrated. This means your body doesn't have enough water to work well — it's not hydrated. This can cause:
   - Blood thickening — you guessed it, the blood gets thicker (more viscous). This makes it harder for the heart to pump the blood around — it has to work harder and beat faster. It also decreases the flow of oxygen to the muscles, so you can't perform as well.
   - An increase in body temperature, as without enough water the body can't sweat effectively. This can cause overheating and maybe even fainting through heat exhaustion.
   - Muscle fatigue and cramps, which could mean you have to stop doing an activity.
   - Slower reactions and poor decision-making, as your brain needs water to function well.
3) Rehydration with water or sports drinks during and after physical activity helps avoid dehydration. This is important in endurance events and hot climates where you sweat more.
4) Sports drinks have sugar in them to replace the energy your muscles have used up. They also contain a bit of salt which helps the water rehydrate you quickly.
5) If you drink too much water, you can become overhydrated. This can lead to headaches, nausea and confusion.

FIBRE

1) You need fibre to keep your digestive system working properly. Good digestion means that your body gets all the nutrients it needs from food, so you're healthy and can do physical activity.
2) There's lots of fibre in fruit and vegetables — another good reason to eat loads of them.

Diet isn't just what you eat — staying hydrated is important too...

Make sure you understand how being dehydrated can have a negative effect on performance.

Section Four — Health, Fitness and Well-being

Diet, Nutrition and Performance

The timing of meals is an important part of a performer's diet. You need to know how your diet can affect your performance and how different activities need different nutrients at different times.

Different Types of Physical Activity Require Different Nutrients

1) The type of physical activity you are doing affects the balance of nutrients you need.
2) If your activity involves long periods of continuous exercise, like competing in a triathlon, you need a diet rich in carbohydrates. This is because carbohydrates provide plenty of energy that is easily available for your muscles. Fat is also an important energy source for endurance athletes as it can provide energy for low to moderate intensity exercise when supplies of carbohydrates are running low.
3) If your activity involves gaining muscle bulk — like sprinting or weightlifting, you need a diet rich in protein in order to build and repair your muscles.
4) Carrying around extra weight as fat can affect performance. So, for many physical activities, you will want a diet that helps keep body fat low.
5) Hydration (the body having the right amount of water) is really important when you're exercising (see p80). It's especially important to take in water during activities where you sweat a lot and have an increased breathing rate for a long period of time.

Organise Your Meals Around Activities

It's not just what you eat — when you eat is really important too if you want to perform well.
1) You should drink to replace lost fluid both during and after an activity (see previous page).
2) You shouldn't eat during exercise, or for a couple of hours before, due to blood shunting:

> When you exercise, blood is redistributed around the body to increase the supply of oxygen to your muscles (see p23).
> This means blood is taken away from your digestive system — which makes it harder for you to digest food, so you end up feeling sick.

3) After exercise, within an hour, you should start eating to replace used energy.

Endurance Athletes use Carbohydrate Loading Before Events

1) Endurance athletes will often increase their carbohydrate intake a few days before an event.
2) They'll also take it easy in training just before the event, so that most of those carbohydrates are not used up.
3) This increases the amount of energy the athlete has stored in their muscles, giving them plenty of energy for the event.

Timing Protein Intake Helps Muscle Growth

1) The body isn't as good at storing protein as it is at storing some other nutrients. This means power athletes, like weightlifters and body-builders, will eat protein regularly so it's available for muscle growth and repair.
2) They might also take in protein at certain times to maximise their muscle growth. E.g. within an hour of doing a workout — when the muscles need to recover and repair themselves, so need protein to rebuild.
3) Also, your body repairs itself while you sleep, so power athletes will make sure they get plenty of protein before bed.

Blood shunting is as pleasant as it sounds...
Make sure you know who can benefit from carbohydrate loading and timing protein intake, and why.

Section Four — Health, Fitness and Well-being

Somatotypes

Somatotype means the basic shape of your body. Your somatotype can affect your suitability for a particular sport. You only need to read this page if you're doing the AQA course.

Somatotypes are Body Types

There are three basic somatotypes — ectomorph, mesomorph and endomorph. Very few people are a perfect example of one of these body types — pretty much everyone is a mixture. You can think of these basic somatotypes as extremes — at the corners of a triangular graph.

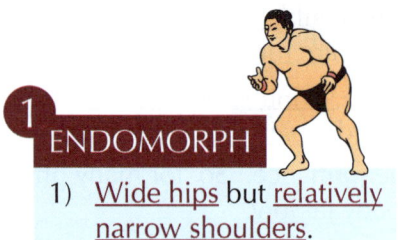

1 ENDOMORPH
1) Wide hips but relatively narrow shoulders.
2) A lot of fat on the body, arms and legs.
3) Ankles and wrists are relatively thin.

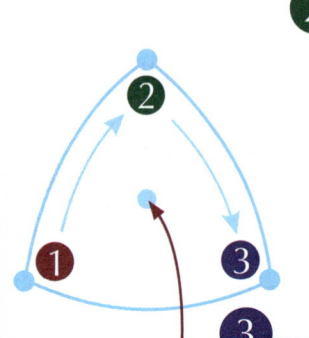

Mr Average would be in the middle of the graph.

2 MESOMORPH
1) Wide shoulders and relatively narrow hips.
2) Muscular body.
3) Strong arms and thighs.
4) Not much body fat.

3 ECTOMORPH
1) Narrow shoulders, hips and chest.
2) Not much muscle or fat.
3) Long, thin arms and legs.

Different Somatotypes suit Different Sports

Certain body types are better suited for certain sports — the right body type can give you an advantage.

Endomorphs are usually best at activities like wrestling and shot-put — where weight and a low centre of mass (see p39) can be an advantage.

E.g. in sumo wrestling, being heavy and having a low centre of mass makes it much harder for your opponent to throw you around the wrestling ring.

Ectomorphs suit activities like the high jump and long-distance running — where being light and having long legs is an advantage. They don't usually suit activities where strength is important.

E.g. high jumpers need to be light so they have less weight to lift over the bar. The taller the jumper, the shorter the distance they (and their centre of mass) have to travel to be able to get over the bar.

Mesomorphs are suited to most types of activity:
1) They're able to build up muscle relatively quickly and easily — which gives them an advantage in any activity where strength is important. E.g. sprinting, tennis, weightlifting...
2) Mesomorphs also have broad shoulders, which make it easier for them to be able to support weight using their upper body. This can be a huge advantage in activities like weightlifting and gymnastics.

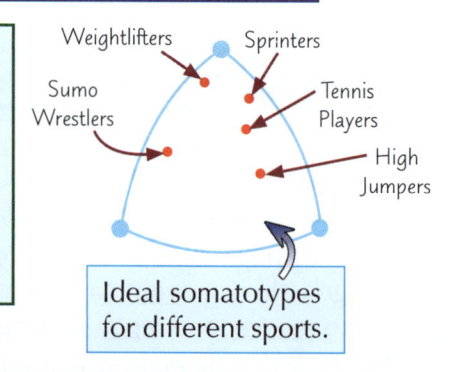

Ideal somatotypes for different sports.

Here's a bunch of long words for you to learn...

REVISION TIP — To remember which somatotype is which, just think that a **M**esomorph is **M**uscular and an ec**T**omorph is **T**hin. So, the one that isn't muscular or thin must be an endomorph.

Section Four — Health, Fitness And Well-being

Optimum Weight

If you're doing the OCR course, skip this page. If you're doing Eduqas, you only need the energy balance bit.

Optimum Weight Depends on Different Things...

Your optimum weight is roughly what you should weigh for good health, based on these four factors that differ from person to person:

1) HEIGHT — The taller someone is, the larger their body, so the higher their optimum weight.
2) BONE STRUCTURE — some people have a larger or more dense bone structure than others. This means their skeleton will be heavier, so their optimum weight will be higher.
3) MUSCLE GIRTH — this is a measurement of the circumference of (the distance around) your muscles when they're flexed. Some people naturally have more muscle than others — they'll have a larger muscle girth and a higher optimum weight.
4) GENDER — men and women naturally have different body compositions. Men usually have larger bone structures and more muscle than women, so men generally have higher optimum weights.

Your Body Mass Index (BMI) score is calculated using your height and weight. A BMI of under 18.5 means underweight, over 25 means overweight and over 30 means obese. BMI doesn't take into account muscle girth or bone structure, so it can incorrectly classify healthy, muscular people as overweight or obese. See page 117 for an example of some BMI data.

Optimum Weight will Vary for Different Sports...

A sportsperson's optimum weight is the weight at which they perform best. Optimum weight will vary depending on the activity or sport — e.g. a sumo wrestler will want to be heavier than a mountain climber.

1) Some sports require competitors to be within a certain weight class — e.g. a boxer's optimum fighting weight needs to be within their weight division.
2) In sports like rugby or American football, players have a large amount of muscle mass because they need strength and power. This means their optimum weight will be higher.
3) Similarly, some sports require performers to be light — e.g. a gymnast needs to hold their own body weight, so being light is an advantage.
4) Endurance athletes will want to be lighter than sprinters as they have to carry their weight for longer. Sprinters need large amounts of muscle to generate power, so have a higher optimum weight.

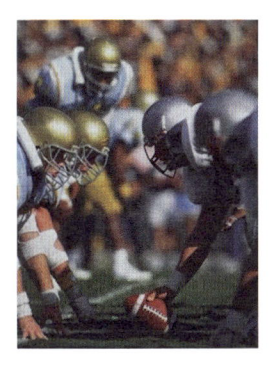

Your Energy Balance controls your Weight

How much energy you need from food depends on how much you use up through bodily processes (like breathing and digestion), daily activities and exercise. This is also affected by your age, height and gender. Your energy balance is the relationship between the energy you take in and the energy you use:

1) If you take in more energy than you use, you have a positive energy balance. Spare energy is stored as fat, which causes you to gain weight.
2) If you don't take in enough food to match the energy you need, you have a negative energy balance. Your body makes up the difference by using up the energy stored in body fat. This causes you to lose weight.
3) If you want to maintain a healthy weight, you need to make sure you balance your energy intake with the energy you use up. This is called a neutral energy balance.
4) Energy from food is measured in calories (Kcal). On average, an adult male needs 2500 calories a day, and an adult female needs 2000 calories a day.

Section Four — Health, Fitness and Well-being

Warm-Up and Worked Exam Questions

There are a lot of facts on the last few pages, so make sure you've got them all with the warm-up and worked exam questions below, and the exam questions on the next two pages.

Warm-Up Questions

1) What percentage of an average person's balanced diet should be made up of carbohydrates?
2) Give one reason why the body needs minerals.
3) Why is fibre an important part of a balanced diet?
4) What is carbohydrate loading? Which type of performer does it benefit?
5) Which somatotype has narrow shoulders, hips and chest?
6) Name a sport that an endomorph is well-suited to play.
7) What weight classification is someone with a BMI of 35?
8) What is meant by 'neutral energy balance'?
9) How many calories does an average adult female need each day?

Worked Exam Questions

1 Explain why a performer taking part in judo would require a higher optimum weight than a gymnast. *(Grade 3-5)*

A gymnast will need to be light, as they have to hold their own body weight.
In judo, being heavy could be an advantage, as it makes the performer harder to throw
to the ground.

[2 marks]

2 Explain how timing of protein intake could improve performance in **one** physical activity or sport. *(Grade 5-7)*

Protein timing is when a performer consumes protein at certain times to maximise
muscle growth — normally one hour after a workout, and just before they go to bed.
This is necessary because protein is not stored well by the body, so intake must be timed
so that protein can be utilised. A weightlifter could use protein timing to help gain
muscle mass which would help them become stronger and lift heavier weights.

[4 marks]

Section Four — Health, Fitness and Well-being

Exam Questions

1 Complete the table below describing the roles of different macronutrients. *Grade 1-3*

Macronutrient	Role in a balanced diet
....	Energy for low-intensity exercise
....	Repairing muscle
Carbohydrates	....

[3 marks]

2 Complete the following statement about energy balance. *Grade 1-3*

Weight gain occurs when more energy is taken in than is used up by the body — this is known as a .... energy balance. To lose weight, more energy must be used up than is taken in — this is known as a .... energy balance.

[2 marks]

3 Chris and Val are both athletes. Chris is a weightlifter and Val is a marathon runner. *Grade 3-5* They want to adapt their diets to improve their performance.

Suggest how each person could adapt their diet, and how this change might help improve their performance.

....
....
....
....

[4 marks]

Section Four — Health, Fitness and Well-being

Exam Questions

4 Maintaining hydration during sport is very important.

(a) State **two** consequences of dehydration. *(Grade 1-3)*

1 ....

2 ....

[2 marks]

(b) Give **one** example of an activity where performers are at a high risk of dehydration. Explain your answer. *(Grade 5-7)*

....

....

[2 marks]

5 Evaluate the importance of carbohydrates and fats for performance in a marathon.

For this question, think about the various roles carbohydrates and fats play in physical activity.

....

....

....

....

....

....

....

....

....

....

....

....

....

....

[9 marks]

Don't forget to come to some sort of conclusion comparing the importance of fats and carbohydrates.

Section Four — Health, Fitness and Well-being

Revision Questions for Section Four

That's it for Section Four. Give yourself a little time to digest all that information, then do these questions...
- Try these questions and tick off each one when you get it right.
- When you've done all the questions for a topic and are completely happy with it, tick off the topic.

Health, Fitness and Well-being (p72-73) ☐

1) Give two physical health benefits of physical activity.
2) What effect does regular aerobic exercise have on blood pressure?
3) Which bone disease can weight-bearing exercise help prevent?
4) How can exercise make you feel good?
5) Give two social health benefits of sport.
6) Physical activity can increase your confidence. Is this a physical, emotional or social benefit?

Lifestyle Choices and a Sedentary Lifestyle (p74-75) ☐

7) How can diet have a positive effect on health?
8) What effect does alcohol have on reaction time?
9) State two health problems that can be caused by smoking.
10) Give one long-term effect of not getting enough sleep.
11) Define a 'sedentary lifestyle'. How is it connected to obesity?
12) What are two health risks associated with a sedentary lifestyle?

Diet and Nutrition (p79-81) ☐

13) What is a 'balanced diet'?
14) Are proteins macronutrients or micronutrients? How about vitamins?
15) Name a macronutrient that provides lots of energy that can easily be used by the body.
16) How does protein help you recover after exercise?
17) Give two reasons why the body needs vitamins.
18) Which mineral is necessary for making red blood cells?
19) Explain what happens to your blood when you become dehydrated.
20) State two effects of overhydration.
21) What role does fibre play in a balanced diet?
22) What type of athlete uses carbohydrate loading?
23) Why might a sprinter have a diet high in protein?

Somatotypes and Optimum Weight (p82-83) ☐

24) Name the three somatotypes and write down their main characteristics.
25) For each somatotype, write down one sport it is suited to.
26) Give three factors that affect optimum weight.
27) What weight classification is someone with a BMI score of 26? Why might this be misleading?
28) If you take in more energy from food than you use up, do you lose weight?
29) How can an athlete maintain a healthy weight?

Section Five — Sport Psychology

Learning Skills

Learning skills and performing them well is really important in PE. If you're doing the AQA or Edexcel course, don't worry about knowing all the characteristics of a skilful movement — they won't come up in your exam.

A Skill is Something You Learn

A 'motor skill' is just a skill that involves movement.

1) Skill is a word we use all the time. Here's what it means in PE:

A SKILL is a learned ability to bring about the result you want with confidence and minimum effort.

2) So a skill is something you've got to learn. You can't be born with a skill, although you might learn it more easily than other people. How easily you learn a skill is based on your ability:

ABILITY is a person's set of characteristics that control their potential to learn a skill.

Different Characteristics make a Movement Skilful

There are some characteristics that make a movement or performance skilful:

PRE-DETERMINED — With any skilled movement, you always have a pre-determined result in mind — you know what you want to do before you start. E.g. if you're passing the ball to someone in hockey you know what type of pass you're going to use and who you want to pass it to.

Check which of these characteristics you need to know for your course.

EFFICIENT — A skilled movement should be efficient and use the minimum amount of energy/time. E.g. a good swimming technique can help you swim faster and for longer.

COORDINATED — Skilled movements are coordinated — they use two or more parts of the body together to get the maximum effect. E.g. a vault in gymnastics requires good arm and leg coordination to produce the necessary lift.

FLUENT AND CONFIDENT — A skilled athlete is able to flow confidently from one skilled movement to another, e.g. punch combinations in boxing.

AESTHETIC — Skilled movements are controlled and look good. In some sports, like gymnastics and figure skating, your skill is judged by the appearance of your movements. Skilled players make skilled movements and techniques look easy, while less skilled players and performers can look awkward and uncoordinated.

EFFECTIVE AND ACCURATE — A skilled athlete can perform a skill accurately to get the result they want.

TECHNICAL — A skilled movement uses the correct technique.

CONSISTENT — Skilled athletes can reliably perform a skill in different conditions.

GOOD DECISION MAKING — Skilled athletes can make good decisions to adapt to their environment, e.g. making tactical decisions to exploit an opponent's weaknesses.

You can describe Skill Level with the Stages of Learning

Beginners and experienced performers of a skill (and people in between) are at different 'stages of learning':

You only need to know this for the Eduqas course.

THE COGNITIVE STAGE	THE ASSOCIATIVE STAGE	THE AUTONOMOUS STAGE
They've just started learning the skill and are still a beginner.	They've learned the techniques involved in the skill, and are focusing on improving them.	They're experienced at performing the skill and can do it almost automatically.

Performers of different skill levels should be coached on their skills in different ways (see pages 94-95).

Skill Classification

This page is all about the different types of skill and how we classify skills. There are quite a few definitions here, so check which ones you need for your course before you look at this page.

There are Different Types of Skill

There are different ways to classify skills:

OPEN VS CLOSED SKILLS

1) An open skill is performed in a changing environment, where a performer has to react and adapt to external factors. E.g. during a football tackle, you need to adapt to things such as the position of other players on the pitch.
2) A closed skill is always performed in the same predictable environment — it's not affected by external factors. E.g. when breaking off in snooker, the conditions are the same every time.

LOW VS HIGH ORGANISATION SKILLS

1) A low organisation skill is one which can easily be broken down into different parts that can be practised separately. E.g. the front crawl stroke in swimming.
2) A high organisation skill is one which can't easily be broken down into different parts that can be practised separately, because the parts of the skill are closely linked. E.g. a cartwheel.

BASIC VS COMPLEX SKILLS

1) A basic skill (or 'simple' skill) is one which doesn't need much concentration to do, e.g. running.
2) A complex skill is one which needs lots of concentration to do, e.g. a volley in football.

SELF- VS EXTERNALLY-PACED SKILLS

1) A self-paced skill starts when a performer decides to start it. Its pace is controlled by the performer.
2) An externally-paced skill starts because of external factors which also control the pace of the skill. E.g. an opponent's actions in football might determine when and how quickly you need to pass the ball.

GROSS VS FINE SKILLS

1) A gross skill involves powerful movements performed by large muscle groups, e.g. the long jump.
2) A fine skill uses smaller muscle groups to carry out precise movements that require accuracy and coordination, e.g. throwing a dart.

You can use a Continuum to Classify Skills

1) Most skills come somewhere in between classifications. You can show this by putting skills on a 'continuum' (or 'scale') with one category on each end.
2) For example, you can compare the "openness" of skills by putting them on a scale like this one:
3) You can also put sport skills on a scale using the other skill classifications, e.g. a scale from basic to complex skills.

CLOSED — Skipping, Throwing a dart, High jump, Catching a cricket ball, Football tackle — OPEN

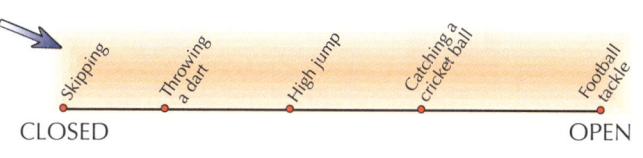

Quick — get learning while there's skill time...

REVISION TASK: Look at the position of 'catching a cricket ball' on the open-closed continuum on this page. Jot down some reasons why you think this skill has been placed at this location on the continuum.

Section Five — Sport Psychology

Practising Skills

To get better at a skill, you need to practise doing it. But first, you need to think about the type of skill and the type of performer learning the skill, so you can decide the best way to improve it.

You need Practice to Improve a Skill

There are different methods you can use to practise skills. Here are six for you to learn:

Massed vs Distributed Practice

MASSED

This means practising the skill continuously without a break. It works well to improve basic skills.

DISTRIBUTED

The breaks can also be used to get feedback on a skill (see p94-95).

This means practising with breaks for rest or mental rehearsal (see p96). It works well to improve complex skills — you might need a break because the skill is difficult.

Fixed vs Variable Practice

FIXED

This means repeating the same technique in one situation over and over again. This makes it useful for practising closed skills, and it's good for beginners to master the basics of a skill. It is sometimes known as doing 'drills'.

VARIABLE

This means repeating the technique in different situations that you might need to use it in. It's useful for practising open skills, and it can work really well for performers as they become more experienced with skills.

Whole vs Part Practice

WHOLE

This means practising the whole technique in one go. It's good for practising basic skills — they're easier to learn all in one go. It works well for experienced performers, since they're more likely to be skilled enough to carry out the entire technique at once.

PART

This means breaking a skill down into parts and practising each bit separately. It's good for improving complex skills that might be difficult to learn all in one go. It works well for beginners — they can practise each part of a skill separately, then put them all together.

REVISION TASK — **Learn this page by practising writing it out...**
Note down a sport skill that could be improved using each of the six practice types on this page.

Section Five — Sport Psychology

Goal Setting

Setting goals and targets can often seem a bit of a hassle. But if you put the effort in and set them properly, not only do you have something to aim for, but reaching your targets can make you feel ace.

Goal Setting can Help you Train

1) Goal setting means setting targets that you want to reach so you can improve your performance.
2) Goal setting helps training by giving you something to aim for, which motivates you to work hard. Also, reaching a goal can boost your confidence and help your emotional well-being (see p73).
3) You can set yourself a performance goal, an outcome goal, or a combination of both:

   PERFORMANCE GOALS — these are based on improving your own personal performance.
   OUTCOME GOALS — these are focused on performing better than other people, e.g. winning.

4) Most of the time, it's better to set performance goals — especially if you're a beginner. Winning might be an unrealistic goal if you're new to a sport, and it can be demotivating if you lose.
5) Also, you can't usually control the result of an outcome goal, as it will depend on how well other people perform.

Goal Setting Should be SMART

When you're setting targets make sure they're SMART.

There are a few different versions of what 'SMART' stands for here — check which one you need for your course.

S ➡ SPECIFIC: Say exactly what you want to achieve.
  1) You need to have a specific target and outline exactly what you need to do to achieve it.
  2) This makes sure you're focused on your goal.
  3) E.g. 'My goal is to swim 1000 m continuously'.

M ➡ MEASURABLE: Goals need to be measurable.
  1) This is so you can see how much you've progressed towards your goal over time — so you stay motivated to train.
  2) E.g. 'My goal is to run 100 m in under 12 seconds'.

'A' can also stand for 'accepted' or 'agreed' — you should agree your goals with your coach.

A ➡ ACHIEVABLE: You need to make sure your targets are set at the right level of difficulty. If a target's too easy, it won't motivate you. If it's too difficult, you might start to feel negative about your performance, and give up.

R ➡ REALISTIC: Set targets you can realistically reach.
  1) This means making sure you have everything you need to be able to fulfil your target.
  2) That could mean being physically able to do something, or having enough resources (time, money, facilities...) to be able to reach your target.
  3) This is so you stay determined during training — if it's not realistic, you could be put off.

'R' can also stand for 'recorded' — you should keep track of your progress.

T ➡ TIME-BOUND/TIME-PHASED/TIMED: Set a deadline for reaching your goal.
  1) You need a time limit to make sure your target is measurable.
  2) Meeting short-term target deadlines keeps you on course to reach your long-term goals in time.
  3) This keeps you motivated — you'll want to train to achieve your goal in time for your deadline.

As well as setting targets, you need to make sure you review them regularly. This is so you can see how much you've progressed towards your goal and what else you need to do to achieve it.

Having goals is a SMART thing...

Make sure you know the reasons for goal setting, what SMART stands for and how it improves performance.

Section Five — Sport Psychology

Warm-Up and Worked Exam Questions

That's the first few pages of this section done, so it's question time. The warm-up questions and worked exam questions will help get you into exam mode before you do the questions on the next page yourself.

Warm-Up Questions

1) What is a performer's 'ability'?
2) Name two characteristics of a skilful movement.
3) At what stage of learning is a performer if they are a beginner — cognitive, associative or autonomous?
4) What is a complex skill?
5) What is the difference between whole and part practice?
6) Give one reason why a performer might want to avoid setting an outcome goal.
7) Why is it important for a target to be achievable?

Worked Exam Questions

1 'SMART' stands for the five principles of goal setting. *(Grade 1-3)*
   Describe the principle that 'S' represents.

   The 'S' in 'SMART' stands for specific, which means a goal should say exactly what the performer wants to achieve.

   [1 mark]

2 Skills can be classified as either high organisation or low organisation. *(Grade 3-5)*
   Explain the difference between a high organisation and low organisation skill, using **one** example of each type of skill from physical activities.

   A high organisation skill cannot easily be broken down into different parts to be practised separately, because the parts of the skill are closely linked. For example, a golf swing must be completed in one whole movement. A low organisation skill can easily be broken down into different parts to be practised separately. For example, a tennis serve can be split into throwing the ball up and the movements with the racket.

   Don't forget to include the examples — they're worth half the marks.   *[4 marks]*

3 Assess the use of distributed practice for improving a somersault. *(Grade 7-9)* Think about the type of skill that a somersault is.

   Distributed practice would be useful for improving a somersault because it is a complex and dangerous skill. Distributed practice is well suited for practising this type of skill, as a performer could use the rest breaks for mental rehearsal or to receive feedback to avoid injuring themselves when performing a somersault.

   [3 marks]

Section Five — Sport Psychology

Exam Questions

1 'Measurable' is one of the principles of goal setting.

   (a) Explain how this principle can be used to improve sports performance. *(Grade 3-5)*

   ....
   ....
   ....
   ....
   [3 marks]

   Layla sets herself a goal to run 5 km in 27 minutes.

   (b) Identify how this goal applies the 'measurable' principle of goal setting. *(Grade 3-5)*

   ....
   ....
   ....
   [1 mark]

   (c) Explain how Layla could apply **two** other principles of goal setting to make her goal more effective. *(Grade 5-7)*

   ....
   ....
   ....
   ....
   [4 marks]

2 Sports skills can be classified using the open-closed continuum. *(Grade 5-7)*
   An example is shown below.

   ```
                      High jump
                         ×
   |─────────────────────────────────────────|
   Closed                                  Open
   ```

   Explain why the high jump may have been placed at this point on the continuum.

   ....
   ....
   ....
   ....
   [3 marks]

Section Five — Sport Psychology

Guidance and Feedback

To learn or improve a skill, you might need some guidance and feedback to help you.

Guidance — How to Perform or Develop a Skill

There are lots of different types of guidance a coach or trainer can give:

Have a look at p89 for definitions of the different skill types.

1) VERBAL — An explanation in words of how to perform a technique.

ADVANTAGES	DISADVANTAGES
1) Can be combined with other types of guidance. 2) Helpful for experienced performers who'll understand any technical language. 3) Can give guidance during a performance. This is especially useful for improving open skills.	1) Less useful for teaching high organisation and complex skills which are difficult to explain. 2) Could be confusing for a beginner if it uses complicated language.

2) VISUAL — Visual clues to help you perform a technique. A coach could use demonstrations or videos and diagrams of a technique to show how it should be performed.

ADVANTAGES	DISADVANTAGES
1) Works well for beginners — they can copy the skill. 2) Can be used to teach low organisation skills — each part of the skill can be shown step by step.	Less useful for teaching complex and high organisation skills — they're more complicated and difficult to copy.

3) MANUAL — When the coach physically moves your body through the technique. For example, a coach might guide your arms when you're practising a golf swing.

ADVANTAGES	DISADVANTAGES
1) You can get the "feel" of a skill before doing it on your own. 2) Works well to teach people of all skill levels.	1) A performer could start to rely on it and not be able to perform a skill without it. 2) Difficult to use with big groups of learners.

Learning by doing an action is known as kinaesthetic learning.

4) MECHANICAL — Guidance given using sport equipment, e.g. a harness in trampolining.

ADVANTAGES	DISADVANTAGES
1) Useful for teaching beginners — they can feel safe while practising a new skill that might normally be dangerous, e.g. a somersault. 2) Helpful for teaching complex and high organisation skills.	1) A learner might be unable to perform the skill without the help of the equipment. 2) Difficult to use in large groups.

Feedback — Finding Out How You Did

1) Feedback can be either intrinsic or extrinsic:

INTRINSIC — you know how well you did the technique because of what it 'felt' like. This works best for experienced performers — they can judge whether or not they've performed well.
EXTRINSIC — someone else tells you or shows you what happened, and how to improve. This is suited to beginners — they don't have the experience or knowledge to accurately assess their own performance.

2) These types of feedback can be either concurrent or terminal:

CONCURRENT FEEDBACK is received during a performance.
TERMINAL FEEDBACK is received after a performance.

3) You can use feedback to work out your strengths and weaknesses and come up with an action plan to improve your performance.

Section Five — Sport Psychology

Using Feedback

More about feedback on this page, and how it's applied when you perform or practise a skill. If you're doing the Edexcel course, you can skip this page and go straight on to the next one.

Feedback can Focus on Different Aspects of a Skill

1) The information in feedback can focus on different parts of a skill or movement. It might focus on:

   KNOWLEDGE OF PERFORMANCE — did you use the correct movements/technique? This can be extrinsic or intrinsic. This type of feedback works well for experienced performers — it helps them to 'fine-tune' a skill that they can already perform.
   KNOWLEDGE OF RESULTS — what was the outcome? This is usually extrinsic and can include data, e.g. your time in a race. This is useful for inexperienced performers — they need to be told whether or not they achieved the right result.

2) Feedback could also focus on what you did well (positive feedback), or what you didn't do well and could improve (negative feedback).

3) It's better to avoid too much negative feedback with beginners — it can put them off learning the skill. Positive feedback is better — it helps them remember which parts of the movement they should repeat.

4) Negative feedback can be useful for experienced performers. It can help to motivate them by setting a goal for them to aim for.

For an example of interpreting feedback data, see p118.

Feedback is part of the Information Processing Model

The information processing model divides the process of performing or practising skills into four stages:

You don't need this bit for the OCR course.

1) INPUT — when you receive information from the environment through your senses, e.g. seeing and hearing what is happening during a game. This stage involves selective attention (see next page).

2) DECISION MAKING — when you decide how to respond to the input. To decide on the best response, you compare what is happening at the time (stored in your short-term memory) with your past experiences of performing the skill (stored in your long-term memory).

4) FEEDBACK — after the output, you receive extrinsic or intrinsic feedback (or both). This helps you to improve the skill next time you perform it.

3) OUTPUT — Your muscles react to messages from the brain telling them what to do to perform the skill.

You can apply this model to analyse a sports skill. For example, when taking a penalty in football:

1) INPUT — You'd need to pay attention to the position of the goalkeeper in front of the net and ignore distractions like noise from the crowd.

2) DECISION MAKING — You'd decide on the best way to perform the penalty by using what you've done in your previous practice of penalties.

3) OUTPUT — Your brain would send information to your muscles to tell them where to aim the shot and how powerfully to kick the ball.

4) FEEDBACK — You'd receive extrinsic feedback, e.g. whether or not you scored the penalty, or your coach telling you what you did right or wrong. You might also get intrinsic feedback. You could learn from this feedback how you could perform a penalty better next time.

Keep going — you're doing really well...

Make sure you learn which types of feedback work best for beginners and more experienced performers.

Section Five — Sport Psychology

Mental Preparation

Who'd have thought it — performing well in sport is about the mind as well as the body...
If you're doing the Edexcel or Eduqas course, you only need to look at the first half of this page.

You can Mentally Prepare for Sport

1) Being mentally prepared is all about being able to get in the 'zone'.
2) It can help you stay focused, confident and motivated, keep control of your emotions and cope with stress so you can perform at your best.
3) There are lots of different techniques to help you mentally prepare:

> 1) MENTAL REHEARSAL is imagining the feeling in the muscles when perfectly performing a skill.
> 2) VISUALISATION involves imagining what an aspect of your performance should look like. It can be used as part of mental rehearsal.
> 3) DEEP BREATHING can help lower your heart rate (which increases when you're anxious) and make you feel more calm.
> 4) IMAGERY is used when you imagine being somewhere or doing something that relaxes you.
> 5) POSITIVE SELF-TALK/THINKING is telling yourself positive things that will motivate you or reassure you that you can perform well.
> 6) SELECTIVE ATTENTION is focusing on important things that will help you perform well, and ignoring things that aren't important.

Techniques 1-5 are also called 'stress-management techniques' — they help lower your arousal level (see below).

4) Practising your skills during a warm-up can also help you mentally prepare (see page 63).

Your Arousal Level shouldn't be Too High or Too Low

1) Your arousal level is how mentally (and physically) alert you are.
2) To perform well you need to have the right arousal level. The relationship between performance and arousal can be shown on an 'inverted-U graph', like this one:
3) The graph shows the 'inverted-U theory', which says that:

> 1) If your arousal level is low, then you're not very excited and you're unlikely to perform well.
> 2) At higher arousal levels, you'll be determined and ready, and should be able to perform your skills well.
> 3) If your arousal level rises too much, you become anxious and nervous. You might become tense, which can cause you to 'choke', so your performance will suffer. You might also become overaggressive.

If you're doing the OCR course, don't worry about this graph — you just need to know the effects of high or low arousal.

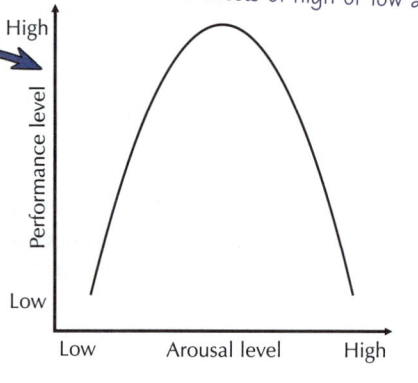

See p89 for the definitions of gross and fine skills.

4) The ideal arousal level varies for different skills in sport.
5) Gross skills require higher arousal levels. E.g. when tackling in football, a higher arousal level will help you commit to putting all of your effort into getting the ball. But if your arousal level is too high, you might end up hurting another player when you tackle them.
6) When performing a fine skill, you need a lower arousal level. E.g. when fielding in cricket, a lower arousal level will help you keep your hands steady to catch the ball. But your arousal level shouldn't be too low — or you won't be alert enough to move into a good position to catch the ball.

Mentally rehearse your exam for guaranteed success...

Being mentally prepared can really help your performance — so it's lucky that there are some handy techniques to help you on your way to being mentally ready for sport. Make sure you learn them all.

Section Five — Sport Psychology

Emotion and Personality

This is the last page to learn in this section — it'll cover types of motivation, aggression and personality. If you're doing the Edexcel or OCR course, you can skip straight on to the questions on the next page.

Motivation makes you Want to Do Well

1) Motivation's about how keen you are to do something.
   It's what drives you on when things get difficult — your desire to succeed.
2) Motivation can be either intrinsic (from yourself) or extrinsic (from outside).

INTRINSIC MOTIVATION
Motivation from the enjoyment and good feelings you get from taking part in physical activity and sport, e.g. pride, high self-esteem.

EXTRINSIC MOTIVATION
Motivation through rewards from other people or sources. This can be tangible (you can touch it, e.g. trophies, money) or intangible (you can't touch it, e.g. applause, praise from a coach).

3) Intrinsic motivation is usually seen as the most effective — you're more likely to try hard in sport and carry on playing it in the long run if you enjoy it.
4) Extrinsic motivation can also be really effective. Rewards or praise about your performance can make you feel good about yourself — so you're more likely to want to perform well again.
5) But if you don't like a sport, extrinsic rewards on their own probably won't motivate you to try very hard at it, or play it regularly. They work better when you're already intrinsically motivated.
6) But some people think that too many extrinsic rewards can actually reduce your intrinsic motivation — so you might start to rely on extrinsic rewards to feel motivated.

Aggression can be Direct or Indirect

You can skip to the revision tip at the bottom of the page if you're doing the Eduqas course.

Aggression doesn't have to be violent — when it's used properly, it can improve your performance in sport.

1) Direct aggression involves physical contact with another person, e.g. pushing against the opposing team in a rugby scrum so you can win the ball.
2) Indirect aggression doesn't involve physical contact — a player gains an advantage by aiming the aggression at an object instead. E.g. a golfer performing a drive would use indirect aggression towards the golf ball to hit it powerfully to the green.

Introverts and Extroverts like Different Sports

The type of sport you like can be affected by your personality. You can describe someone as an introvert or an extrovert based on what their personality is like — most people are somewhere in between.

INTROVERTS are shy, quiet and thoughtful — they like being alone.
1) Introverts usually prefer sports that they can do on their own.
2) They tend to like sports where they'll need fine skills, high concentration and low arousal.
3) For example, archery, snooker and athletics are all suited to introverts.

EXTROVERTS are more sociable — they're talkative and prefer being with other people.
1) Extroverts might get bored when they're alone, so they usually prefer team sports.
2) They also tend to like fast-paced sports that need gross skills and low concentration.
3) For example, hockey, rugby and football are well-suited to extroverts.

I hope you're feeling motivated for your PE exams...

REVISION TIP There's a handy way to remember what 'intrinsic' and 'extrinsic' mean. 'Intrinsic' starts with 'in', so it comes from inside you. 'Extrinsic' starts with 'ex', just like 'exit', so it comes from outside.

Section Five — Sport Psychology

Warm-Up and Worked Exam Questions

Section Five is nearly done — so check you've taken in the last few pages by doing some questions. Make sure you understand the answers below before you try the exam questions on the next page.

Warm-Up Questions

1) Give one advantage of verbal guidance.
2) Where does extrinsic feedback come from?
3) Give one reason why feedback involving knowledge of performance is effective for experienced performers.
4) Describe the 'output' stage of the information processing model.
5) What is meant by 'arousal level'?
6) Who is more likely to play rugby — an extrovert or an introvert?

Worked Exam Questions

1 Define the term **mechanical guidance**. *Grade 1-3*

   Mechanical guidance is when a performer is given help with performing a skill through the use of sports equipment.

   [1 mark]

2 Explain the difference between intrinsic and extrinsic motivation. *Grade 1-3*

   Intrinsic motivation comes from a performer's positive feelings they get from doing something, whereas extrinsic motivation comes from an outside source.

   [2 marks]

3 Explain why extrinsic feedback is important to a beginner. *Grade 3-5*

   Extrinsic feedback comes from a coach or other person, which is useful for a beginner as they aren't knowledgeable enough to give themselves feedback, so they need someone else to tell them what they are doing right or wrong.

   [3 marks]

4 Describe, using **one** example, how indirect aggression could improve performance in a sport. *Grade 5-7*

   Indirect aggression could be used during a tennis serve to allow a player to aim their aggression at the ball to hit it powerfully across the court.

   [2 marks]

Section Five — Sport Psychology

Exam Questions

1   Explain the benefits of mental rehearsal for performance in physical activity and sport. *Grade 1-3*

....

....

[2 marks]

2   A coach might use verbal and mechanical guidance to teach sporting skills. *Grade 7-9*

Assess the relative importance of these guidance types when teaching a group of beginners how to swim.

   (i)   Verbal guidance

   ....

   ....

   ....

   [3 marks]

   (ii) Mechanical guidance

   ....

   ....

   ....

   [3 marks]

3   Use the stages of the information processing model to analyse how a footballer tackles an opponent.

To get all six marks, you need to show knowledge of the stages of the information processing model, apply them to a football tackle, and analyse how each stage would help a footballer tackle someone.

....

....

....

....

....

....

....

....

[6 marks]

Section Five — Sport Psychology

Revision Questions for Section Five

Section Five has come to an end, so let's see how much you've learned.
- Try these questions and tick off each one when you get it right.
- When you've done all the questions for a topic and are completely happy with it, tick off the topic.

Skills and Practice (p88-90) ☑
1) Explain what is meant when a movement is described as 'pre-determined'.
2) What is the difference between an open and a closed skill?
3) Which type of skill can be broken down into separate parts?
4) Which type of skill needs lots of concentration to perform?
5) Which type of skill has its pace controlled by the person performing it?
6) Give two examples of an open skill.
7) What is the difference between massed and distributed practice?
8) Explain the difference between fixed and variable practice.

Goal Setting (p91) ☑
9) Why might a performer set themselves a goal?
10) What is the difference between performance and outcome goals? Why are performance goals better?
11) What do the letters in SMART stand for?
12) Explain the meaning and benefits of each element of SMART.
13) Why should you review your targets and goals regularly?

Guidance and Feedback (p94-95) ☑
14) What is guidance?
15) What is verbal guidance and why is it more suited to more experienced performers?
16) What is visual guidance? Why is it effective for teaching low organisation skills? Why is it less effective for teaching high organisation skills?
17) Give an example of manual guidance.
18) What is mechanical guidance?
19) What disadvantage do manual and mechanical guidance have in common?
20) What is feedback?
21) Explain the difference between intrinsic and extrinsic feedback.
22) Explain what is meant by:
    a) Concurrent feedback
    b) Terminal feedback
23) What is the difference between knowledge of performance and knowledge of results?
24) Describe the four stages of the information processing model.

Mental Preparation, Emotion and Personality (p96-97) ☑
25) How might an athlete mentally prepare for a performance?
26) Explain the 'inverted-U theory'.
27) Explain why intrinsic motivation is usually more effective than extrinsic motivation.
28) Explain the difference between direct and indirect aggression.
29) What type of sport do introverts usually enjoy? Give an example.

Section Five — Sport Psychology

Section Six — Sport, Society and Culture

Influences on Participation

Participation rates are how many people take part in sport or other physical activities. Whether you participate in sports, and the type of sports you play, can be affected by lots of different factors...

People Influence the Activities you do

FAMILY

1) Parents might encourage their children to take up sports, or discourage them.
2) If your parents or siblings play sport, or are interested in it, you're familiar with sport from a young age. You may also have more opportunities to take part.

FRIENDS

1) You're influenced by the attitudes of people your own age (your peers), especially your close friends...
2) For example, if all your mates play football, you're likely to play football with them. If your mates say that sport is rubbish and don't play it, you might do less sport.

ROLE MODELS

People who excel in their sport can become role models for their sport and inspire people to be like them. This encourages more people to participate in their sport.

The media can help create role models — see p108.

Your Gender may Influence whether you do an Activity

Although things are getting better, there's still a real gender divide in participation. Surveys carried out by Sport England show that, overall, fewer women participate regularly in sport than men.

1) This may be because many women's events have a lower profile than men's, as they get less media coverage. This has meant that in many sports there are fewer female role models to inspire younger generations to take up the sport.
2) Less media coverage also means there is less sponsorship available for women's sport, meaning there are fewer opportunities and less money for women to do sport at a high level.
3) Gender tagging — outdated attitudes about some things being "women's activities" and others being "men's activities" — might also affect what sports you decide to take up.
4) This includes ridiculous gender stereotypes about it 'not being feminine' to get sweaty or muddy, or to play sports where you need aggression. Similarly, stereotypes about masculinity may also mean boys are expected to play more aggressive sports or mocked for enjoying activities seen as less 'manly'.

Ethnicity and Religion can have an Effect too

1) Sometimes your religious beliefs or ethnic background can influence the physical activity you do.

> E.g. many Muslim women keep their bodies covered up. This may mean they're less likely to participate in activities such as swimming because of the clothing that's expected to be worn.

2) Religious festivals and days may impact on when you can play sport. For example, some Christians won't play sport on a Sunday because it's the Sabbath, so could not join a Sunday league team.
3) Racism and racial abuse used to be a huge problem in sport. Campaigns against racism, such as the Let's Kick Racism Out Of Football campaign, have helped to raise awareness of the problem. Also, punishments for players and fans who are racist are now much more severe than they used to be.
4) Governing bodies have also tried to help create more positive role models to inspire and engage younger generations to participate.
5) Policies like the 'Rooney Rule' in American football, which says that teams must interview at least one ethnic minority candidate for any head coaching job, are also helping to create more opportunities.

Influences on Participation

Another page of influences on participation — so many influences, so little time... Disability can influence what activities you do, and so can your job, where you live and how much money you have...

Disability can Influence how Active you are

1) Having a disability can limit the physical activities you can do. Studies show that participation rates for disabled people are lower than they are for non-disabled people.
2) The opportunities in sport and access to sporting facilities for disabled people used to be few and far between.
3) Nowadays, there are many schemes set up to give disabled people more opportunities to exercise and take part in activities within their physical limits. These schemes focus on:
   - Adapting sports so that they're more accessible for disabled people — e.g. wheelchair basketball or handcycling.
   - Creating new sports specifically for disabled people — like boccia (a game like bowls that can be played from a wheelchair) and goalball (a game like handball that blind people can play).
   - Including disabled people in activities alongside non-disabled people. This helps to challenge stereotypes about disabled people as well as giving disabled people the opportunity to enjoy a wide range of activities.
4) Disabled sporting events are now given a lot more media coverage than they once were. The Paralympics now gets extensive media coverage, like the Olympics.
5) This media coverage is helping to change people's attitudes towards disability and sport.
6) It's also helping create many more disabled role models (like Dame Tanni Grey-Thompson and Ellie Simmonds), which encourages more disabled people to get active.

Your Socio-Economic Group can also have an Effect

1) Socio-economic groups are just a fancy way of grouping people based on how much money they have, where they live and the type of job they do.
   "Working class", "middle class" and "young professional" are all examples of socio-economic groups.
2) Studies seem to show that, in general, people in lower socio-economic groups are less likely to regularly take part in sport. The kinds of activities people do can also be affected by their socio-economic group.

- Most sports cost money. This means that some people can't afford to take part.
- Lots of sports — like horse riding, skiing, sailing and even cycling — require specialist equipment and clothing. This can be very expensive, so could prevent people from taking part.
- Some sports require special facilities — like ski slopes or ice rinks. If you don't live in an area with these sorts of facilities, you won't easily be able to do those sports.
- If you don't have access to a car or good public transport to get to the facilities, this makes it a lot harder to participate. You'll be more likely to do a more accessible sport like football or basketball.
- If you work shifts or irregular hours it can be hard to join clubs or groups that meet in the evenings or at the weekend.
- Playing sport can also require a lot of free time. If you work long hours, or have family commitments like caring for children, you might just not have the time.

We're all under the influence...

There really are a lot of different factors that influence whether or not someone takes part in physical activity. Make sure you learn all of the ones covered on the last two pages. And, as if that wasn't enough, there are still three more factors to learn on the next page... Keep at it though, you're nearly there.

Section Six — Sport, Society and Culture

Influences on Participation

That's right, it's another page of influences on participation. Just like the rest of them, there's a bunch of facts to get your head around. So, buckle up, get comfortable and set your brain to 'memorise'...

Age can Limit the Activities you can do

1) Some sports are more popular than others with different age groups.
2) Most people aged 16-30 have loads of choice for physical activity.
3) People over 50 are more physically limited in the sports they can choose. They tend to do less strenuous activities like walking or swimming.
4) Some sports, such as weightlifting or endurance events, can potentially damage a young person's body. Competitions in these sorts of activities often have a minimum age restriction.
5) Young people often have more spare time to do sport. As people get older and have careers and families, there's less time available for playing sport.

PE in Schools can have a big effect on Participation

If you're doing the Edexcel course, you don't need to know this bit.

PE in schools plays a big role in shaping people's feelings towards sport and exercise:

1) PE classes and after-school activities are a way for students to try out lots of different sports. This allows students to become familiar with lots of activities, which might encourage regular participation. It's really important that schools offer a wide range of activities, so there's something for everyone. This will encourage more students to join in and enjoy sport:
   - Some students are put off by PE at school because they find it awkward or embarrassing.
   - Allowing students to choose what activities they would like to do, and listening to students' suggestions about improving PE, can make students more willing to take part.
   - Some students do not enjoy the competitive nature of sport, so offering non-competitive activities in PE is a good idea — e.g. fitness classes or yoga.
   - Schools can also bring in outside agencies to help with coaching and sports development.
2) Having a really good PE teacher, or sport's coach at a club, can really help to inspire people too. The flip side of this is that a bad experience in PE could end up putting you off sports and exercise.
3) The facilities a school has available can limit what activities it can offer. Also, grimy old changing rooms and equipment can mean some students just aren't inspired to join in with PE at all.
4) In PE you should learn physical literacy. This means you have basic skills like running, jumping, throwing, catching and swimming that you can use as a starting point for learning lots of new activities and sports. These skills allow you to go on and take part in physical activity throughout your life.

Even the Environment has an effect

This bit is just for the OCR course.

1) If you live nowhere near mountains and snow, the opportunities to compete in many winter sports will be few and far between.
2) In very hot and very cold climates, it might not be possible to be outside and active for long periods of time, which can affect participation in sports.
3) Pollution levels can force people to remain indoors, which makes it harder to participate in a lot of sports.
4) The layout of a city can dramatically affect participation in running, cycling and other outdoor activities — without pavements, cycle lanes and green spaces like parks, there is nowhere to do these things.
5) Really mountainous regions may struggle to have flat areas for creating pitches, so participation in many team sports can be difficult.

Section Six — Sport, Society and Culture

Influences on Participation

You need to know about ways of improving participation rates, and how to interpret data about participation.

Learn these Three Strategies for Encouraging Participation

There are three main ways of improving participation rates: promotion, provision and access:

PROMOTION

1) Participation can be promoted through advertising campaigns — like Sport England's This Girl Can campaign launched in 2015, which challenges stereotypes about women in sport.
2) Big sporting events, like the London Olympics in 2012, help to create role models and promote active lifestyles. Media coverage of events like the Paralympics and the Women's World Cup in football can also help inspire higher participation rates and challenge stereotypes.
3) More locally, clubs and facilities can be promoted to local residents through local advertising, so they know what's available in their area.

PROVISION

1) Providing facilities and well-trained staff can help to encourage more people to take up sports and activities.
2) It's important that these facilities cater to a wide range of people by offering plenty of variety — including offering a range of activities for disabled and elderly folk.
3) Leisure centres provide a wide range of classes and activities, and have trained staff and coaches to help all kinds of people be active and healthy.
4) PE classes and clubs after school help provide students with opportunities to participate in sport and exercise (see p103).

ACCESS

1) Having access to facilities can be a problem, especially in rural areas. Also, sometimes it can be difficult for families without a car to get involved in lots of sporting activities.
2) The government can help by providing good public transport links. Organisations like Sport England help clubs buy minibuses and other methods of transportation. Some disabled people may also require specialist equipment, like ramps, to be able to use these methods of transport.
3) Access can be improved by clubs and facilities being reasonably priced, so people can afford to use them.

You'll Need to Interpret Data about Participation Rates

In the exam, you'll need to be able to analyse graphs showing participation rates for different sports and activities.

1) You may get asked to compare activities, e.g. to say which activity has increased or decreased most from one point to another.
2) The bigger the difference between these two points, the bigger the increase or decrease.
3) For example, the graph on the right shows that:
   - Participation in running increased more than football or cycling from 07/08 to 10/11.
   - Participation in football decreased more than cycling or running from 11/12 to 12/13.

An increase means going up, so the second point is higher than the first.

A decrease means going down, so the second point is lower than the first.

Graph showing the number of English people aged 16 or over who participated at least once a week.

Promotion, provision and access — the key to improving participation...

Make sure you're comfortable with analysing graphs, because this is another topic you could get a data question on in the exam. The only way to get good at it is to practise until graphs no longer seem scary...

Section Six — Sport, Society and Culture

Warm-Up and Worked Exam Questions

There are so many things that can influence whether or not you participate in sport it's tough to remember all of them. Test yourself with these questions to check you've got all the details stored in your memory.

Warm-Up Questions

1) How can role models improve participation rates?
2) Explain how your family can influence whether you play sport.
3) Give one way that your religious beliefs might affect the sports you do.
4) Give two ways that school PE lessons might influence your attitude towards exercise.
5) Give one effect that the environment where you live can have on which sports you play.
6) Give two ways of improving access to sporting facilities.

Worked Exam Questions

1 Give **one** way that schools can encourage students to enjoy sport and physical activity. *(Grade 1-3)*

A school could allow students to choose from a range of activities.

There are loads of answers you could give, but you only need to put one to get the mark. *[1 mark]*

2 Explain, using **one** example, how age can affect the level of participation in a sport. *(Grade 3-5)*

Some sports, like weightlifting, place the body under a lot of strain. This means that children should not participate, as their bodies are not developed enough to withstand it. Similarly, weightlifting would not be an appropriate sport for the elderly, as the risk of injury will be too high.

You get 1 mark for the example of a sport and 2 marks for the explanation. *[3 marks]*

3 Discuss possible influences that may affect women's participation in physical activity. *(Grade 5-7)*

Women may have fewer female role models to inspire them to do an activity, due to a lack of media coverage of women's sports. Also, women may receive less encouragement to play some, traditionally male, sports because of sexist attitudes. Promotional campaigns run by organisations such as Sport England could help to encourage participation by challenging these outdated stereotypes.

You're asked to discuss the influences, so you need to think about both positive and negative influences. You'll get one mark for each influence. *[3 marks]*

Section Six — Sport, Society and Culture

Exam Questions

1 Which one of the following is a socio-economic influence on whether someone participates in sport?

    A   Sexism ☐

    B   Religious beliefs ☐

    C   Cost ☐

    D   Racism ☐

[1 mark]

2 Studies show that participation rates in physical activity and sport are lower for disabled people than they are for non-disabled people.

Give **two** possible reasons for the lower participation rates amongst disabled people.

1 ....

2 ....

[2 marks]

3 **Figure 1** shows participation rates for three activities in England.

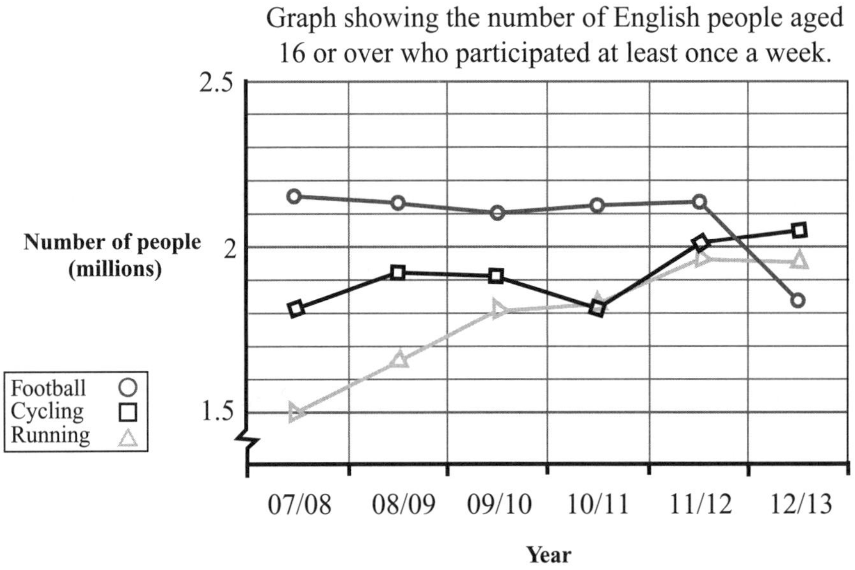

Graph showing the number of English people aged 16 or over who participated at least once a week.

Football ○
Cycling ☐
Running △

Figure 1

Analyse the data in **Figure 1**.

(a) Identify the sport that saw the greatest increase in participation from 07/08 to 12/13.

....

[1 mark]

(b) Explain what you think will happen to the participation rate in cycling in 13/14.

....

....

....

[2 marks]

Section Six — Sport, Society and Culture

Commercialisation of Sport

Lots of people are raking in the cash from sport these days. This is the commercialisation of sport, and the next three pages are all about it. Lots of this money comes from the media and through sponsorship.

Commercialisation Means Making Money

1) The commercialisation of sport is all about making money from it.
2) A lot of money comes from sponsorship — if people are going to see it, companies will put their name on it, whether it's a person, team, league, stand, trophy, mascot or ball. This is great advertising for the sponsor. As well as money, sponsors might also provide equipment, clothing or facilities.
3) Money also comes from the media — organisations involved in mass communication — like television companies, radio broadcasters and newspapers.
4) The media pay so they can cover the sport, which means people will buy their newspaper or watch their TV show. Some companies sell sport on TV, or over the Internet, as a subscription package too.
5) Broadcasting sports on television and the Internet means it now reaches an even larger, global audience — this is known as the globalisation of sport. This all makes sponsorship even more valuable.
6) Social media gives fans new ways to interact with their favourite sports stars and teams. This keeps sponsors of those teams and players in the public eye, which promotes them even more.
7) Sports also make money through selling tickets to events, and merchandise.

You'll Need to Interpret Data About Commercialisation

It's another one of those fun data bits. In your exam you could be asked to interpret data about the commercialisation of sport.

1) For example, the graph on the right shows the total amount spent each year on shirt sponsorship (that's companies paying to have their logo on the front of a team's shirt) in the Premier League.
2) The graph shows that every year since 2010, spending on shirt sponsorship in the Premier League has increased.
3) So there's an upward trend in spending on shirt sponsorship — and if the graph carried on past 2015, you'd expect it to keep on going upwards.
4) You can also see that the biggest increases in spending were from 2011 to 2012 and from 2014 to 2015 — shown by the line going up more steeply.

A graph showing the amount spent on shirt sponsorship in the Premier League between 2010 and 2015.

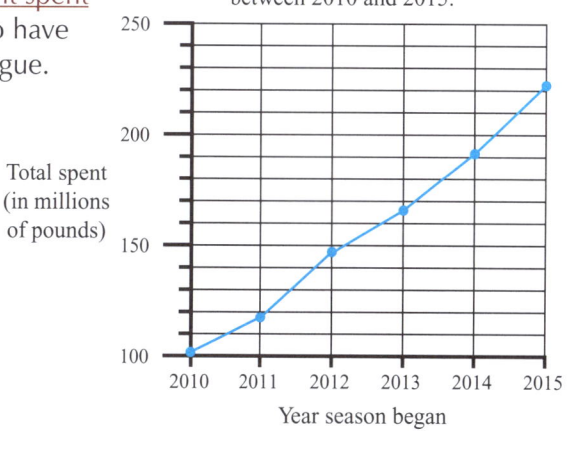

Show me the money...

It's really important that you understand what sponsorship is and why companies pay so much money to do it. The media is another key player in the commercialisation of sport. Make sure you know why, then turn the page for more info on how sport, the media and sponsorship are all connected.

Section Six — Sport, Society and Culture

Commercialisation of Sport

This page covers the links between sport, the media and sponsorship in more detail.
This can be quite tricky, so take your time and read through each of the boxes below really carefully.

Sport, the Media and Commercialisation are all Connected

Sport, the media and sponsorship have grown to depend on one another — this is called the 'golden triangle'. There are advantages and disadvantages to this relationship for the sponsor, the sport, the players, the spectators and the officials.

SPONSORSHIP AND SPORT

1) Sponsorship deals mean companies can associate their name with the prestige of successful sportspeople and teams. This is an effective form of advertising, which helps the sponsor to make more money.
2) These deals mean big money for sport — which can be spent on development, e.g. of a new stadium or facilities. This benefits the players and the spectators. This money can also pay for technology to help officials (see p110).
3) Sponsorship money also means players and officials can be paid good wages, and players can train full-time. This benefits everyone, because they will perform better.

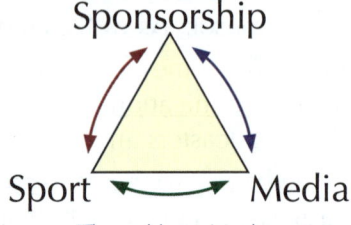

The golden triangle

SPONSORSHIP AND THE MEDIA

1) The more media coverage a sport gets, the more people watch it. This makes sponsorship more valuable, as it can reach a larger audience.
2) This increases the likelihood of sponsorship and means the sport and players can demand more money for their sponsorship deals.

SPORT AND THE MEDIA

1) The media pay for the rights to cover sporting events, which provides investment for sports to develop at lower levels.
2) Media coverage makes more people aware of the sport, so more people may play it or watch it.
3) Media coverage of elite players and athletes can create role models who inspire people to play.
4) This can make players into superstars. But, the downside is that players are hounded by the media and their private lives are all over the news.
5) Also, the media can hold so much power over sport that they'll change things:
   - The number of games played, or the timings of matches, might be changed so more matches can be shown. This risks injury to players through lack of rest, and might mean spectators miss a game because it's not at a convenient time.
   - Also, rules may be changed — e.g. the tiebreaker set was brought into tennis to make matches shorter so they were easier to fit into TV schedules.
6) Being able to watch on TV or the Internet, rather than going to the game, can save fans money. However, fewer fans buying tickets means losses in ticket sales for the sport and a poorer atmosphere at the stadium for spectators.
7) The media's analysis of refereeing decisions puts sports officials under a lot of pressure.
8) Media analysis of games can also educate spectators, so they understand the sport better.

The golden triangle — every bit as wealthy as it sounds...

REVISION TASK: Draw out the golden triangle diagram from the top of this page. Around the outside write two advantages of each of the relationships. For example, along the bottom of the triangle you would put two advantages of the relationship between sport and the media.

Section Six — Sport, Society and Culture

Commercialisation of Sport

Sponsorship can be a little complicated. You need to know that it has its downsides and that not all types of sponsor are suitable. Read on to find out about this dark side of sponsorship...

Sponsorship Isn't All Great

There can be drawbacks to sponsorship for teams and individuals:

1) Sometimes, the money is only available for the top players and teams, so benefits the elite — not the sport as a whole.
2) It could all turn nasty — if an athlete gets injured, loses their form or gets a bad reputation they could lose their sponsorship deal. Bad behaviour by an athlete reflects badly on the sponsor too and could damage the company's reputation.
3) Sometimes athletes have to fulfil contracts with their sponsor — they might have to turn up at a special event or appear in a TV advert (even if they don't want to).
4) Athletes can get into trouble with their sponsor if they're spotted using another company's products.
5) If a team really needs a sponsor's money, this puts the sponsor in a position of power. This means they can influence the team's playing style or team selection.
6) In some sports where there are breaks in play, adverts will be shown. The game won't be allowed to restart until the advert break is finished, which can be quite boring for spectators in the stadium.

One bad story can mean the end for an athlete's sponsorship deals...

Some Sponsors are Inappropriate

Sponsorship brings in loads of money, but you have to be careful not to promote the wrong image, especially in youth sports:

1) Cigarette and tobacco companies aren't allowed to sponsor sports in the EU. This is because their products are harmful and unhealthy.
2) Alcoholic drinks companies are allowed to sponsor some sports, but this can be bad as it gives alcohol a false image of health. The same is true for unhealthy food companies.
3) Also, as sport is watched by children, advertising alcohol and fast food could be encouraging young people to drink or eat unhealthily.

In the past, it was common for cigarette companies to sponsor sporting events and teams. Nowadays, this is seen as unacceptable.

Sponsorship — sometimes it comes at a price...

EXAM TIP: If you get a question about the impact of sponsorship in the exam, you'll need to weigh up the pros and cons, especially when it comes to fast-food and alcohol companies. Also, make sure to take note of the age group mentioned in the question — for example, it might be okay for an alcohol company to sponsor an adult event, but not to sponsor a youth one.

Section Six — Sport, Society and Culture

Technology in Sport

There's loads of technology used in sport and you need to know all about it for the AQA and Eduqas courses.

Technology can help Players to Perform Better

1) Lots of the technology used today is designed to help athletes perform better at their sports. This benefits spectators as well as performers, as new levels of sporting excellence are achieved.
2) New materials are used to make sports equipment and clothes more effective — from shoes to swimming costumes to tennis rackets. This helps players reach new levels of performance.
3) Improvements to training facilities, like all-weather pitches, mean that training doesn't have to stop for bad weather. This means more time can be spent training, so performances will improve.
4) There have also been developments to make sports safer, like better protective clothing and better playing surfaces. Also, medical technology can help athletes recover from injuries quickly and safely.
5) Video footage and 3D modelling software can be used by coaches to analyse an athlete's movement. This can be done to a very high degree of accuracy, so an athlete's technique can be fine-tuned. In events like the 100 m sprint, where winning may come down to a few milliseconds, this level of accuracy is really important.
6) All this technology is expensive though. This can mean that only people with lots of money can compete at the highest level.
7) There is a worry that technology can give athletes an unfair advantage over their competitors. If sport becomes less about the abilities of the athletes and more about the technology they're using, it kind of stops being interesting for spectators.

Technology can help Officials to make Correct Decisions

Many sports now make use of technology during matches to help referees and umpires.

1) Hawk-Eye (tennis) — Hawk-Eye uses a set of six cameras to track and predict the path of the ball. It's used so that players can challenge the decision of whether shots are in or out.
2) Decision Review System (DRS) (cricket) — players are allowed to challenge an umpire's decision and have it reviewed by the third umpire, who uses various bits of technology (including Hawk-Eye) to decide whether the on-field umpire was correct or not.
3) Television Match Official (TMO) (rugby union) — the TMO is an extra official who watches video replays. The referee on the pitch can consult with the TMO to help them make key decisions.
4) Goal-line technology (football) — there are cameras pointed at each goal that are used to tell whether or not the ball has crossed the goal line.

ADVANTAGES

1) All these systems help to make the sport more fair, which benefits spectators and players by avoiding the frustration of wrong decisions.
2) They help officials to make valid and reliable decisions, even in marginal situations. This lessens the pressure on them.
3) The DRS in cricket has shown that the umpires are right most of the time. This has led to increased respect for umpires.
4) Sponsors can use the breaks in play that some of these technologies cause to show adverts.

DISADVANTAGES

1) These systems are expensive to install, so are only used at the top end of sporting leagues.
2) The fact that things can be reviewed could undermine the authority of the officials on the pitch. This could lead to players contesting every decision the referee makes.
3) Referring to a video replay can sometimes take a long time. Some people worry that these breaks disrupt the flow of play and can also be boring for spectators.

Section Six — Sport, Society and Culture

Sporting Behaviour

The next two pages are about good and bad behaviour in sport. First up, we have sportsmanship and gamesmanship. Sportsmanship is good sporting behaviour — gamesmanship is behaviour that seems unfair.

Sportsmanship is About Being Fair and Humble

Being a good sportsperson is more than just playing by the rules. You also have to show good 'sportsmanship' (even if you lose) and uphold the 'contract to compete'.

> **Sportsmanship means being honest, sticking to the rules and treating your opponents with respect.**

> **The contract to compete is an unwritten agreement between competitors to respect the 'spirit of the game'.**

You only need to know this for the AQA course.

1) This means no rubbing it in the opposition's face if you win. And no going off in a huff if you lose.
2) It also means observing the etiquette of an activity — following unwritten rules and conventions. E.g.:

- In cricket, a batsman might choose to 'walk' if they think they've been caught out — even if the umpire has ruled them not out.
- In football, players will kick the ball out of play if a member of the other team goes down injured.
- In cycling, if someone has a mechanical problem with their bike (e.g. a puncture), the other riders will not take advantage by speeding up until the problem is fixed.
- In many sports, competitors will shake hands before and after the game, to show that they respect their opponents.

Gamesmanship is About Bending The Rules

Gamesmanship is sort of like the opposite of sportsmanship, because it feels as if it goes against the 'spirit of the game':

> **Gamesmanship is gaining an advantage by using tactics that seem unfair, but aren't against the rules.**

1) Gamesmanship is not actually cheating — but it can come quite close. A lot of the techniques are about breaking up the flow of a game, or distracting your opponents:

- Time-wasting in football is when players deliberately faff about. This runs down the clock and breaks up the flow of the game.
- In tennis, some players make loud grunting or shrieking noises when they hit the ball to try to intimidate or distract their opponent.
- In basketball, a manager might call a timeout just as the opposition win a free throw. This is to try and make them overthink the shot.

2) Gamesmanship does not normally result in punishment for the players, although if it is taken too far referees might get involved.

Sportsmanship's the good one, gamesmanship's the bad one...

I know, it's easy to get confused between sportsmanship and gamesmanship. Just remember that sportsmanship is about 'being a good sport', and you can't go wrong.

Section Six — Sport, Society and Culture

Sporting Behaviour

Now you're moving into the murkier waters of deviance. This is actually a bit more straightforward than the types of behaviour on the previous page — deviance just means breaking the rules or behaving badly.

Deviance is Breaking The Rules

If you commit deviance, this means you've broken the rules.

> Deviance is behaviour that goes against the moral values or laws of the sport.

1) Sometimes it involves cheating to gain an advantage:

   > Using performance-enhancing drugs or blood doping are both deviance because they give you an unfair advantage.

   See p68 for more about performance-enhancing drugs.

   > 'Professional fouls', like tripping someone to get ahead of them, are also deviance.

2) Other times it's being overly violent and aggressive:

   > Cuban taekwondo athlete Angel Matos was banned from the sport for life after deliberately kicking a referee.

   See p120 for an example of data about ethical issues in sport...

   > Boxer Mike Tyson and footballer Luis Suarez have both been in trouble for biting their opposition.

3) Most forms of deviance happen more at the higher levels of a sport because there is so much at stake — e.g. the money and the fame brought about through the commercialisation of sport (see p107).

4) Violence in sport can happen because players are frustrated with the result, or with decisions made by the referee. It can also come from players being overly emotional or competitive.

Referees Help to Stop Players Committing Deviance

Deviance is punished by sports officials to discourage players from doing it:

Referees make sure that the rules are followed.

1) For deviance like fouling an opponent, the referee or umpire may punish players by removing them from the field of play temporarily — the 'sin bin', or permanently — a red card or disqualification.
2) For really serious offences, like using performance-enhancing drugs or biting, players may be banned from competing. There could also be a hefty fine.

One man's deviance is another man's sport...

Violence in sport can be a little confusing. Some sports, like rugby or boxing, allow pretty violent interactions between players — as long as these are within the rules they're not deviance. However, if you behaved the same way in a badminton match, it would definitely be deviance. You just need to get it clear in your head that deviance is about breaking rules. And biting? Well that's just never okay...

Section Six — Sport, Society and Culture

Spectator Behaviour

Big sporting events draw big crowds. This has both advantages and disadvantages. Make sure you learn them and also what can be done to prevent hooliganism. You only need this page if you're doing the AQA course.

Spectators create an Atmosphere

1) Crowds at sporting events create an atmosphere and this adds to the excitement, making the event more enjoyable for spectators and players.
2) Also, this can create a 'home-field advantage' — the 'home' team perform better because they're in familiar surroundings with more fans supporting them. This can also intimidate the opposition.
3) However, sometimes all those spectators can put pressure on the performers, who end up performing worse because they are nervous and afraid to make mistakes.
4) Having spectators at sporting events for younger people (like youth leagues in football) can put more pressure on the kids who are taking part. This can discourage children from taking up activities, so can negatively affect participation rates (see pages 101-104).
5) At big events, it takes a lot of planning and money to make sure spectators are safe. With large groups there's the chance of crowd trouble and hooliganism...

Hooliganism is when fans Become Aggressive

Hooliganism is rowdy, aggressive and sometimes violent behaviour of fans and spectators of sport. You need to know what causes hooliganism and how it can be prevented.

CAUSES

1) Rivalries between fans. These rivalries might be built up by the press and the media so they seem even more important. This hype can cause fans to take the match too seriously.
2) Some fans might have been drinking, or even taking drugs, which can fuel aggression and violence.
3) Frustration with decisions made by officials, or just frustration with how the match is going, can lead to spectators getting angry.
4) Some people see hooliganism as a display of masculinity, or a way of fans proving themselves to be macho. Peer pressure can make people feel they have to join in. There could also be a 'gang mentality', where people feel less responsible for their actions because they're in a group.

METHODS OF PREVENTION

1) Kick-offs can be made earlier for games where it's likely there will be trouble. This leaves less time between the pubs opening and the start of the game, so fans will be less drunk during the game. Alcohol restrictions can also be brought in to control buying alcohol within the stadium.
   - However, fans often get round this by drinking more before they go to the game. Also, having earlier kick-offs can make it inconvenient for travelling fans to get to the game.
2) Making every stadium 'all-seated' so fans don't have to stand. This is safer because people are less packed together. It's also easier for stewards and police to get to troublemakers.
3) Fans can be segregated (sat in separate sections) to stop fighting inside the ground. Sometimes home and away fans enter and leave the ground at different times.
   - This doesn't help prevent violence outside of the stadium though, and it can mean it takes longer for fans to get into or out of the stadium, which is annoying for the fans.
4) The number of police and stewards at games can be increased, which boosts security in the ground. Also, video surveillance and other technology can be used to monitor crowds.
   - It can be very expensive to install all this technology and pay extra police and stewards.
5) For fans who have committed hooliganism in the past, there are banning orders and travel restrictions, e.g. confiscating passports. This means that the worst offenders aren't at games.
6) There have been lots of campaigns to educate fans about the harm that's caused by hooliganism.

Section Six — Sport, Society and Culture

Warm-Up and Worked Exam Questions

There's a wide range of topics covered in the last few pages. Use this page of questions to check you've got it all, then go back and re-read anything you're stuck on before trying the exam questions on the next page.

Warm-Up Questions

1) What is meant by the commercialisation of sport?
2) Name four different types of media that feature sport.
3) Media coverage can only have a positive impact on sport. True or false?
4) Give one possible disadvantage of sponsorship for a player.
5) How can improvements in technology help a player to avoid injury.
6) What is the difference between gamesmanship and sportsmanship?
7) Give one example of deviance in sport.
8) List two advantages for the home team of having a large crowd at a football match.

Worked Exam Questions

1   Give **two** examples of technology brought in to support officials during a match. *(Grade 1-3)*

   Hawk-Eye in tennis and goal-line technology in football.

   [2 marks]

2   Define the **contract to compete**. *(Grade 1-3)*

   The contract to compete is an unwritten agreement between competitors to respect the 'spirit of the game'.

   [1 mark]

3   Evaluate the use of early kick-offs as a method of preventing hooliganism. *(Grade 5-7)*

   Early kick-offs mean that there is less time between pubs and bars opening and the start of the game, so fans will have less time to drink in them before going to the game. This should help to reduce rowdy behaviour. However, it cannot prevent fans from drinking at home before they attend the game, so may not be entirely effective. An early kick-off can also be a serious inconvenience for travelling fans, who might end up missing the start of the match or decide not to go at all.

   [3 marks]

   Evaluating means judging whether the effects of early kick-offs are positive or negative.

Section Six — Sport, Society and Culture

Exam Questions

1 Which one of the following is an example of deviance? *(Grade 1-3)*

    A Trying to distract an opponent by grunting or shrieking in tennis ☐
    B Timing the intake of protein to maximise muscle growth ☐
    C Time-wasting in football ☐
    D Deliberately tripping a player as they run down the pitch in hockey ☐

[1 mark]

2 Most sports players display sportsmanship. *(Grade 1-3)*

  (a) Define **sportsmanship**.

....
....
[1 mark]

  (b) Give **one** example of sportsmanship in a sport of your choice.

....
....
[1 mark]

3 Give **one** advantage and **one** disadvantage of sponsorship for sport as a whole. *(Grade 3-5)*

Advantage

....
....

Disadvantage

....
....
[2 marks]

4 Explain how increased media coverage of the Paralympics could affect sponsorship of the athletes involved. *(Grade 5-7)*

....
....
....
....
[3 marks]

Section Six — Sport, Society and Culture

Revision Questions for Section Six

That's Section Six done and dusted — time to put all that knowledge to the test.
- Try these questions and tick off each one when you get it right.
- When you've done all the questions for a topic and are completely happy with it, tick off the topic.

Influences on Participation (p101-104)

1) Give one way that your family and friends might influence your participation in sport.
2) How can your gender influence what sports you participate in?
3) How can the media help improve participation rates amongst the disabled?
4) What is meant by a socio-economic group?
5) Outline one way that the amount of money you have could affect your participation in sport.
6) Describe two ways that your age can limit your participation in physical activities.
7) What is meant by 'physical literacy'?
8) Give two ways that the environment you live in can affect what sports you take part in.
9) Explain how sports participation rates can be improved by promotion, provision and access.
10) How do you spot an increase in a participation rate on a line graph?

Commercialisation of Sport (p107-109)

11) What does 'commercialisation' mean?
12) Give one effect of increased media coverage on a sport.
13) Give one advantage and one disadvantage of sponsorship for a sport.
14) If a sports team gets media coverage, what might happen to the value of their sponsorship deals? Give a possible reason for this happening.
15) How can increased media coverage increase participation in a sport?
16) Why do companies sponsor sports?
17) Give one way an athlete could lose their sponsorship deal.
18) Which of these cannot sponsor an EU football team: a) a car manufacturer, b) a tobacco company?
19) Give an advantage and a disadvantage of a brewery sponsoring a youth games tournament.

Technology in Sport (p110)

20) Outline three ways technology can help an athlete perform better.
21) Give an advantage and a disadvantage of using technology to help officials during a match.

Sporting and Spectator Behaviour (p111-113)

22) Give a definition and an example of:
    a) Sportsmanship
    b) Gamesmanship
    c) Deviance
23) Is time-wasting in football an example of gamesmanship or deviance? What about a 'professional foul'?
24) Is deviance more likely or less likely to happen in the higher levels of sport? Why?
25) Name one possible punishment an athlete could face if they're caught blood-doping.
26) Give a definition of hooliganism. Name one thing that can cause hooliganism.

Section Six — Sport, Society and Culture

Section Seven — Using Data

Using Data

You've got to be comfortable with interpreting data displayed in graphs and tables. Luckily for you, these five pages will go through how you do it. And you thought you could get away from maths by taking PE...

There Are Two Different Types of Data

You can collect two different types of data — qualitative data and quantitative data:

Qualitative data describes something — it will be in words.

1) Qualitative data can be collected through observation — e.g. 'the team played well', 'the athlete is strong' or 'the weather was cold'.
2) Or you can interview people. E.g. asking an athlete how they're feeling before a race might give you answers like "confident" or "well-prepared".
3) It's less easy to analyse than data in numbers.

Quantitative data measures something — it will be in numbers.

1) Quantitative data measures things — e.g. 'time taken to finish a race' or 'weight of an athlete'.
2) All the fitness tests (see pages 41-45) give quantitative data, as the results are numbers. You can also use surveys or questionnaires to collect quantitative data.
3) Quantitative data can be represented in tables and graphs, and analysed easily.

You need to be able to Plot a Bar Chart from a Table

In the exam you might be asked to plot a bar chart using a table of data. You might know how to do this already, but it never hurts to go over it again. Below is a bar chart for the following data on BMI:

Number of students with each Body Mass Index (BMI) rating

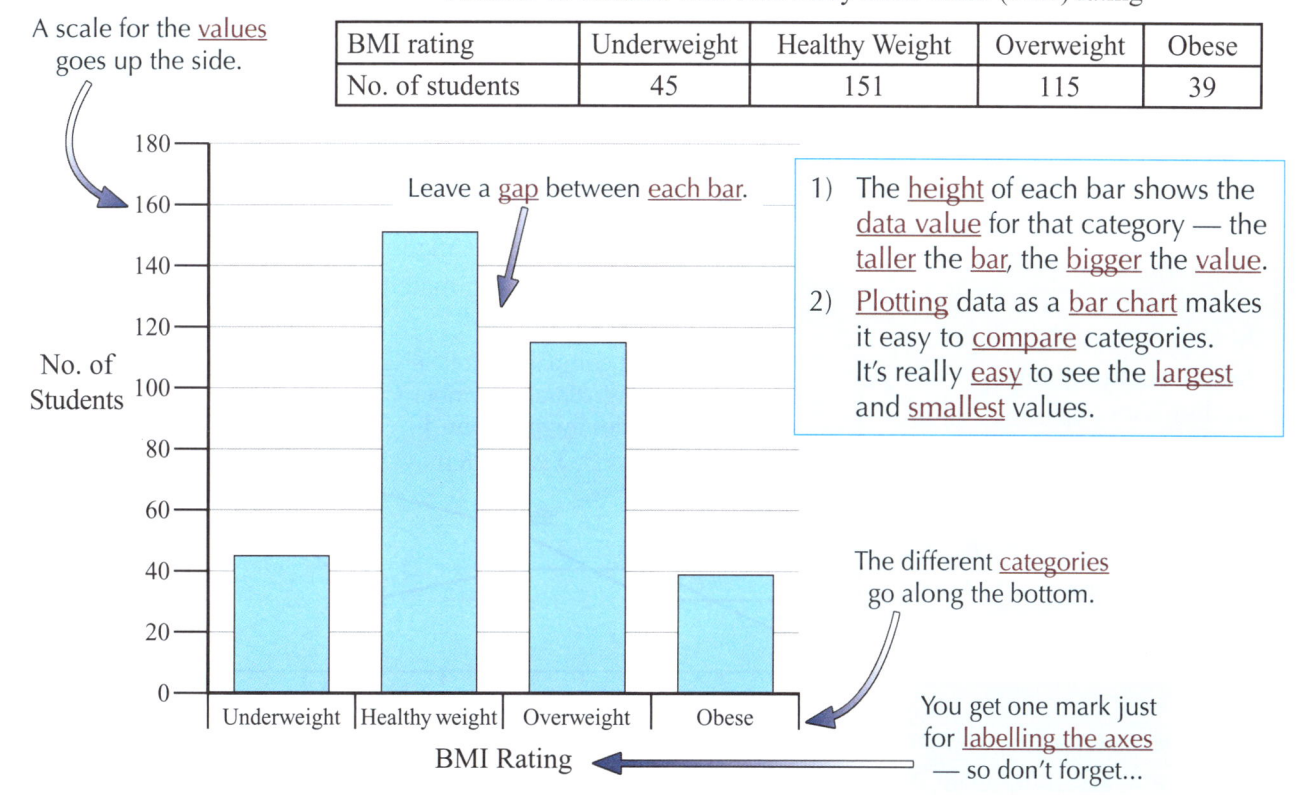

BMI rating	Underweight	Healthy Weight	Overweight	Obese
No. of students	45	151	115	39

A scale for the values goes up the side.

Leave a gap between each bar.

1) The height of each bar shows the data value for that category — the taller the bar, the bigger the value.
2) Plotting data as a bar chart makes it easy to compare categories. It's really easy to see the largest and smallest values.

The different categories go along the bottom.

You get one mark just for labelling the axes — so don't forget...

Quantitative is numbers — qualitative is words...

REVISION TIP: It's easy to mix up 'qualitative' and 'quantitative', so check you're using the right word. The best way to remember the difference is 'quantitative' sounds like 'quantity', which means 'number of'.

Using Data

This page is all about line graphs — you need to know how to plot them and how to analyse them. Often, line graphs are used to show how something is changing over time, to help you spot trends.

You can Plot a Line Graph from a Table

In the exam, you might be asked to plot a line graph from a table. Just like with the bar charts on the previous page, you might know how to do this already — but there's no harm in going over it again.

Riyad's results for the standing stork test

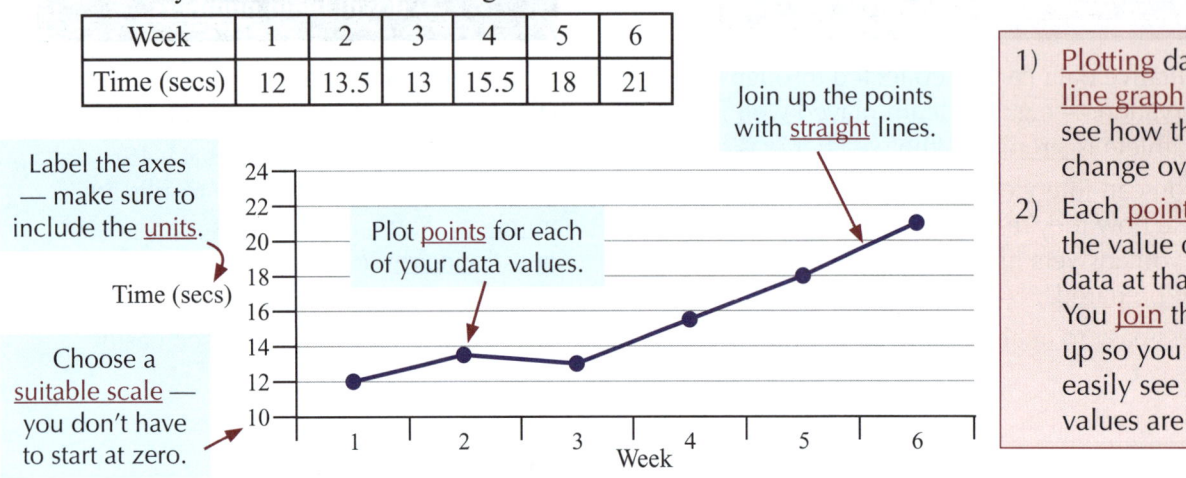

Week	1	2	3	4	5	6
Time (secs)	12	13.5	13	15.5	18	21

Label the axes — make sure to include the units.

Choose a suitable scale — you don't have to start at zero.

Plot points for each of your data values.

Join up the points with straight lines.

1) Plotting data as a line graph lets you see how things change over time.
2) Each point shows the value of the data at that time. You join the points up so you can easily see how the values are changing.

Analyse Graphs to spot Trends

To analyse a graph you can talk about increases and decreases, and highest and lowest values. This can also help you to spot trends and make predictions.

A trend is when a graph is generally going up or down over time.

Here's an example of how data on performance can be analysed as part of feedback (see p94-95), to help a performer improve.

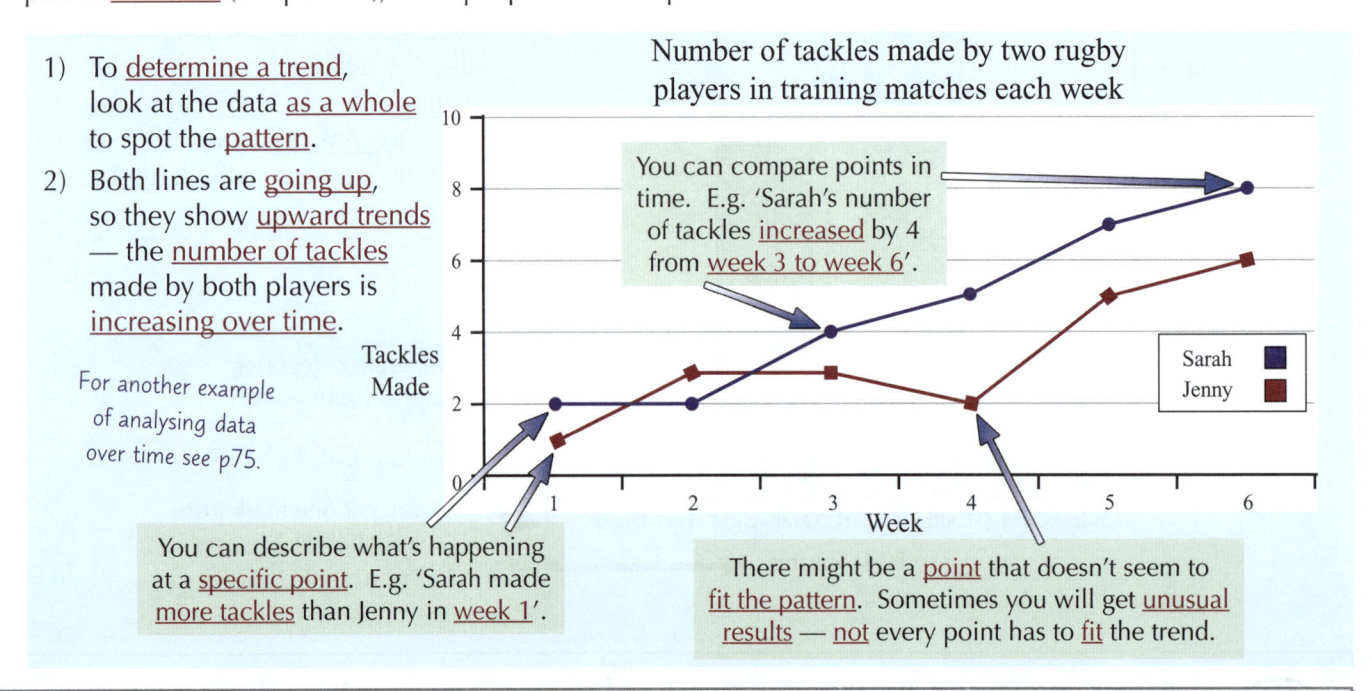

1) To determine a trend, look at the data as a whole to spot the pattern.
2) Both lines are going up, so they show upward trends — the number of tackles made by both players is increasing over time.

For another example of analysing data over time see p75.

Number of tackles made by two rugby players in training matches each week

You can compare points in time. E.g. 'Sarah's number of tackles increased by 4 from week 3 to week 6'.

You can describe what's happening at a specific point. E.g. 'Sarah made more tackles than Jenny in week 1'.

There might be a point that doesn't seem to fit the pattern. Sometimes you will get unusual results — not every point has to fit the trend.

Revision trends — amount of knowledge is increasing over time...

If you can analyse graphs and spot trends, you'll breeze through any graph questions in the exam.

Section Seven — Using Data

Using Data

Using data to help you evaluate and plan fitness training is really important, so here's a whole page on it. You need to understand what the data is showing you as well as use your knowledge about physical fitness.

You can Analyse your Fitness over Time

1) You can measure the effect of your training by doing regular fitness tests, and comparing the data you get over time.
2) You need to be able to describe what the data shows, and say what this means about the training — i.e. if it's working or what changes are needed.
3) Here's an example of the kind of thing you might see in the exam:

Bryan is doing a training programme to improve his cardiovascular fitness and his muscular endurance...

Bryan's Fitness Test Results

Fitness Test	Weeks					
	1	2	3	4	5	6
Cooper 12-minute Run (distance in m)	1450	1490	1530	1600	1640	1690
One-Minute Sit-up test (no. of sit-ups)	45	46	45	46	44	45

The Cooper's Run data shows that Bryan is doing better at the Cooper 12-minute Run Test each week — he is running further in 12 minutes. So the training is improving Bryan's cardiovascular fitness.

The sit-ups data shows that the number of sit-ups Bryan can do is staying about the same, so the training is not improving his abdominal muscular endurance. This means Bryan may want to change his training programme to include more exercises that help improve his abdominal muscular endurance.

For more on fitness testing and training methods, see Section Three.

You can also look at national averages or ratings tables to understand how your scores in fitness tests compare with others in your age group or gender. For an example of this, see page 46.

Bar Charts can show Fitness Data

Remember that on a bar chart the heights of the bars show the data values. This means you can spot trends by looking at how the heights of the bars change over time.

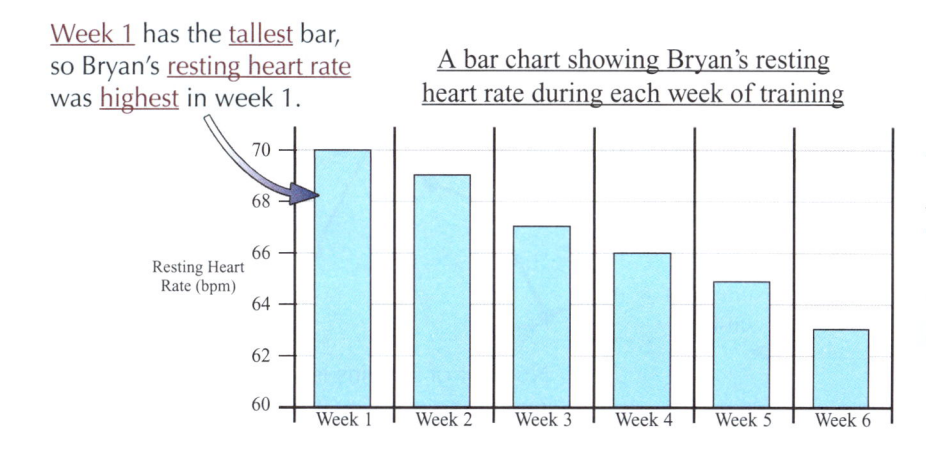

Week 1 has the tallest bar, so Bryan's resting heart rate was highest in week 1.

A bar chart showing Bryan's resting heart rate during each week of training

The trend here is that Bryan's resting heart rate is decreasing each week. This means that his cardiovascular fitness must be improving, as his heart is pumping blood more efficiently.

The key to understanding fitness tests is understanding data...

It's really important that you get confident with using data about fitness to evaluate how effective an exercise programme is. Have another look over pages 41 to 45 to check you know all the fitness tests.

Section Seven — Using Data

Using Data

The first half of this page will look at pie charts, which are used to show proportions. The second half is all about how to analyse data to decide whether a decision has been effective or not.

You can Look at Data for Large Groups of People

You can also use data to understand what's going on for large groups of people.

For examples of using data to understand trends on a large scale, see pages 75, 104 and 107.

1) Pie charts are a good way to compare different categories.
2) The amount of the whole chart a section takes up tells you the percentage in that category — the whole chart represents 100% (everybody).
3) These charts show that the netball club is almost entirely female, the football club is mostly male, and the badminton club is 50% male and 50% female.

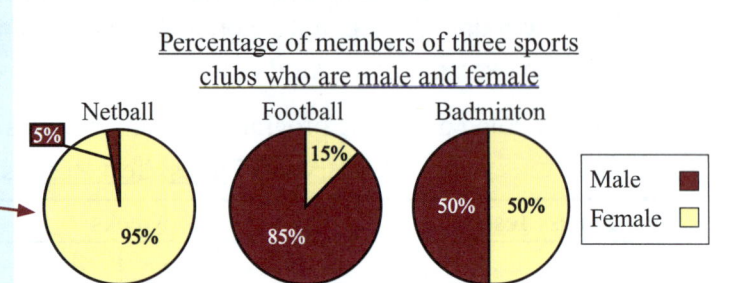

Percentage of members of three sports clubs who are male and female

Netball: 5% / 95%
Football: 15% / 85%
Badminton: 50% / 50%

Male ■ Female ☐

Remember, percentages tell you the proportion of people in a category, not the actual number.

You can use Data to see the Effects of something

You might be asked to use data to assess the effectiveness of a decision.

EXAMPLE

1) Organisers of a regional Rugby Union tournament were becoming concerned at the high number of players being sin-binned during the competition. A player is sent to the 'sin-bin' for repeatedly breaking the rules or for a really bad foul.
2) From 2012, the organisers introduced a fine for the player being sin-binned to try and discourage players from foul play.
3) The table below shows the number of 'sin-bins' awarded at the tournament each year, from 2007 to 2015. You can analyse this data to see whether or not the fine has been effective:

Total number of sin-bins awarded each year → The fine is introduced here.

Year	2007	2008	2009	2010	2011	2012	2013	2014	2015
No. of 'sin-bins'	8	7	12	13	15	10	8	7	6

4) The fine will have been effective if it has led to fewer sin-bins.
5) As there has been a decrease in sin-bins awarded every year since the introduction of the fine, it looks like the fine has been effective.
6) Plotting a line graph of the data makes it easier to see the patterns.

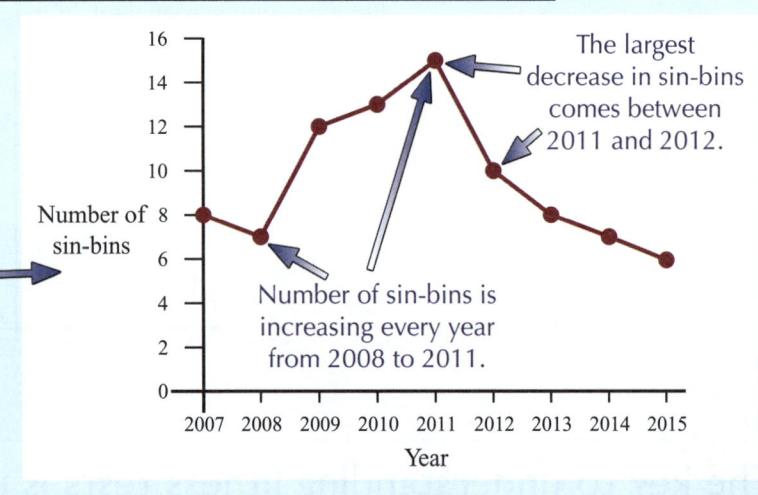

The largest decrease in sin-bins comes between 2011 and 2012.

Number of sin-bins is increasing every year from 2008 to 2011.

Section Seven — Using Data

Using Data

More ways to use data in training. Heart rate data is useful for working out how long you're exercising at different intensities for, and data collected about performance can help you check you're achieving your goals.

Heart Rate Data can be used to work out Exercise Intensities

By analysing data about someone's heart rate during exercise, you can work out how long they worked in each target zone for. Check back on page 52 for more information about training target zones. E.g.:

Joanna is 45 years old, so her maximum heart rate is 220 − 45 = 175.
This means the lower threshold of her aerobic target zone is 0.6 × 175 = 105 bpm,
and the lower threshold of her anaerobic target zone is 0.8 × 175 = 140 bpm.

A graph of Joanna's heart rate (bpm) during exercise.

Anaerobic target zone starts

Aerobic target zone starts

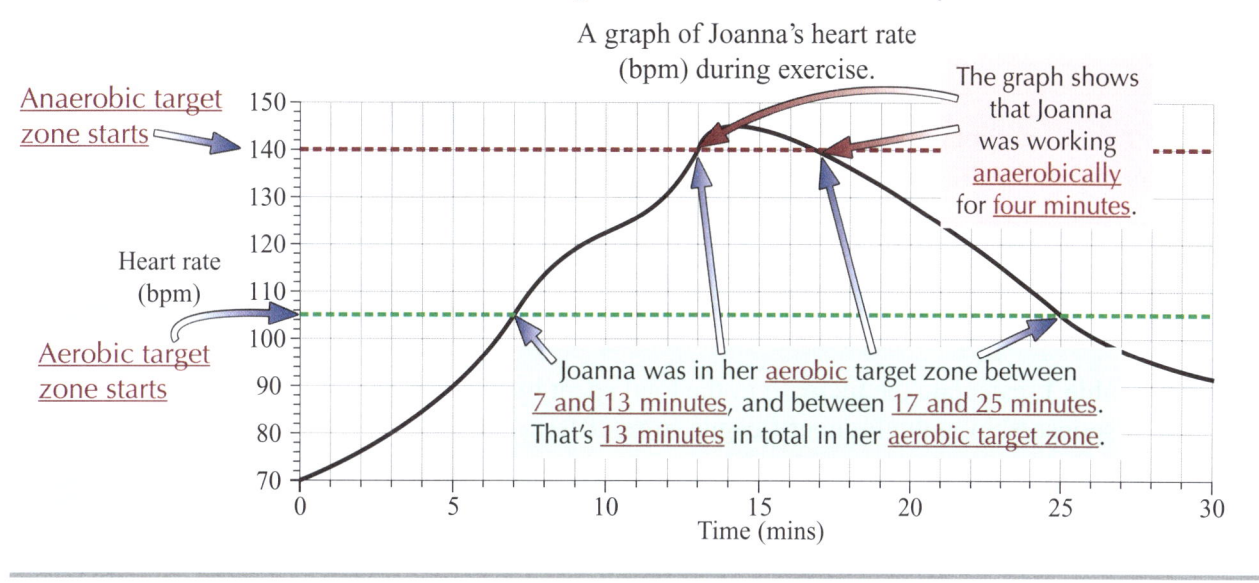

The graph shows that Joanna was working anaerobically for four minutes.

Joanna was in her aerobic target zone between 7 and 13 minutes, and between 17 and 25 minutes. That's 13 minutes in total in her aerobic target zone.

Data can be used to help Monitor your Progress

Check back to page 91 to read about goal setting and SMART targets.

Data about your performances in training can help you to see whether or not you're on track to meet your goals. This is one of the reasons your targets need to be measurable. E.g.:

Nadège has just started cycling and she wants to improve her average speed. She sets herself a goal to increase her average speed by 4 km/h in 12 weeks.

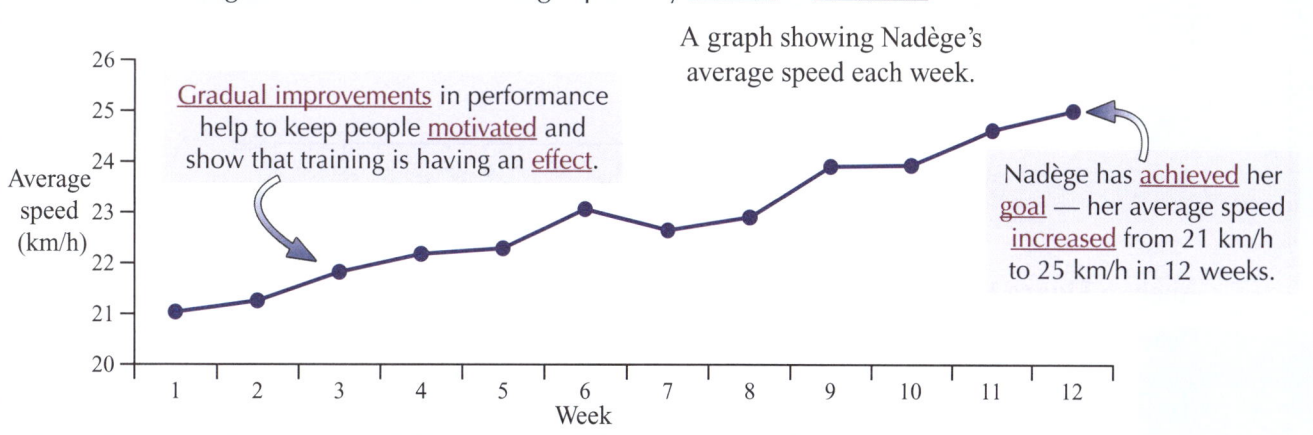

A graph showing Nadège's average speed each week.

Gradual improvements in performance help to keep people motivated and show that training is having an effect.

Nadège has achieved her goal — her average speed increased from 21 km/h to 25 km/h in 12 weeks.

Having a goal to aim for helps motivate people to keep training. In turn, this means that they are far more likely to achieve their goal — because they are sticking to their training regime. It's a win-win situation...

EXAM TIP — If it helps, don't be afraid to draw on the graph...

If you get a question where you need to use a graph to work out when someone was in the different training target zones, it might help if you draw the thresholds of the zones on the graph.

Section Seven — Using Data

Warm-Up and Worked Exam Questions

Data crops up all over PE, so it's important that you get to grips with everything covered in this section. Go through the warm-up and worked exam questions carefully before you try the exam style questions.

Warm-Up Questions

1) Give two ways of collecting quantitative data.
2) Describe how an upward trend would be shown on a line graph.
3) What can fitness testing data tell you about a training programme?

Worked Exam Questions

1 **Table 1** shows the total spent by companies on shirt sponsorship in the Premier League from 2010 to 2015. *Grade 3-5*

Year season began	2010	2011	2012	2013	2014	2015
Total spent (millions of pounds)	100.45	117.5	147.1	165.75	191.35	222.9

Table 1

Using **Table 1**, calculate the increase in the total spent by companies on shirt sponsorship in the Premier League from 2010 to 2015.

£222.9 million − £100.45 million = £122.45 million

[1 mark]

2 **Figure 1** shows the percentage of adults that were obese by gender from 1993 to 2013. *Grade 5-7*

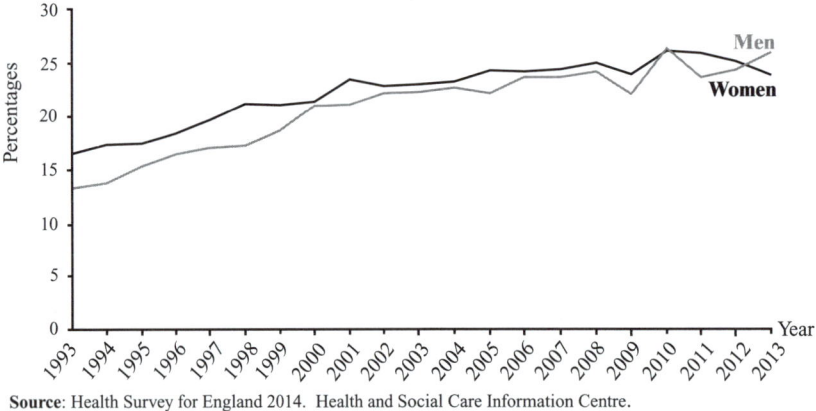

Source: Health Survey for England 2014. Health and Social Care Information Centre.

Figure 1

Analyse **Figure 1**.
Describe the changes in obesity rates for men and women between 2009 and 2013.

In 2009 the obesity rate for men was lower than the rate for women, but in 2010 the rate for men increased sharply and men had a higher obesity rate than women. The obesity rate for men decreased between 2010 and 2011, before rising again for two years. However, the obesity rate for women consistently fell between 2010 and 2013.

[4 marks]

Section Seven — Using Data

Exam Questions

1 Amir has been following a training programme. [Grade 3-5]

Table 1 shows the results of two different fitness tests that Amir has done in each week of his training programme.

Fitness Test	Week					
	1	2	3	4	5	6
Sit and reach test (cm)	5.0	5.0	5.5	6.0	6.5	7.0
One minute sit-up test (no. of sit-ups)	25	25	24	25	24	25

Table 1

Analyse the data in **Table 1** and describe the trends for each of the fitness tests.

....

....

....

[2 marks]

2 **Table 2** shows the numbers of yellow cards awarded each year at a five-a-side football tournament.

Year	2009	2010	2011	2012	2013	2014	2015
No. of yellow cards	6	7	10	11	8	9	12

Table 2

(a) Complete the graph below to display the data in **Table 2**. Label the axes and join up the points to make a line graph. [Grade 3-5]

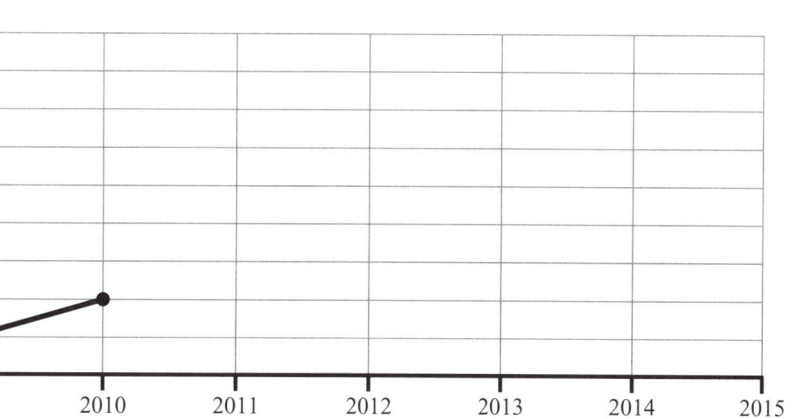

[2 marks]

From 2013 the organisers of the tournament brought in a fine for anyone receiving a yellow card, to try to encourage fair play.

(b) Analyse the data in **Table 2** to determine whether the fine has been successful. Justify your answer. [Grade 5-7]

....

....

[2 marks]

Section Seven — Using Data

Revision Questions for Section Seven

That's it for Section Seven. Now put your data skills to the test with these revision questions...
- Try these questions and tick off each one when you get it right.
- When you've done all the questions for a topic and are completely happy with it, tick off the topic.

Using Data (p117-121)

1) Describe the difference between quantitative and qualitative data.
2) Give two ways of collecting qualitative data.
3) Do fitness tests give qualitative or quantitative data?
4) Look at the bar chart below. Which BMI category contains the highest number of students? Which contains the lowest?

Number of students with each Body Mass Index (BMI) rating

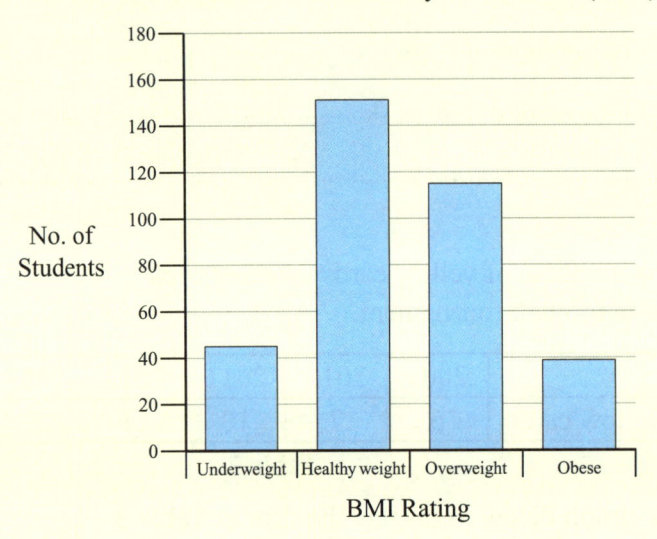

5) What is a 'trend'?
6) Look at the line graph below. How many sin-bins were awarded in 2009? How many more were awarded in 2011?

Total number of sin-bins awarded each year

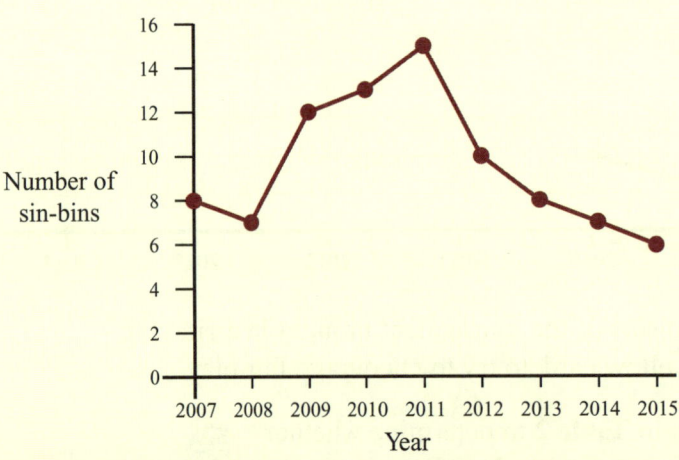

7) Give one way that data on performance in training can improve the effectiveness of a training programme.

Section Seven — Using Data

Practice Papers

Once you've been through all the questions in this book, you should be starting to feel prepared for the final exams. As a last bit of preparation, here are two practice exam papers for you to try — both papers contain a mixture of multiple-choice, short-answer and extended writing questions. Paper 1 will test you on the topics in Sections 1-3 and 7 of this book, and Paper 2 will test you on the topics in Sections 4-7. So even if your course only has one exam, try both papers so you get some practice with all of the topic areas.

Candidate Surname	Candidate Forename(s)

Centre Number	Candidate Number	Candidate Signature

GCSE

Physical Education
Paper 1

Practice Paper
Time allowed: 1 hour 30 minutes

You are **allowed** to use a calculator.

Instructions to candidates
- Use **black** ink to write your answers.
- Write your name and other details in the spaces provided above.
- Answer **all** questions in the spaces provided.
- In calculations show clearly how you worked out your answers.

Information for candidates
- The marks available are given in brackets at the end of each question.
- There are 80 marks available for this paper.

Advice
- Carefully read each question before answering it.
- Try to answer every question.
- If you have time after finishing the paper, go back and check your answers.

Practice Paper 1

Answer ALL the questions.

Write your answers in the spaces provided.

You must answer some questions with a cross in a box ☒. If you change your mind about an answer, put a line through the box ☒, then mark your new answer with a cross ☒.

1   (a) Which one of the following bones is found in the lower leg?

   ☐ **A** Clavicle
   ☐ **B** Ulna
   ☐ **C** Tibia
   ☐ **D** Femur

[1]

(b) Which one of the following muscles is responsible for flexion at the knee?

   ☐ **A** Quadriceps
   ☐ **B** Hamstrings
   ☐ **C** Hip flexors
   ☐ **D** Gluteus maximus

[1]

(c) Which one of the following describes a third class lever system?

   ☐ **A** The load is between the fulcrum and effort
   ☐ **B** The fulcrum is between the effort and load
   ☐ **C** The effort is at the end of the lever
   ☐ **D** The effort is between the fulcrum and load

[1]

(d) Identify the type of movement that would occur in the sagittal plane.

   ☐ **A** Flexion
   ☐ **B** Abduction
   ☐ **C** Rotation
   ☐ **D** Adduction

[1]

Practice Paper 1

(e) Which one of the following fitness tests measures cardiovascular endurance?

- [ ] A Cooper 12-minute run test
- [ ] B Vertical jump test
- [ ] C 30 m sprint test
- [ ] D One rep max test

[1]

(f) Which one of the following methods of training can be used to improve both aerobic and anaerobic fitness?

- [ ] A Continuous training
- [ ] B Resistance training
- [ ] C Plyometric training
- [ ] D Circuit training

[1]

Hanif is a 22-year-old basketball player. He has just taken the vertical jump test.

Table 1 shows ratings for the vertical jump test for adult athletes.

Gender	Excellent	Above Average	Average	Below Average	Poor
Male	>70 cm	56-70 cm	41-55 cm	31-40 cm	<31 cm
Female	>60 cm	46-60 cm	31-45 cm	21-30 cm	<21 cm

Table 1

(g) Which one of the following is the correct rating for Hanif, given that he scored 61 cm in the vertical jump test?

- [ ] A Poor
- [ ] B Average
- [ ] C Above Average
- [ ] D Excellent

[1]

[Total 7 marks]

Practice Paper 1

2 Tendons are part of the musculo-skeletal system.

Explain the role of tendons in movement of the skeleton.

....

....

....

....

....

....

....

[Total 2 marks]

3 **Figure 1** shows an athlete preparing to jump during plyometric training.

Figure 1

Analyse, using **one** example, how **one** of the antagonistic muscle pairs in the body enables the athlete to jump.

....

....

....

....

....

....

....

[Total 3 marks]

Practice Paper 1

4 Describe what it means for a lever to have a mechanical advantage.

....

....

....

....

[Total 2 marks]

5 Explain how blood can be redistributed around the body during exercise.

....

....

....

....

....

....

[Total 3 marks]

6 Assess the positive and negative impact on performance of using anaerobic respiration during a swimming race.

(i) Positive

....
....
....
....
....
....
....

[3]

(ii) Negative

....
....
....
....
....
....
....

[3]
[Total 6 marks]

7   Explain how an increase in both breathing rate and heart rate provides
    the muscles with the oxygen they need during physical activity and sport.

    ....

    ....

    ....

    ....

    ....

    ....

    ....

    [Total 4 marks]

8   **Figure 2** shows a diver standing on their toes in preparation for a dive.

    Figure 2

    (a) Classify the lever being used in **Figure 2**.

        ....
        [1]

    (b) Explain your answer.

        ....

        ....

        ....
        [1]
        [Total 2 marks]

Practice Paper 1

9 Jack uses a heart rate monitor during a 50-minute training session with his running club. **Figure 3** shows his heart rate values during the session.

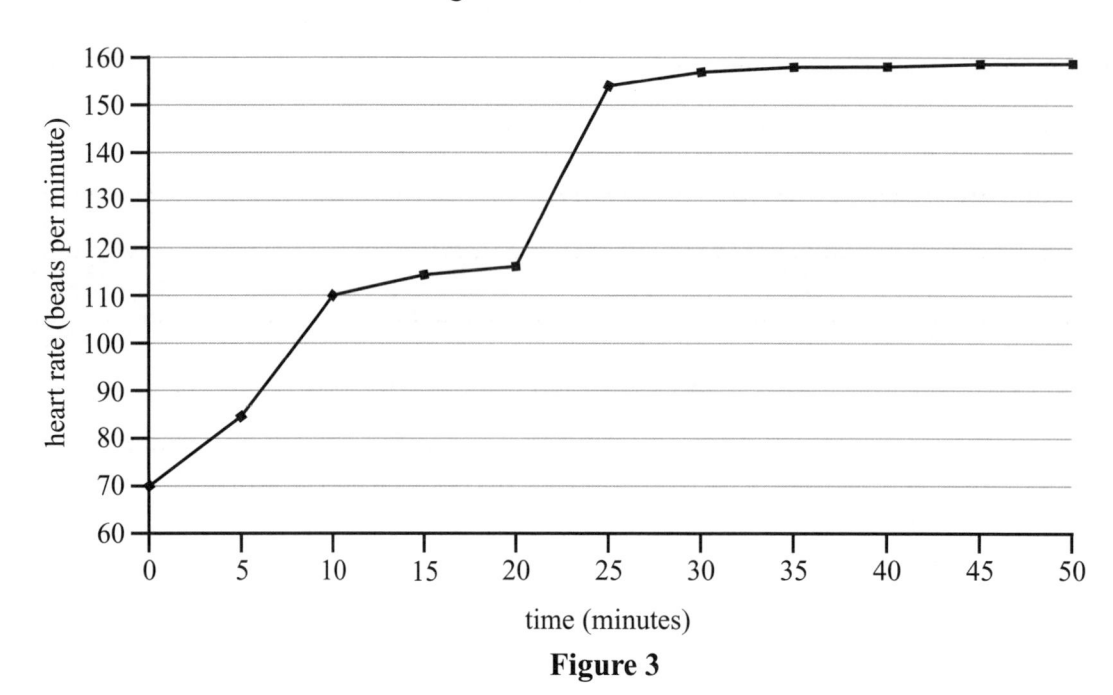

Figure 3

Using **Figure 3**, analyse Jack's heart rate at the following times to suggest what may have happened in his training session during those times. Justify your answers.

(i) Between 0 and 20 minutes.

....

....

....

[2]

(ii) Between 20 and 50 minutes.

....

....

....

[2]
[Total 4 marks]

10 Explain how the long-term effects of regular exercise on the heart would benefit an endurance athlete's performance.

....

....

....

....

....

....

....

[Total 3 marks]

11 **Figure 4** shows a tennis player using a third class lever system at the shoulder to swing the tennis racket and hit the ball.

Figure 4

Analyse how this third class lever system affects the tennis player's performance.

....

....

....

....

....

....

[Total 3 marks]

Practice Paper 1

12 Explain how a high level of flexibility can improve a long jumper's performance.

....
....
....
....
....
....
....

[Total 3 marks]

13 The sit and reach test and the vertical jump test are two fitness tests.

Assess the importance of each of these fitness tests for a beach volleyball player.

(i) Sit and reach test

....
....
....
....
....
....
....

[3]

(ii) Vertical jump test

....
....
....
....
....
....
....

[3]

[Total 6 marks]

Practice Paper 1

14 Hannah has been using the Illinois agility run test and the 30 m sprint test to monitor how her training is going. **Table 2** shows the results of her fitness tests.

Fitness Test	Week 1	Week 3	Week 5	Week 7	Week 9
Illinois agility run test	22 s	20.7 s	20.2 s	19.4 s	18.5 s
30 m sprint test	5.60 s	5.55 s	5.45 s	5.40 s	5.40 s

Table 2

(a) Describe how to carry out the Illinois agility run test.

....
....
....
....
[2]

(b) Analyse the data in **Table 2** to determine the trends for both fitness tests.

....
....
....
....
[2]

Hannah would like to improve her power.

(c) Identify **one** training method she could use to improve this component of fitness.

....
[1]
[Total 5 marks]

Practice Paper 1

15 Matthew plays for his school hockey team.
To improve his performance, Matthew trains by jogging for half an hour twice a week.

(a) Discuss whether his training applies the training principle of specificity.

....
....
....
....
....
....
....
[4]

After a month of training, Matthew finds that his fitness is no longer improving because he is not achieving overload.

(b) Using the FITT principles, outline how Matthew could alter his training to achieve overload.

....
....
....
....
....
....
....
....
[4]
[Total 8 marks]

16 Weight training can be used to improve strength and muscular endurance.

(a) Explain how weight training can be used to improve muscular endurance.

....

....
[2]

(b) Give **one** advantage and **one** disadvantage of weight training.

Advantage

....

....

Disadvantage

....

....
[2]
[Total 4 marks]

17 Evaluate the importance of muscular endurance and agility for performance in netball.

....

....

....

....

....

....

....

....

....

....

....

....

....

....

....
[Total 6 marks]

18 Evaluate the extent to which an increase in tidal volume would allow a midfielder in football to perform well during a match.

[Total 9 marks]

TOTAL FOR PAPER = 80 MARKS

Candidate Surname		Candidate Forename(s)	

Centre Number	Candidate Number	Candidate Signature

GCSE

Physical Education
Paper 2

Practice Paper
Time allowed: 1 hour 30 minutes

You are **allowed** to use a calculator.

Instructions to candidates
- Use **black** ink to write your answers.
- Write your name and other details in the spaces provided above.
- Answer **all** questions in the spaces provided.

Information for candidates
- The marks available are given in brackets at the end of each question.
- There are 80 marks available for this paper.

Advice
- Carefully read each question before answering it.
- Try to answer every question.
- If you have time after finishing the paper, go back and check your answers.

Practice Paper 2

Answer ALL the questions.

Write your answers in the spaces provided.

You must answer some questions with a cross in a box ☒. If you change your mind about an answer, put a line through the box ☒, then mark your new answer with a cross ☒.

1 (a) Which one of the following describes a key role of carbohydrates in a balanced diet?

☐ A Carbohydrates are used for muscle repair
☐ B Carbohydrates are the main source of energy for the body
☐ C Carbohydrates provide the body with nutrients such as omega-3 and omega-6
☐ D Carbohydrates are used by the body to help protect vital organs

[1]

(b) Which one of the following is **false**?

☐ A A sedentary lifestyle can lead to emotional health problems such as depression
☐ B Agility may decrease as a result of a sedentary lifestyle
☐ C A sedentary lifestyle can have consequences for social health
☐ D Someone who exercises once a month does not have a sedentary lifestyle

[1]

(c) Which one of the following describes intrinsic feedback?

☐ A Feedback from how a performance feels to the performer
☐ B Feedback that contains only positive comments
☐ C Feedback from the audience at an event
☐ D Feedback that a coach gives to a performer

[1]

(d) Which one of the following describes manual guidance?

☐ A When a learner uses sport equipment to help them learn a skill
☐ B When a coach physically moves a learner's body through a technique
☐ C When a learner watches someone else perform a technique before practising it
☐ D When a learner listens to an explanation of how to perform a technique

[1]

Practice Paper 2

Alison takes part in very little physical activity because her nearest sports centre is five miles away and she doesn't own a car. Public transport links to the sports centre are also very poor.

(e) Which one of the following types of influence has affected Alison's participation in physical activity?

☐ A   Disability
☐ B   Age
☐ C   Gender
☐ D   Socio-economic

[1]

(f) Which one of the following is an example of gamesmanship?

☐ A   Time-wasting in football
☐ B   Using performance-enhancing drugs
☐ C   Deliberately tripping an opponent in football
☐ D   Blood doping

[1]

(g) **Figure 1** shows data on the frequency of alcohol consumption in the years 2005 to 2014.

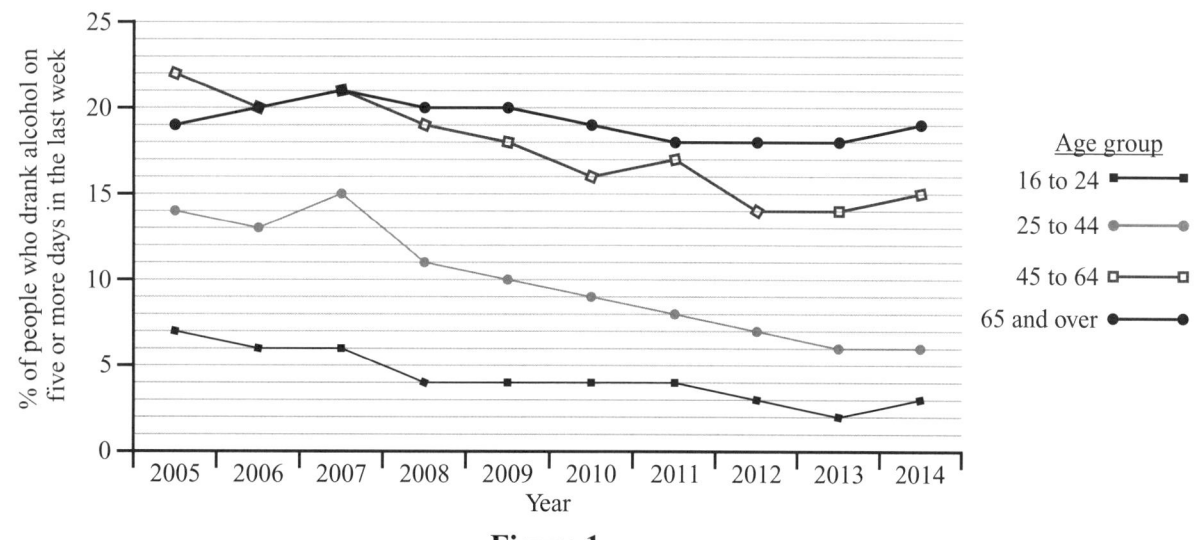

Figure 1

Using **Figure 1**, identify the age group that saw the largest **decrease** in the percentage who drank alcohol on five or more days, between 2005 and 2014.

☐ A   16 to 24
☐ B   25 to 44
☐ C   45 to 64
☐ D   65 and over

[1]

[Total 7 marks]

Practice Paper 2

2 Exercise can improve physical, emotional and social health and well-being.

(a) Give **one** example of a physical benefit of exercise.

....

....
[1]

(b) Explain **one** way that exercise can improve emotional health.

....

....

....
[2]

(c) Exercise can help you to learn the skills of teamwork and cooperation. State whether this is a physical, emotional or social benefit of exercise.

....
[1]

[Total 4 marks]

3 Explain how a sedentary lifestyle can lead to an increased risk of heart disease and osteoporosis.

....

....

....

....

....

....

....

[Total 4 marks]

4 Water is one of the nutrients required for a balanced diet.

(a) Complete the following statements about the effects of dehydration.

Dehydration can cause the blood to become .... It can also cause your

body temperature to ....

[2]

(b) Give **one** way that exercise causes the body to lose water.

....

....

[1]

(c) Explain **two** ways that dehydration can negatively affect performance in a 5-mile running race.

1 ....

....

2 ....

....

[4]

[Total 7 marks]

5 The optimum weights of a rugby player and a hockey player are different.

(a) State which sport will have the higher optimum weight.

....

[1]

(b) Explain why two rugby players in the same team might have different optimum weights.

....

....

....

[2]

(c) Explain how a hockey player could manipulate their energy balance to increase how much they weigh.

....

....

....

[2]

[Total 5 marks]

Practice Paper 2

6 Sports skills can be classified using the basic-complex continuum.
An example is shown below.

Football pass — marked with X toward the basic end of a continuum line between Basic and Complex.

Justify the position of the football pass at this point on the continuum.

....
....
....
....
....
....

[Total 3 marks]

7 Variable and fixed practice can be used to improve performance in sport.

Assess the importance of these practice types for improving performance in tennis.

(i) Variable practice

....
....
....
....

[3]

(ii) Fixed practice

....
....
....
....

[3]
[Total 6 marks]

8 Amanda sets herself a goal to complete an 80-mile bike ride in four months' time.

Analyse how the application of one of the principles of SMART in Amanda's goal will help her to achieve her goal.

....
....
....
....
....
....

[Total 3 marks]

9 A coach uses manual guidance when teaching a gymnast to perform a cartwheel on the beam. Give **one** advantage and **one** disadvantage of the coach using this guidance type.

Advantage

....
....

Disadvantage

....
....

[Total 2 marks]

Practice Paper 2

10 **Figures 2a and 2b** show data on participation rates in swimming and football between 07/08 and 14/15.

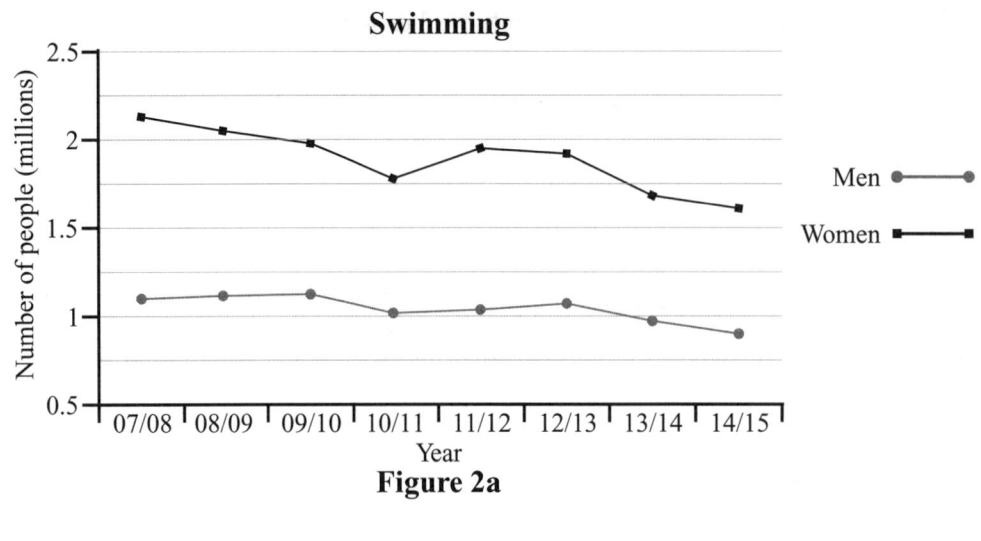

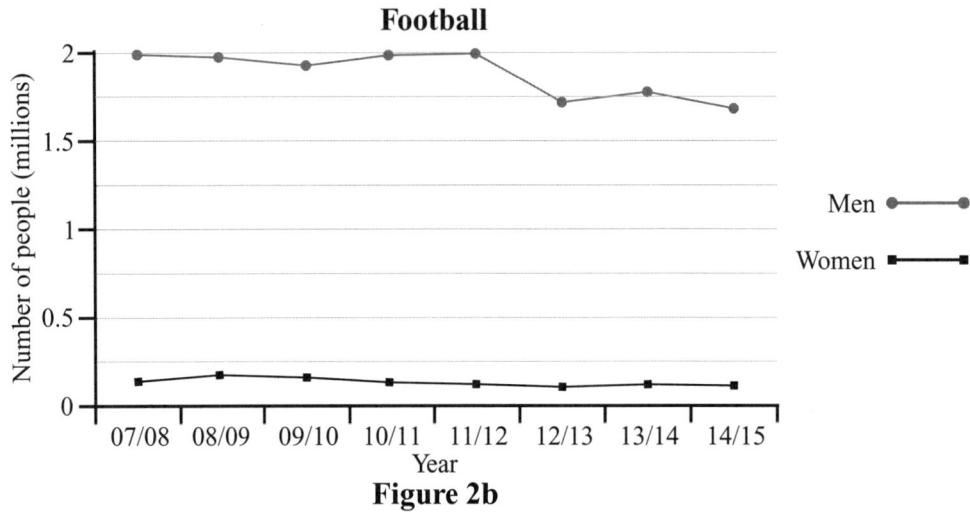

Swimming

Figure 2a

Football

Figure 2b

(a) Analyse **Figure 2a** to determine the trend in participation in swimming between 2007 and 2015.

....
[1]

(b) Analyse **Figures 2a** and **2b** to determine the differences in participation levels between men and women in swimming and football. Give **one** possible reason for these differences in each sport.

Swimming

....

....

....
[2]

Football

....

....

....
[2]

[Total 5 marks]

11 Studies by Sport England have shown that people from some ethnic groups
are more likely to participate in physical activity than others.

   (a) Explain **one** reason why an individual's ethnicity can affect their participation in sport.

   ....
   ....
   ....
   ....
   [2]

   (b) Give **one** other personal factor, besides ethnicity or gender,
   that can affect an individual's participation in sport.

   ....
   [1]
   [Total 3 marks]

12 Sponsorship, sport and the media have grown to rely on one another.

   (a) Outline **one** way that sponsorship could have a positive effect on a sports team.

   ....
   ....
   ....
   ....
   [3]

   (b) Give **one** example of an inappropriate sponsor for an under-16s badminton tournament.

   ....
   [1]

   (c) Explain your answer to part (b).

   ....
   ....
   ....
   [2]
   [Total 6 marks]

Practice Paper 2

13 Assess the positive and negative impact of increased media interest in a sport.

(i) Positive impact

....
....
....
....
[3]

(ii) Negative impact

....
....
....
....
[3]
[Total 6 marks]

14 Some sportspeople display gamesmanship while competing.

(a) Define **gamesmanship**.

....
....
[1]

(b) Assess the impact of elite performers demonstrating gamesmanship in high profile sports, such as cricket.

....
....
....
....
....
....
[3]
[Total 4 marks]

Practice Paper 2

15 Analyse how carbohydrates, fats and proteins would benefit the training and performance of a basketball player.

....
....
....
....
....
....
....
....
....
....
....
....
....
....
....

[Total 6 marks]

16 Outline what visual and mechanical guidance are and justify their use when coaching a group of beginners in trampolining.

[Total 9 marks]

TOTAL FOR PAPER = 80 MARKS

Answers

A note about marks and grades
The answers and mark schemes given here should be used mainly for guidance, as there may be many different correct answers to each question — don't panic if your answers are a bit different. The grade stamps are a rough guide to the level of difficulty of each question, and should not be used to predict the grade you'll get in the real exams.

Section One — Anatomy and Physiology

Page 12 (Warm-Up Questions)
1) Vital Organs.
2) E.g. The tibia. It is used when the lower leg flexes and extends to kick a football.
3) E.g. The vertebral column protects the spinal cord.
4) E.g. The shoulder. It allows flexion, extension, adduction, abduction, rotation and circumduction.
5) Ligaments, tendons and cartilage
6) E.g. Synovial fluid lubricates joints to allow them to move more easily.
7) The gastrocnemius
8) Antagonistic muscle pair
9) Eccentric
10) Type I

Page 13 (Exam Questions)
1 (a) A Deltoid *[1 mark]*
        B Triceps *[1 mark]*
        C Latissimus dorsi *[1 mark]*
   (b) Quadriceps *[1 mark]*
2 E.g. In position A, the biceps are contracting and the triceps are relaxing *[1 mark]* to flex the elbows *[1 mark]*. In position B, the triceps are contracting and biceps are relaxing *[1 mark]* to extend the elbows *[1 mark]*.

Page 19 (Warm-Up Questions)
1) Pulmonary
2) Arteries
3) Red
4) Trachea
5) Exhaled air
6) E.g. Tidal volume is the volume of air breathed in or out during one breath, whereas vital capacity is the greatest volume of air that can possibly be breathed in after breathing out as much as possible.

Page 20 (Exam Questions)
1 **D** Alveoli *[1 mark]*
2 E.g. The cardiovascular system releases heat by shunting blood closer to the skin's surface *[1 mark]*. This allows a performer to exercise for long periods without overheating *[1 mark]*.
3 E.g. Arteries have thick, muscular walls *[1 mark]*, which allows them to carry blood flowing at high pressure *[1 mark]*.
4 E.g. The thin walls of alveoli allow gases to pass through them easily *[1 mark]*. This makes it easier for oxygen to pass from the alveoli into the blood in the capillaries surrounding them *[1 mark]* and for carbon dioxide to pass from the blood in the capillaries into the alveoli *[1 mark]*.
5 E.g. Red blood cells carry oxygen *[1 mark]*, so a high number of red blood cells would lead to more oxygen being delivered to the muscles during exercise *[1 mark]*. This is very important for an endurance athlete, as it would allow them to work aerobically for long periods *[1 mark]*.

Page 26 (Warm-Up Questions)
1) Aerobic
2) The ATP-PC energy system is used during the first few seconds of exercise.
3) Oxygen debt is the amount of oxygen needed to remove lactic acid and recover after exercising using anaerobic respiration.
4) Exercise causes an increase in breathing rate.
5) Stroke volume increases during exercise.
6) Cardiac output = heart rate × stroke volume
7) Any **one** from:
   - Muscle hypertrophy/increased muscle strength/increased muscular endurance
   - Increased bone density/stronger bones
   - Improved posture
   - Stronger ligaments
   - Stronger tendons
   - Increased flexibility of joints
8) Cardiac hypertrophy is when the heart muscle gets bigger and stronger.

Pages 27-28 (Exam Questions)
1 (a) E.g. Anaerobic respiration happens when the muscles need more oxygen than the body can provide *[1 mark]*.
   (b) E.g. The by-product of anaerobic respiration is lactic acid *[1 mark]*, which gradually builds up and causes fatigue in muscles. This could negatively affect performance, as a performer would need to slow down or stop their activity to recover *[1 mark]*.
2 (a) Any **one** from: e.g.
        - Increased lung capacity
        - Increased strength of diaphragm
        - Increased strength of external intercostal muscles
        - Increase in number of alveoli in lungs
        - Increased vital capacity
        - Increased maximum tidal volume and minute ventilation
        [1 mark available]
   (b) E.g. Breathing rate and heart rate may remain high after exercise has stopped in order to keep taking in large amounts of oxygen and delivering it to the muscles to repay oxygen debt *[1 mark]* by removing waste products such as lactic acid *[1 mark]*.
3 E.g. The performer's heart rate was much higher throughout workout A *[1 mark]*, which suggests that they exercised at a higher intensity than in workout B *[1 mark]*.
4 (a) E.g. Arm muscles *[1 mark]* and leg muscles *[1 mark]*.
   (b) E.g. The muscles in the arms and legs would be working while swimming *[1 mark]*, so they would need more oxygenated blood *[1 mark]* in order to release the extra energy needed for swimming movements *[1 mark]*.
        You could also have said that the muscles in the arms and legs would release more waste products, such as carbon dioxide or lactic acid, so they would need extra blood to remove them.
5 *This mark scheme gives examples of some points you might have made in your answer. You can still get full marks if you haven't written every individual point below, as long as the points you have made are detailed enough and you meet all three assessment objectives.*

   To meet assessment objective one, you will need to show knowledge of aerobic and anaerobic respiration, for example:
   - Aerobic respiration uses glucose and oxygen to release energy.
   - Aerobic respiration is needed for activities that require endurance.
   - Anaerobic respiration uses glucose to release energy, but doesn't use oxygen.

   To meet assessment objective two, you will need to include examples of when aerobic and anaerobic respiration would be needed during a 50-mile cycling race, for example:
   - Cycling for 50 miles would take several hours, so aerobic respiration would be needed for the majority of the race.
   - Anaerobic respiration would be needed for high-intensity parts of the race, for example, when cycling on a steep gradient.
   - Anaerobic respiration would be used for short bursts of speed on the bike.

   To meet assessment objective three, you will need to evaluate the importance of aerobic and anaerobic respiration for performance in a 50-mile cycling race, for example:
   - A cyclist in a 50-mile race would want to mainly use aerobic respiration to ensure they can maintain a good performance throughout the race.
   - The cyclist may want to avoid cycling at speeds where anaerobic respiration is needed too often, as this would cause muscle fatigue, leading to a drop in performance.

- In conclusion, both types of respiration are important to achieve good overall performance in a 50-mile cycling race, as the performer must balance endurance with speed.

[9 marks available in total]

Section Two — Movement Analysis

Page 33 (Warm-Up Questions)

1) Muscles
2) E.g. At the ankle, when standing on the toes.
3) E.g.

   It doesn't matter if your diagram has the load and effort the opposite way around — as long as the fulcrum is closer to the load than it is to the effort.
4) Third class levers have a mechanical disadvantage because the effort is between the load and fulcrum, so their effort arm is always shorter than their weight arm.
5) The transverse plane divides the body into top and bottom.
6) Longitudinal (or 'vertical' if you're doing the Edexcel or Eduqas course)

Page 34 (Exam Questions)

1. (i) Frontal plane *[1 mark]* and sagittal axis (or 'frontal axis' if you're doing the OCR course) *[1 mark]*.
   (ii) Sagittal plane *[1 mark]* and transverse axis (or 'frontal axis' if you're doing the Edexcel or Eduqas course) *[1 mark]*.
   (iii) Transverse plane *[1 mark]* and longitudinal axis (or 'vertical axis' if you're doing the Edexcel or Eduqas course) *[1 mark]*.
2. (a) Second class *[1 mark]*
   (b) Second class levers have a mechanical advantage, so can move large loads *[1 mark]* with a small effort from the muscles *[1 mark]*. This allows the performer to easily raise their entire body weight onto their toes *[1 mark]*.

Section Three — Physical Training

Page 47 (Warm-Up Questions)

1) E.g. Exercise is a form of physical activity done to maintain or improve health or fitness.
2) A gymnast holding a hand stand.
3) E.g. A high level of flexibility decreases the chances of pulling or straining muscles.
4) E.g. Body composition is the percentage of body weight made up of muscle, bone and fat.
5) Agility is more important for a football player.
6) E.g. A gymnast needs good balance to keep themselves stable on the beam.
7) E.g. Reaction time is the amount of time it takes to move in response to a stimulus.
8) Power is a combination of strength and speed.
9) E.g. The Harvard step test, the multi-stage fitness test and the Cooper 12-minute run test.
   You could also have said the Cooper 12-minute swim test.
10) E.g. The standing jump test and the vertical jump test
11) Body fat percentage/body composition
12) E.g. Many of the tests do not test specific sporting actions. They do not tell you how an athlete will perform under pressure in a competition. Some tests are submaximal, so the real maximum is an unknown.
    You might have also said that fitness test scores can improve through practising them without the relevant components of fitness improving.

Pages 48-49 (Exam Questions)

1. **D** Cardiovascular Endurance *[1 mark]*
2. **A** Good *[1 mark]*

3. Muscular endurance is the ability to repeatedly use your voluntary muscles over a long time without getting tired *[1 mark]*. Good muscular endurance would benefit a runner's performance as they would be able to run for a long time without getting tired *[1 mark]*.
4. E.g. The sit and reach test to measure flexibility. The student should sit on the floor with their legs straight out in front of them against a box. Then they reach as far forward as they can, and an assistant measures the distance reached in centimetres. The distance reached is a measure of their flexibility.
   E.g. The ruler drop test to measure reaction time. The tester holds a ruler vertically, with the 0 cm mark in line with the top of the student's thumb. The tester drops the ruler, and the student must try to catch it. The distance that the ruler falls before the student catches it is a measure of their reaction time.
   [6 marks available in total — 1 mark for each named test of flexibility, reaction time or muscular endurance and 2 marks for a complete description of each test, or 1 mark for a partial description].
5. (a) E.g. Eric could compare his fitness test score to national averages to understand where he ranked *[1 mark]*.
   Eric could use fitness testing to monitor his progress, so he would know whether his training was effective *[1 mark]*.
   (b) E.g. The Cooper 12-minute run test measures cardiovascular fitness (aerobic endurance) *[1 mark]*, whereas the 30 m sprint test measures maximum sprint speed over a short distance *[1 mark]*. The triathlon is an endurance event that requires a high level of cardiovascular fitness, so the Cooper 12-minute test is more suitable for Eric *[1 mark]*.
   (c) Eric's training is not improving his cardiovascular fitness *[1 mark]*.
6. *This mark scheme gives examples of some points you might have made in your answer. You can still get full marks if you haven't written every individual point below, as long as the points you have made are detailed enough and you meet all three assessment objectives.*
   To meet assessment objective one, you will need to show knowledge of cardiovascular fitness and power, for example:
   - Good cardiovascular fitness means you can exercise the whole body for a long time.
   - Power is the ability to do strength actions with speed.

   To meet assessment objective two, you will need to include examples of how these components of fitness could impact a long-jumper's performance, for example:
   - A long jumper only has to run for a short amount of time, so will not need to exercise aerobically for a long time during a competition.
   - During a long jump, both the sprint up to the board and the take-off from the board require lots of power.

   To meet assessment objective three, you will need to make judgements about the importance of these components of fitness for a long-jumper, for example:
   - Cardiovascular fitness is not the most important component of fitness for a long jumper as they only have a short sprint before they jump.
   - Power is very important for a long jumper as it allows them to sprint quickly and jump explosively from the board.

Page 53 (Warm-Up Questions)

1) A Personal Exercise Programme. It is designed to improve health, a particular component of fitness or fitness in general.
2) Overload is working the body harder than it would normally work.
3) E.g. A training programme should be carefully monitored to ensure that overload is being achieved.
4) E.g. To give your muscles the chance to adapt, and to repair the damage caused by physical activity.
5) Both

Page 54 (Exam Questions)

1. (a) They are likely to have decreased *[1 mark]*.
   (b) Athletes need to leave enough time to allow the body to repair itself, which reduces the risk of injury and allows adaptations which increase fitness to take place *[1 mark]*. However, athletes should not rest too much so that their fitness level drops due to reversibility *[1 mark]*.
2. Fatima should spend more time training anaerobically *[1 mark]* as weightlifting requires short bursts of maximal effort, so is an anaerobic activity *[1 mark]*.
3. (a) Specificity means matching training to the activity and components of fitness you want to improve *[1 mark]*.
   (b) E.g. Lucy could apply specificity to her training by making sure that most of her training involves running long distances without taking breaks *[1 mark]*.

Answers

Page 60 (Warm-Up Questions)

1) Fartlek training is a type of continuous training that involves changing the intensity of the exercise over different intervals.
2) A rep is one single completed movement, whereas a set is a group of reps.
3) E.g. Weight training and plyometric training.
4) E.g. It takes a long time to set up.
5) E.g. Endurance athletes, because the increase in red blood cells helps them to perform aerobically for longer.
6) E.g. Active stretching means using your own muscles to hold the stretch position. Passive stretching means using equipment or an assistant to help you hold the stretch position.
7) Strength, muscular endurance and cardiovascular endurance.
8) Pre-season (preparation) and post-season (transition).

Pages 61-62 (Exam Questions)

1 **C** Fartlek training *[1 mark]*
2 **A** Plyometric training *[1 mark]*
3 Resistance training can be used to improve strength, muscular endurance and **power**. To improve strength, a **high** weight is used, with a **low** number of reps.
   [3 marks available in total — 1 mark for each correct word or phrase]
   You would still get marks for using different words that mean the same thing as 'high' and 'low' here, e.g. if you wrote 'large' and 'small' instead.
4 (a) E.g. Continuous training *[1 mark]*, as it improves cardiovascular and muscular endurance, which are both important for cross-country *[1 mark]*.
       Interval training or fartlek training would also be okay here.
   (b) E.g. Continuous training doesn't need much equipment to do *[1 mark]*.
       E.g. Continuous training can be boring as there is no variety in the training *[1 mark]*.
5 E.g. Interval training *[1 mark]* because there are alternating periods of higher- and lower-intensity exercise shown on the graph *[1 mark]*.
   You could have also interpreted the graph as showing fartlek training or circuit training, as both also involve alternating periods of different intensity exercise.
6 *This mark scheme gives examples of some points you might have made in your answer. You can still get full marks if you haven't written every individual point below, as long as the points you have made are detailed enough and you meet all three assessment objectives.*
   To meet assessment objective one, you will need to show knowledge of interval training and continuous training, for example:
   • Interval training involves alternating periods of high- and low-intensity exercise.
   • Continuous training involves training at a constant rate without any rests.
   • Interval training can improve both aerobic and anaerobic fitness.
   To meet assessment objective two, you will need to include examples of how these training methods could impact a basketball player's performance, for example:
   • Basketball often requires sudden spurts of fast movement to beat an opponent to the ball. Interval training can help prepare the player for this by combining slower jogs with quicker sprints within one training session.
   • Continuous training improves cardiovascular fitness, which will help the basketball player to use their muscles continuously throughout a game.
   • Continuous training does not improve anaerobic fitness, so does not help prepare the basketball player for when they may need to sprint.
   To meet assessment objective three, you will need to make judgements about the suitability of these training methods for a basketball player, for example:
   • Interval training is better suited to the conditions of a basketball game, with its constantly changing pace. Therefore interval training is a crucial part of a basketball player's training.
   • Continuous training is an important part of a basketball player's training as it improves cardiovascular fitness and helps to prepare them for constantly moving throughout the game.
   • In conclusion, both types of training can be used effectively by a basketball player, however it would be sensible for a basketball player to also use weight and plyometric training to develop the strength and power they need.

Page 69 (Warm-Up Questions)

1) E.g. To ensure that it is safe for a performer to take part in a new training programme.
2) Any **one** from: e.g.
   • It prepares the muscles that are going to be used during an activity.
   • It helps with mental preparation by focusing the performer on the activity and getting them "in the zone".
3) Any **one** from: e.g.
   • Leave enough recovery time
   • Eat and rehydrate
   • Complete a cool-down
   • Take an ice bath
   • Get a sports massage
4) Any **one** from: e.g.
   • Golfer's Elbow
   • Tennis Elbow
5) Simple, compound, stress and greenstick.
6) E.g. Ice helps reduce swelling and internal bleeding.
7) Any **one** from: e.g.
   • Nausea
   • Weakness
   • Low blood pressure
   • Cramp
   • Heart Failure

Page 70 (Exam Questions)

1 E.g. Jogging lightly increases heart rate *[1 mark]* which increases muscle temperature, so muscles are less likely to be injured *[1 mark]*.
2 (a) E.g. She can ensure students are wearing the correct protective clothing, like shin pads and gum shields *[1 mark]*. She can also inspect the pitch before they play to make sure that it's in good condition *[1 mark]* and she can referee the match *[1 mark]*.
   (b) E.g. Refereeing the game ensures that rules are followed *[1 mark]*. This reduces the chance of injury because it discourages players from committing fouls or carrying out dangerous actions that could injure other players *[1 mark]*.
       Inspecting the pitch makes sure that there aren't any tripping, slipping or other hazards *[1 mark]*. This reduces the risk of injury, as it makes players less likely to fall, or be cut by litter on the pitch, while playing *[1 mark]*.
3 Blood doping is where an athlete injects blood or takes EPO to increase the number of red blood cells in their bloodstream *[1 mark]*. This increases the oxygen supply to their muscles *[1 mark]* which can improve their performance in aerobic activities *[1 mark]*.

Section Four — Health, Fitness and Well-being

Page 76 (Warm-Up Questions)

1) It can lower blood pressure.
2) E.g. Exercise can create a feeling of having achieved something, for example, if a goal is achieved. This would lead to an increase in self-esteem as a performer would have a higher opinion of themselves and feel more confident.
3) E.g. Social well-being is about having friends, believing you have some worth in society and having food, clothing and shelter.
4) High alcohol consumption can raise blood pressure.
5) Nicotine
6) E.g. Being overweight can reduce flexibility, speed and agility, which would have a negative effect on performance.

Pages 77-78 (Exam Questions)

1 **A** It raises heart rate and blood pressure *[1 mark]*
2 **D** Regular exercise can help to increase self-esteem *[1 mark]*
3 Exercise increases the level of endorphins and **serotonin** in your brain, which may make you feel happier and help to reduce the risk of depression. *[1 mark for the correct word]*
4 E.g. Exercise helps to improve your insulin sensitivity *[1 mark]*. This means you are less likely to become insulin-resistant, so are less likely to get type-2 diabetes *[1 mark]*.
   You could also have written about how exercise helps you maintain a healthy weight which significantly reduces the risk of diabetes.

5 (a) 26% *[1 mark]*
(b) E.g. The overall trend is that the proportion of people who smoke in Great Britain is decreasing over time *[1 mark]*.
6 (a) E.g. A sedentary lifestyle is a lifestyle that involves little or no physical activity *[1 mark]*.
(b) E.g. Joint damage *[1 mark]*
E.g. Osteoporosis *[1 mark]*
(c) E.g. Regular exercise helps to maintain a healthy weight *[1 mark]*, which reduces the amount of strain placed on joints, helping to prevent damage to them *[1 mark]*.
E.g. Regular exercise can improve the body's ability to repair and strengthen bones *[1 mark]*, which helps to prevent osteoporosis as bones are less likely to become fragile *[1 mark]*.

Page 84 (Warm-Up Questions)

1) 55-60%
2) E.g. Minerals help to keep bones and teeth strong.
3) E.g. Fibre helps to keep the digestive system working properly.
4) E.g. Carbohydrate loading is when a performer increases their carbohydrate intake a few days before a competition, so they have plenty of energy stored in their muscles. It benefits endurance athletes, as they need plenty of energy to last the duration of their event.
5) Ectomorph
6) E.g. Wrestling
7) Obese
8) E.g. A neutral energy balance occurs if someone takes in the same amount of energy as they use up.
9) 2000

Pages 85-86 (Exam Questions)

1

Nutrient	Role in a balanced diet
Fat	Energy for low-intensity exercise
Protein	Repairing muscle
Carbohydrates	**Energy for all intensities of exercise**

[3 marks available — 1 mark for each correct entry]

2 Weight gain occurs when more energy is taken in than is used up by the body — this is known as a **positive** energy balance. To lose weight, more energy must be used up than is taken in — this is known as a **negative** energy balance.
[2 marks available in total — 1 mark for each correct word]

3 Chris may eat more protein *[1 mark]* in order to build up his muscles *[1 mark]*. Val may eat more carbohydrates *[1 mark]* to provide her with the energy that she requires for long distance runs *[1 mark]*.

4 (a) Any **two** from: e.g.
• Blood thickening
• Headaches
• Increase in body temperature/heat exhaustion
• Muscle cramps
• Fainting
[2 marks available in total]

(b) E.g. Performers would be at a high risk of dehydration during an endurance event like marathon running *[1 mark]* because this event lasts a very long time, so performers lose a lot of water through sweating and heavy breathing *[1 mark]*.

5 *This mark scheme gives examples of some points you might have made in your answer. You can still get full marks if you haven't written every individual point below, as long as the points you have made are detailed enough and you meet all three assessment objectives.*
To meet assessment objective one, you will need to show knowledge and understanding of the roles of fats and carbohydrates in physical activity, for example:
• Fats can be used as energy for low-intensity exercise.
• Carbohydrates can be used as energy for any intensity of exercise.
• Carbohydrate loading is used to increase stores of carbohydrates in the muscles in the days before an event.
To meet assessment objective two, you will need to include examples of how these nutrients affect performance in a marathon, for example:
• A marathon runner would use carbohydrates for energy for the majority of the race, as they are the main energy source for the body.
• A diet too high in fats could cause a marathon runner to gain weight. This would negatively affect their performance in the marathon by reducing their cardiovascular fitness and their speed by increasing the amount of weight they need to carry.
• Fats can be used as an energy source for low-intensity activity, so could be used when running very slowly during a marathon.
To meet assessment objective three, you will need to evaluate the importance of each nutrient for performance in a marathon, for example:
• Carbohydrates are an essential energy source in a marathon because they can provide energy for all parts of the race, including moderate- and high-intensity parts such as a sprint-finish.
• However, fats still provide a vital function in a balanced diet and help the body to function properly, and can be used as energy in the race if supplies of carbohydrates run out.
• In conclusion, a diet with some fat and plenty of carbohydrates, as well as the use of carbohydrate loading, will help provide essential fuel for performance in a marathon.
[9 marks available in total]

Section Five — Sport Psychology

Page 92 (Warm-Up Questions)

1) A performer's ability is their set of characteristics that control their potential to learn a skill.
2) Any **two** from:
• pre-determined
• efficient
• coordinated
• fluent
• confident
• aesthetic
• effective
• accurate
• technical
• consistent
• good decision making
3) Cognitive
4) A skill that requires lots of concentration to do.
5) Whole practice is practising a whole technique at once, whereas part practice is practising the parts of a technique separately.
6) E.g. It might be difficult for a performer to achieve an outcome goal, as it will depend on how well other people perform.
7) A target needs to be achievable because if it is too difficult, a performer may begin to feel negative about their performance, and give up trying to achieve their goal.

Page 93 (Exam Questions)

1 (a) E.g. If a goal is measurable, then a performer can see how much they have progressed towards achieving it *[1 mark]*. This can help to motivate a performer to continue training hard *[1 mark]* so that their performance will continue to improve *[1 mark]*.
(b) It specifies a time and a distance, both of which can be accurately measured *[1 mark]*.
(c) E.g. Layla could make her goal time-bound by setting a deadline for when she wants to achieve it, for example, within two months *[1 mark]*. This will help increase her motivation to train, as she will know how much she needs to improve in a certain amount of time *[1 mark]*.
Layla could also make sure her goal is achievable by comparing the time in which she can currently run 5 km with the time she wants to achieve *[1 mark]*. This will make sure her goal isn't too difficult for her to achieve, so that she will stay motivated to continue training *[1 mark]*.

2 E.g. A closed skill is one that is performed without having to adapt to any external factors *[1 mark]*. The high jump is partially closed, as the jump itself can be practised repeatedly and is usually the same under any conditions *[1 mark]*. However, it is not a completely closed skill, as the run up to the jump can be affected by external factors such as the weather *[1 mark]*.

Page 98 (Warm-Up Questions)

1) Any **one** from: e.g.
   - It can be combined with other guidance types.
   - It's useful for explaining techniques to experienced performers, as they will understand the language used.
   - It can be given during a performance.
2) Extrinsic feedback comes from a source that is not the performer, for example, a coach or teammate.
3) E.g. Knowledge of performance can help an experienced performer to improve specific aspects of a skill that they can already perform.
4) The output stage is when a skill is performed. This is done by the brain sending messages to the muscles to tell them how to move.
5) Someone's arousal level is how mentally and physically alert they are.
6) An extrovert is more likely to play rugby than an introvert.

Page 99 (Exam Questions)

1 E.g. Mental rehearsal involves imagining the feeling of a perfect performance in the muscles *[1 mark]*, which can help a performer to focus and boost their confidence, so they are able to perform well *[1 mark]*.

2 (i) E.g. Verbal guidance can involve a coach giving instructions or descriptions of a skill in words *[1 mark]*, which would be useful for providing instructions to beginners while they are in the pool *[1 mark]*. However, beginners could find this type of guidance confusing if a coach were to use technical language that they were not familiar with *[1 mark]*.

   (ii) E.g. Mechanical guidance involves the use of equipment in order to guide a learner through performing a skill, such as armbands or floats in swimming *[1 mark]*. This would be very useful for beginners, who may find it daunting to be in the swimming pool unaided *[1 mark]*, as the use of floats or armbands could help to give them confidence in new swimming skills *[1 mark]*.

3 *This mark scheme gives examples of some points you might have made in your answer. You can still get full marks if you haven't written every individual point below, as long as the points you have made are detailed enough and you meet all three assessment objectives.*
   To meet assessment objective 1, you will need to show knowledge of the four stages of the information processing model, for example:
   - The four stages of the information processing model are input, decision making, output and feedback.

   To meet assessment objective 2, you will need to apply each stage to the skill of tackling in football, for example:
   - The input is the player seeing their opponent running with the ball.
   - Decision making is the player deciding how to tackle.
   - Output is the tackle that is performed.
   - Feedback is information about how the tackle was performed.

   To meet assessment objective 3, you will need to analyse how a footballer tackling an opponent would use each stage of the information processing model, for example:
   - During the input stage, the footballer will receive information such as how fast their opponent is running and which direction they are going in. They may use selective attention to block out distractions, such as noise from the crowd, so they can focus on tackling their opponent.
   - During the decision making stage, the footballer will access their long-term memory to refer to previous experiences of performing different types of tackle successfully. They will then access their short-term memory to compare these previous experiences with what is happening in the game at the time, before deciding how to tackle.
   - During the output stage, information is sent from the footballer's brain to the muscles in their legs, such as the hamstrings and quadriceps, telling them how to carry out the tackle.
   - The feedback stage involves the footballer receiving either intrinsic feedback from themselves, or extrinsic feedback from their coach or teammates. For example, whether they gained possession of the ball, whether the tackle was painful and whether they used the correct technique.

   [6 marks available in total]

Section Six — Sport, Society and Culture

Page 105 (Warm-Up Questions)

1) E.g. Role models can inspire people to take up a sport.
2) E.g. Your parents might encourage you to take up sports, which will give you more opportunities to participate. Also, your siblings might play or be interested in sport, so you are familiar with it from a young age and so are more likely to play it yourself.
3) E.g. Religious beliefs about the Sabbath may prevent someone playing sport on certain days. This could limit the opportunities they have to participate in a particular sport.
4) E.g. Having the chance to try out a range of activities might help you to find a sport you enjoy and encourage you to exercise. If you dislike competitive sports, some PE lessons might put you off doing exercise.
5) E.g. If you live near mountains and snow, you may be more likely to take up winter sports such as skiing and snowboarding.
6) E.g. Making sure that facilities are reasonably priced, and that there are good public transport links to the facilities.

Page 106 (Exam Questions)

1 **C** Cost *[1 mark]*

2 Any **two** from: e.g.
   - There may be fewer opportunities through lack of facilities and equipment.
   - They may face discrimination or stereotypes about disabled people which may discourage them from taking part.
   - The lack of media coverage of disabled sporting events compared to other sporting events may mean there are fewer role models to inspire people to take part.

   [2 marks available in total]

3 (a) Running *[1 mark]*
   (b) E.g. Participation in cycling will increase in 13/14 *[1 mark]* because it has increased each year since 10/11, so you would expect the trend to continue *[1 mark]*.

Page 114 (Warm-Up Questions)

1) The commercialisation of sport means making money from it.
2) E.g. Newspapers, television, radio and the internet.
3) False
4) E.g. They may have to appear in adverts, even if they don't want to.
5) E.g. Better protective clothing, playing surfaces and medical technology can all help players to avoid injury.
6) E.g. Gamesmanship means using tactics that seem unfair to gain an advantage, whereas sportsmanship means respecting your opponent, sticking to the rules and playing fairly.
7) E.g. Using performance-enhancing drugs.
8) E.g. Crowds can create a good atmosphere which can make the game more enjoyable for the players, and can create a 'home-field advantage' for the home team.

Page 115 (Exam Questions)

1 **D** Deliberately tripping a player as they run down the pitch in hockey *[1 mark]*

2 (a) E.g. Sportsmanship means being honest, sticking to the rules and treating your opponents with respect *[1 mark]*.
   (b) E.g. In football, players will kick the ball out of play if an opposition player is injured *[1 mark]*.

3 E.g. Sponsorship brings in lots of money that can be spent on developing the sport *[1 mark]*.
   E.g. The money brought in through sponsorship may only benefit those at the top of a sport, and not the sport as a whole *[1 mark]*.

4 E.g. Increased media coverage of the Paralympics means that it reaches a wider audience *[1 mark]*. This means that the value of sponsorship deals for the athletes involved may increase *[1 mark]*, as a larger audience means that sponsors can advertise to more people *[1 mark]*.

Section Seven — Using Data

Page 122 (Warm-Up Questions)

1) E.g. Fitness testing and surveys.
2) E.g. An upward trend would be shown on a line graph by the data points generally going up and the line sloping upwards from left to right.
3) E.g. Fitness testing data can tell you whether or not training is having an effect on the desired component of fitness.

answers

Page 123 (Exam Questions)

1. E.g. Amir's score in the sit and reach test has increased each week after week 2, so he is reaching a little further each week *[1 mark]*. Amir's score has stayed almost constant each week in the one minute sit-up test, so the number of sit-ups he can do is neither increasing nor decreasing *[1 mark]*.

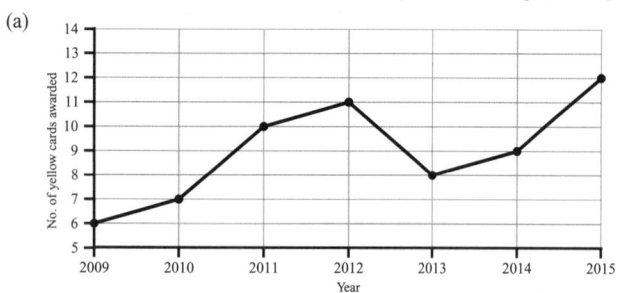

2. (a)
    [2 marks available in total — 1 mark for correctly plotting the points and joining them with straight lines and 1 mark for labelling the axes]

   (b) E.g. The fine was initially successful but its effectiveness seems to have worn off *[1 mark]* because there was a decrease in the number of yellow cards awarded in 2013, but in 2015 the number of yellow cards awarded was higher than in 2012 *[1 mark]*.

Practice Papers

Pages 125-138 (Practice Paper 1)

1. (a) **C** Tibia *[1 mark]*
   (b) **B** Hamstrings *[1 mark]*
   (c) **D** The effort is between the fulcrum and load *[1 mark]*
   (d) **A** Flexion *[1 mark]*
   (e) **A** Cooper 12- minute run test *[1 mark]*
   (f) **D** Circuit training *[1 mark]*
   (g) **C** Above Average *[1 mark]*

2. E.g. Tendons attach muscle to bone *[1 mark]*. When muscles contract, the tendons pull the bones to move the skeleton *[1 mark]*.

3. E.g. The antagonistic muscle pair at the knee works to push the athlete's body weight off the floor *[1 mark]* as the quadriceps contract *[1 mark]* and the hamstrings relax *[1 mark]*.

   To explain what the muscle pair does to help the athlete to jump, you could have said that it moves the knee from flexion to extension instead.
   The antagonistic muscle pair at the knee isn't the only one you could have written about — there's also the pair at the hip (the gluteus maximus and hip flexors), or at the ankle (the gastrocnemius and tibialis anterior).

4. A lever with a mechanical advantage can move a large load with a small effort *[1 mark]*. However, it only allows a small range of movement *[1 mark]*.

5. E.g. Blood is redistributed around the body when the arteries supplying the working muscles vasodilate *[1 mark]* and arteries supplying inactive areas of the body vasoconstrict *[1 mark]*. This causes the amount of blood flowing to the muscles used during exercise to increase *[1 mark]*.

6. (i) E.g. Anaerobic respiration can release energy very quickly for short periods *[1 mark]*, allowing a performer to sprint through the water *[1 mark]*. This makes it very useful during races of a short distance, or in parts of longer races, such as a sprint finish *[1 mark]*.

   (ii) E.g. Anaerobic respiration releases lactic acid as a by-product *[1 mark]*, which would eventually lead to muscle fatigue *[1 mark]*, so it can't be sustained for a long period *[1 mark]*.

7. E.g. An increase in breathing rate would increase the rate that oxygen is delivered into the lungs *[1 mark]*. An increase in heart rate would increase the rate that blood passes through the capillaries in the lungs and is delivered to the muscles *[1 mark]*. Therefore, when both breathing rate and heart rate increase, oxygen can diffuse much more quickly from the lungs into the bloodstream *[1 mark]* and then be delivered to the muscles to be used to release energy *[1 mark]*.

8. (a) Second class *[1 mark]*
   (b) E.g. The load is the diver's body weight, which is in the middle of the lever arm, therefore it is a second class lever *[1 mark]*.

9. (i) E.g. He may have been jogging lightly to warm up *[1 mark]* because his heart rate increases for 10 minutes, then stays at a moderate rate *[1 mark]*.

   (ii) E.g. He may have increased his running speed and then continued to run at this speed *[1 mark]*, because his heart rate increases very quickly and stays elevated to this level between 20 and 50 minutes *[1 mark]*.

10. E.g. Regular exercise makes the heart stronger and increases the size of its ventricles, therefore increasing maximum stroke volume and cardiac output *[1 mark]*. This would increase the amount of oxygenated blood reaching the muscles of an endurance athlete *[1 mark]*, meaning they would be able to exercise more intensely and for longer *[1 mark]*.

11. E.g. The third class lever used by the tennis player allows her to move the tennis racquet quickly *[1 mark]* and through a large range of movement *[1 mark]* in order to generate lots of power with the swing *[1 mark]*.

12. E.g. Flexibility is the amount of movement possible at a joint *[1 mark]*. Having a high level of flexibility in, for example, the hip joint, would help a long jumper to reach their legs further *[1 mark]*, and therefore jump a greater distance *[1 mark]*.

13. (i) E.g. The sit and reach test measures flexibility of the back and lower hamstrings *[1 mark]*, which could be useful for a beach volleyball player if they need to reach high to serve or dive for the ball *[1 mark]*. However, it is not the most important fitness test for a beach volleyball player, as flexibility of the shoulders is much more important for most actions in beach volleyball *[1 mark]*.

    (ii) E.g. The vertical jump test measures power of the leg muscles *[1 mark]*, therefore it is a useful fitness test for a beach volleyball player *[1 mark]* as they would need power in their legs to jump high when spiking the ball *[1 mark]*.

14. (a) E.g. A course must be set out using cones, and the person taking the test must start the course by lying down at the first cone. They must then run as quickly as possible around the course, weaving around the cones first in one direction, then the other, before running to the final cone.
    [2 marks for a complete description, 1 mark for a partial description]

    (b) E.g. The time taken to complete the Illinois agility run test is decreasing, which means her agility is increasing *[1 mark]*. Her time on the 30 m sprint test is decreasing, which means she is running faster *[1 mark]*.

    (c) Any **one** from:
    - Plyometric training
    - Resistance/weight training
    - Circuit training
    [1 mark available]

15. (a) E.g. Matthew's training applies specificity in some ways, as it focuses specifically on training the muscle groups in the legs, which are used constantly throughout a hockey match *[1 mark]*. It will also improve his cardiovascular fitness, which will enable him to move continuously throughout the match without becoming tired *[1 mark]*. However, it does not completely apply specificity, as jogging will not improve the skills that are specific to hockey, such as shooting accurately at the goal *[1 mark]*. Also, it will not improve other important components of fitness needed for hockey, such as strength in his arms, or his anaerobic fitness, which would be needed to sprint down the hockey pitch *[1 mark]*.

    (b) E.g. Matthew could increase the frequency of his training sessions, for example, by going jogging three or four times a week *[1 mark]*. He could increase the intensity of his training sessions by jogging at a faster speed *[1 mark]*. He could increase the time spent on each training session, perhaps by jogging for 45 minutes instead of 30 *[1 mark]*. Finally, he could vary the type of training that he does, for example, by including weight training to improve the strength in his legs *[1 mark]*.

16. (a) E.g. To improve muscular endurance with weight training, a low weight, below 70% of one rep max, should be used with a high number of repetitions *[1 mark]*. Overload is produced by gradually increasing the number of repetitions *[1 mark]*.

    (b) E.g. Weight training can be easily adapted to focus on different muscle groups needed for different activities *[1 mark]*.
    E.g. Weight training can be dangerous if a participant has poor technique *[1 mark]*.

17. *This mark scheme gives examples of some points you might have made in your answer. You can still get full marks if you haven't written every individual point below, as long as the points you have made are detailed enough and you meet all three assessment objectives.*

    To meet assessment objective one, you will need to show knowledge of muscular endurance and agility, for example:

- Muscular endurance is the ability to use the body's muscles for a long time without becoming tired.
- Agility is the ability to change body position or direction quickly and with control.

To meet assessment objective two, you will need to include examples of when muscular endurance and agility would be needed in netball, for example:
- A netball player would need good muscular endurance to be able to use their leg and arm muscles for the duration of a netball match.
- A netball player would need agility to move quickly around the court in order to find space to receive a pass or to mark an opponent.
- Agility is required in netball once in possession of the ball in order to change body position quickly when aiming passes towards teammates.

To meet assessment objective three, you will need to evaluate the importance of muscular endurance and agility for performance in netball, for example:
- Good muscular endurance would be important for overall performance in netball, as it would prevent a player's muscles from fatiguing towards the end of a match. This would allow them to continue to run quickly around the court and pass and shoot the ball powerfully.
- Agility is very important for many aspects of a netball match, such as intercepting and making passes.
- In conclusion, both good muscular endurance and agility would benefit performance in netball. However, a netball player may also want to focus on improving other components of fitness. For example, improved hand-eye coordination would mean they could shoot more accurately, and therefore score more goals.

[6 marks available in total]

18 *This mark scheme gives examples of some points you might have made in your answer. You can still get full marks if you haven't written every individual point below, as long as the points you have made are detailed enough and you meet all three assessment objectives.*

To meet assessment objective one, you will need to show knowledge and understanding of tidal volume, for example:
- Tidal volume is the volume of air breathed in or out during one breath.
- Increased tidal volume brings more oxygen into the lungs.
- Increased tidal volume removes more carbon dioxide from the lungs.

To meet assessment objective two, you will need to include examples from a football match that would impact on the need for a midfielder to have an increased tidal volume, for example:
- A slight increase in tidal volume would help a midfielder to meet the increased oxygen demand in the muscles, and so release the energy needed to jog around the pitch throughout the match.
- A large increase in tidal volume would help a midfielder to remove lactic acid from the muscles and recover from oxygen debt after sprinting up the pitch.
- An increase in tidal volume would be less beneficial to a midfielder during actions such as taking a penalty, as this action would not require much extra energy to be released in the muscles and therefore would not lead to much of an increase in oxygen demand.

To meet assessment objective three, you will need to make judgements about the extent to which an increase in tidal volume will allow a midfielder to perform well in a football match, for example:
- An increase in tidal volume would be necessary to bring in extra oxygen and remove extra carbon dioxide, as running around the pitch for 90 minutes would increase the rate of respiration in the muscles.
- Other changes would also be necessary to meet the increased oxygen demand in the muscles, for example, increased heart rate, stroke volume and breathing rate.
- In conclusion, without an increase in tidal volume, a midfielder would be unable to remain active for the total duration of a match. However, this change alone would be insufficient to meet the demands of the match, therefore other physiological changes would also be necessary.

[9 marks available in total]

Pages 139-150 (Practice Paper 2)

1 (a) **B** Carbohydrates are the main source of energy for the body *[1 mark]*
   (b) **D** Someone who exercises once a month does not have a sedentary lifestyle *[1 mark]*
   (c) **A** Feedback from how a performance feels to the performer *[1 mark]*
   (d) **B** When a coach physically moves a learner's body through a technique *[1 mark]*
   (e) **D** Socio-economic *[1 mark]*
   (f) **A** Time-wasting in football *[1 mark]*
   (g) **B** 25 to 44 *[1 mark]*

2 (a) E.g. Improved efficiency of the cardiovascular system *[1 mark]*.
       There are lots of other benefits that you could put here, like improved body tone, increased strength, increased flexibility and better posture.
   (b) E.g. Exercise increases the level of endorphins in your brain *[1 mark]*. This helps you to feel good, so can help prevent depression *[1 mark]*.
       You could also have explained how exercise helps to reduce stress, or how it helps improve confidence and gives a sense of achievement.
   (c) Social *[1 mark]*

3 E.g. A sedentary lifestyle can lead to an increase in body fat, which can cause fatty deposits to build up in arteries *[1 mark]*. These deposits restrict blood flow, increasing the risk of coronary heart disease *[1 mark]*. Osteoporosis is when bones have become fragile *[1 mark]*. A sedentary lifestyle means that bones become less dense, because they are involved in less weight-bearing exercise, which increases the risk of osteoporosis *[1 mark]*.

4 (a) E.g. Dehydration can cause the blood to become **thicker**. It can also cause your body temperature to **increase**.
       [2 marks available in total — 1 mark for each correct word]
       You will still get the marks for using other words that mean the same thing — e.g. if you say 'more viscous' instead of 'thicker'.
   (b) Any **one** from: e.g.
       - Exercise causes heavier breathing.
       - Exercise causes increased sweating.
       [1 mark available]
   (c) E.g. Dehydration can cause muscle fatigue, which makes muscles tired and painful *[1 mark]*. This would mean a runner would be unable to perform as well, as they would be forced to either run more slowly or stop completely *[1 mark]*.
       Dehydration can cause an increase in body temperature, as the body isn't able to produce as much sweat *[1 mark]*. This could make a runner feel faint and unable to continue running *[1 mark]*.

5 (a) Rugby *[1 mark]*
   (b) E.g. The rugby players' optimum weights are also affected by their height, bone structure, muscle girth and the position they play *[1 mark]*. So, for example, the players could have different optimum weights because they are a different height *[1 mark]*.
   (c) E.g. The energy balance is the relationship between the amount of energy you get from food and the amount of energy you use up *[1 mark]*. To increase weight, the hockey player's energy intake (from food) would need to be greater than the amount of energy they use up, giving them a positive energy balance *[1 mark]*.

6 E.g. A basic skill is one that does not require much concentration to complete *[1 mark]*. Therefore, a football pass is basic in some respects as it involves the simple action of kicking *[1 mark]*. However, it is not right at the 'basic' end of the continuum because it has some aspects that are complex, such as aiming the pass precisely towards a teammate *[1 mark]*.

7 (i) E.g. Variable practice is important in tennis because tennis involves mainly open skills *[1 mark]*. Variable practice will provide practice in many different match situations — for example, allowing a player to react to different types of shot *[1 mark]* — which will provide realistic practice and therefore help improve their performance in a real match *[1 mark]*.
   (ii) E.g. Fixed practice is less important in tennis as there are fewer closed skills in the sport, although it still plays an important role in coaching a player's serve *[1 mark]*. Fixed practice would only provide repeated practice of skills in the same situations *[1 mark]*, so would not provide realistic practice for many of the skills needed in a match *[1 mark]*.

8 E.g. Amanda's goal applies the time-bound principle by saying that she wants to achieve her goal in four months *[1 mark]*. Having a deadline will help motivate her to train *[1 mark]* and will therefore improve her fitness and performance so she will be more likely to achieve her goal *[1 mark]*.

9 E.g. Manual guidance works well for beginners to get the feel of a complex skill before trying to perform it on their own *[1 mark]*.
   E.g. The gymnast may begin to rely on the manual guidance and be unable to perform a cartwheel on the beam without the coach's help *[1 mark]*.

10 (a) The trend is that participation in swimming is decreasing *[1 mark]*.
   (b) E.g. More women participate in swimming than men *[1 mark]*. This could be because there are more female role models in swimming than male role models *[1 mark]*. E.g. More men participate in football than women *[1 mark]*. This could be because women have faced discrimination for wanting to play football *[1 mark]*.

11 (a) E.g. For some people from certain ethnic groups there may be a lack of role models in sport *[1 mark]*. This could lead some people to be less inspired to participate in sport themselves *[1 mark]*.

(b) Any **one** from: e.g.
- Age
- Socio-economic group
- Disability
- Attitudes of family/friends
- Experiences in PE at school
- The environment you live in

[1 mark available]

12 (a) E.g. Sponsorship of a team would mean that they would have more money *[1 mark]*. They could spend this money on improved equipment *[1 mark]*, which may help them to improve their performance *[1 mark]*.

(b) E.g. An alcoholic drinks company *[1 mark]*.

(c) E.g. As it is a youth tournament, the participants are young so may be impressionable *[1 mark]*. This means that the company's sponsorship might make them more likely to start underage drinking, which would have a negative impact on their health *[1 mark]*.

13 (i) E.g. Increased media coverage can have a positive impact on a sport by increasing awareness of the sport and helping it to reach a wider audience *[1 mark]*. This could lead to an increase in participation in the sport *[1 mark]* and increased ticket revenues from more people coming to watch events *[1 mark]*.

(ii) E.g. Increased media coverage of a sport could have a negative impact as the media may come to have too much control over the sport *[1 mark]*. As the sport becomes increasingly reliant on the money brought in through media coverage, this puts the media companies in a position of power *[1 mark]* which could lead to the media dictating when and how many games are played, and maybe even changing the rules of the sport *[1 mark]*.

14 (a) E.g. Gamesmanship is gaining an advantage by using tactics that seem unfair, but aren't against the rules *[1 mark]*.

(b) E.g. Elite performers demonstrating gamesmanship could be bad for the sport as it could lead to more occurrences of gamesmanship at lower levels of the sport *[1 mark]*. This is because elite performers are role models and cricket is a high-profile sport *[1 mark]*, so their behaviour will gain lots of media attention and may inspire others to behave in the same way *[1 mark]*.

15 *This mark scheme gives examples of some points you might have made in your answer. You can still get full marks if you haven't written every individual point below, as long as the points you have made are detailed enough and you meet all three assessment objectives.*

To meet assessment objective one, you will need to show knowledge of the functions of carbohydrates, fats and proteins, for example:
- Carbohydrates are the main source of energy for the body.
- Fats provide some energy for the body.
- Proteins help the body to build and repair muscles.

To meet assessment objective two, you will need to include examples of when a basketball player would need carbohydrates, fats and proteins, for example:
- Carbohydrates would provide energy throughout a basketball match or training session for exercise at any intensity.
- Fats could provide energy for low-intensity periods of the match.
- Proteins would be used to repair and build muscle between training sessions.

To meet assessment objective three, you will need to analyse how carbohydrates, fats and proteins would benefit a basketball player's training and performance, for example:
- Carbohydrates would benefit a basketball player's training and performance as they would allow them to run and sprint around the court. They would also provide energy for powerful movements, such as jumping to shoot at the hoop.
- Fats would benefit a basketball player's performance, as they would provide energy to allow them to continue using their muscles at the end of a match if carbohydrate stores were to run out.
- Proteins would benefit a basketball player by helping them to build stronger muscles which will improve performance.

[6 marks available in total]

16 *This mark scheme gives examples of some points you might have made in your answer. You can still get full marks if you haven't written every individual point below, as long as the points you have made are detailed enough and you meet all three assessment objectives.*

To meet assessment objective one, you will need to show knowledge and understanding of visual and mechanical guidance, for example:
- Visual guidance involves being shown visually how to perform a skill.
- Mechanical guidance involves the use of equipment to help a learner perform a skill.

To meet assessment objective two, you will need to apply your knowledge of these guidance types to a group of beginners in trampolining, for example:
- Visual guidance could be used to demonstrate how basic bounces on the trampoline should look.
- Mechanical guidance could include the use of a harness to guide the learners through a somersault on the trampoline.

To meet assessment objective three, you will need to justify the use of these guidance types with a group of beginners in trampolining, for example:
- Visual guidance would be useful for the beginners who aren't familiar with different trampolining skills.
- Visual guidance would be useful for beginners as they would be able to copy basic skills, such as bouncing, from demonstrations.
- Mechanical guidance can be very useful for a learner in trampolining, as it can increase their confidence at performing dangerous or complex skills.
- Mechanical guidance works well to teach high organisation skills, and is therefore well suited for teaching trampolining, as many of the skills in the sport can be classified as high organisation.
- It may be best for visual guidance to be used initially so that the beginners become familiar with what trampolining skills should look like, before using mechanical guidance to help them learn the skill.

[9 marks available in total]

Glossary

abduction	Movement away from an imaginary centre line through the body.
ability	A person's set of characteristics that control their potential to learn a skill.
adduction	Movement towards an imaginary centre line through the body.
aerobic respiration	When the body releases energy using glucose and oxygen. Carbon dioxide and water are produced as by-products (waste).
agility	The ability to change body position or direction quickly and with control.
alveoli	Small air bags in the lungs where gases are exchanged.
anaerobic respiration	When the body doesn't have enough oxygen to release energy aerobically, so it just uses glucose. Lactic acid is produced as a by-product (waste).
antagonistic muscle pair	A pair of muscles that work together to bring about movement. As one muscle contracts (the agonist or prime mover) the other relaxes (the antagonist).
anticipatory rise	When heart rate increases before exercise has started.
arousal	A person's level of mental and physical alertness.
ATP-PC	The anaerobic energy system used in the muscles during the first few seconds of exercise.
axis of movement	An imaginary line that the body or a body part can move around.
balance	The ability to keep the body's centre of mass over a base of support.
balanced diet	The best ratio of nutrients to match your lifestyle.
basic skill	A simple skill which doesn't need much concentration to do, e.g. running.
blood cell	A component of blood. There are red blood cells (which carry oxygen and carbon dioxide) and white blood cells (which fight disease).
blood pressure	How strongly the blood presses against the walls of blood vessels.
blood vessel	Part of the cardiovascular system that transports blood around the body. The three main types are arteries, veins and capillaries.
body composition	The percentage of body weight made up by fat, muscle and bone.
body mass index (BMI)	A score used to determine whether a person is underweight, overweight, obese or of a normal weight. It's calculated using their height and weight.
breathing rate	The number of breaths taken each minute.
calorie	A unit used to measure the amount of energy in food. It's often shortened to Kcal.
cardiac output	The volume of blood pumped by each ventricle in the heart per minute.
cardio-respiratory system	The combination of the cardiovascular and respiratory systems working together to get oxygen into the body tissues and carbon dioxide out of them.
cardiovascular endurance/fitness	The ability of the heart and lungs to supply oxygen to the muscles, so that the whole body can be exercised for a long time. It can also be called aerobic endurance, aerobic power or stamina.
cardiovascular system	The organs responsible for circulating blood around the body.
circumduction	Movement of a limb, hand or foot in a circular motion.
closed skill	A skill performed in a predictable environment — it's not affected by external factors.

Glossary

commercialisation	The commercialisation of sport means the transformation of sport into something people can make money from, e.g. through sponsorship.
complex skill	A skill which needs lots of concentration to do, e.g. a volley in football.
concentric contraction	A type of muscle contraction where a muscle contracts and shortens.
connective tissue	Body tissue that holds other body tissues (e.g. muscles and bones) together. Cartilage, ligaments and tendons are types of connective tissue.
contract to compete	An unwritten agreement between competitors to respect the 'spirit of the game'.
cool-down	Light exercise and stretching done after exercise to return your body to normal.
coordination	The ability to use two or more parts of the body together, efficiently and accurately.
coronary heart disease	When fatty deposits build up in the arteries around the heart, which restrict the flow of blood.
data	Information — in words or numbers. Data can be quantitative (numbers) or qualitative (words).
delayed onset of muscle soreness (DOMS)	Soreness in the muscles in the days after exercise.
deviance	Behaviour that goes against the moral values or laws of the sport.
diffusion	The process of substances (e.g. oxygen) moving from a place where there is a higher concentration to a place where there is a lower concentration.
dorsi-flexion	Flexion at the ankle by lifting the toes.
eccentric contraction	A type of muscle contraction where a muscle contracts and lengthens.
effort arm	The distance between the fulcrum and the effort in a lever system.
exercise	A form of physical activity done to maintain or improve health and/or fitness.
expiratory reserve volume (ERV)	The amount of extra air that can be breathed out after breathing out normally.
extension	Opening a joint, e.g. straightening the leg at the knee.
externally-paced skill	A skill that starts because of external factors which also control the pace of the skill.
feedback	Information received about a performance either during it (concurrent feedback) or after it (terminal feedback). It can be intrinsic (from yourself) or extrinsic (from other sources).
fine skill	A skill using small muscle groups for precise movements requiring accuracy and coordination.
fitness	The ability to meet the demands of the environment.
flexibility	The amount of movement possible at a joint.
flexion	Closing a joint, e.g. bending the arm at the elbow.
gamesmanship	Gaining an advantage by using tactics that seem unfair, but aren't against the rules.
gross skill	A skill involving powerful movements performed by large muscle groups.
guidance	Information or help in learning a skill. Guidance can be visual, verbal, manual or mechanical.
health	A state of complete physical, mental and social well-being and not merely the absence of disease or infirmity.

Glossary

heart rate	The number of times your heart beats in one minute. It is measured in beats per minute (bpm).
high organisation skill	A skill which can't easily be broken down into different parts that can be practised separately, because the parts of the skill are closely linked. E.g. a cartwheel.
hooliganism	Rowdy, aggressive and sometimes violent behaviour of fans and spectators of sport.
hydration	Having the right amount of water for the body to function properly. If you have too little water, you're dehydrated.
inspiratory reserve volume (IRV)	The amount of extra air that can be breathed in after breathing in normally.
isometric contraction	When a muscle stays the same length as it contracts.
isotonic contraction	When a muscle changes length as it contracts.
joint type	The main types of joint are ball and socket, hinge, condyloid and pivot. Each type allows a different range of movement.
lactic acid	A waste product produced during anaerobic respiration, making the muscles feel tired (fatigued).
lever system	A system that allows the body's muscles to move the bones in the skeleton. A lever system can be first, second or third class, and is made up of a lever arm, effort, fulcrum and load.
low organisation skill	A skill which can easily be broken down into different parts that can be practised separately. E.g. the front crawl stroke in swimming.
mechanical advantage	When a lever can move a large load with a small amount of effort from the muscles.
mechanical disadvantage	When a lever requires a large effort from the muscles to move a small load.
the media	Organisations involved in mass communication — e.g. through television, radio, newspapers and the Internet.
minute ventilation	The volume of air breathed in or out in one minute. It can also be called 'minute volume'.
muscle fibre	One of the fibres that make up the muscles in the body. There are three main types: type I, type IIA and type IIX. Each type is suited to a different intensity of exercise.
muscular endurance	The ability to repeatedly use the muscles over a long time, without getting tired.
musculo-skeletal system	The combination of the muscular and skeletal systems working together to allow movement.
obesity	Having a lot more body fat than you should.
open skill	A skill performed in a changing environment, where a performer has to react and adapt to external factors.
optimum weight	Roughly what you should weigh for good health, based on your gender, height, bone structure and muscle girth. It can also be affected by the kind of activity or sport you do.
overload	Working your body harder to increase fitness levels over time.
PEP	Personal Exercise Programme. A training programme that's designed to suit a specific person and improve their health, fitness or performance.
performance	How well a task is completed.
plane of movement	An imaginary flat surface used to describe the direction of a movement. The body or a body part moves in a plane. There are three planes you need to know: sagittal, transverse and frontal.
plantar-flexion	Extension at the ankle by pointing the toes.

Glossary

power	A combination of speed and strength.
practice	When a skill is repeated to improve it. The types of practice are massed, distributed, fixed, variable, whole and part.
reaction time	The time taken to move in response to a stimulus.
residual volume	The amount of air left in the lungs after the most possible air has been breathed out.
resistance/load arm	The distance between the fulcrum and the load in a lever system.
respiratory system	The organs in the body used for breathing.
rotation	Movement of the body or a body part in a clockwise or anticlockwise motion.
sedentary lifestyle	A lifestyle where there is little, irregular or no physical activity.
self-paced skill	A skill that starts when a performer decides to start it. The performer also controls the pace of the skill.
SMART	The five principles of goal setting.
socio-economic group	A way of grouping people based on their job, how much money they have and where they live, e.g. 'working class' is a socio-economic group.
somatotype	A person's body type based on their body shape and the amount of muscle and fat they have. The main somatotypes are endomorph, mesomorph and ectomorph.
speed	The rate at which someone is able to move, or to cover a distance in a given amount of time.
spirometer trace	A graph produced by a spirometer machine which can be used to measure lung volumes.
sponsorship	When a company pays to associate their name with some part of a sport, including individual sportspeople. It's usually done to make money.
sportsmanship	Being honest, sticking to the rules and treating your opponents with respect.
stage of learning	How experienced someone is at performing a skill. The stages are cognitive, associative and autonomous.
strength	The amount of force that a muscle or muscle group can apply against a resistance. It can be broken down into different types: maximal, static, explosive and dynamic.
stroke volume	The volume of blood pumped with each heartbeat by each ventricle in the heart.
synovial joint	Where two or more bones are joined together in a joint capsule containing synovial fluid.
tidal volume	The amount of air that is breathed in or out in one breath.
training season	One of the three parts of the year with different training aims depending on whether it's before, during or after the period when sport competition takes place.
trend	When a graph is generally going up or down over time.
vertebral column	The bones (vertebrae) making up the spine/spinal column. The vertebral column has five regions: cervical, thoracic, lumbar, the sacrum and the coccyx.
vital capacity	The most air you can possibly breathe in after breathing out the largest volume of air possible.
warm-up	Preparing your body for exercise. It's made up of three main phases: light exercise, stretching and practice actions.

Index

30 m sprint test 43

A
abdominal curls 42
abdominals 8
abduction 6, 8-10, 32
ability 88
abrasions 66
active stretching 58
adaptations 51
adduction 6, 8-10, 32
advertising 107-109
aerobic
  exercise 21
  respiration 21
  target zone 52
  training 55-59
aerobic endurance/power 37
aerobics 59
aggression 97
agility 39, 43
agonists 10
air 17
alcohol 74
alternate hand throw test 44
alveoli 16, 25, 74
anabolic steroids/agents 68
anaerobic
  exercise 21
  respiration 21
  target zone 52
  training 55-57, 59
antagonistic muscle pairs 10
antagonists 10
aorta 14
arousal 96
arteries 15, 23, 25, 72
arterioles 15
atria 14
average ratings (fitness tests) 41, 46
axes (of movement) 32

B
balance 39, 44
balanced diet 74, 79
ball and socket joints 6
bar charts 117, 119
beta blockers 68
biceps 8, 10, 30
bleep test 41
blood 14, 15
  pressure 23, 25, 45, 72, 74, 75
  vessels 15, 23
blood doping 68, 112
body composition 38, 45, 55
body density test 45
body fat 38, 75, 81, 83
Body Mass Index (BMI) 83
Bodypump™ 59
bone density 25, 72
bones 4, 5
  injuries 67
breathing 16, 17
breathing rate 22, 25
bronchi 16
bronchioles 16

C
calories 45, 83
cancer 74, 75
capillaries 15, 16, 25
carbohydrate loading 81
carbohydrates 21, 65, 79, 81
carbon dioxide 16, 17, 24
cardiac muscle 8
cardiac output 23-25
cardio-respiratory system 16, 24, 25, 59
cardiovascular endurance/fitness 25, 37, 41, 45, 55-59
cardiovascular system 14, 15, 23, 24
cartilage 7, 66
centre of mass 39
cholesterol 72, 75
cilia 74
circuit training 57
circumduction 6, 8
commercialisation 107-109
components of fitness 37-40
concentration gradient 16, 24
concentric contractions 11
concussion 67
condyloid joints 6
connective tissues 7
continuous training 55
contract to compete 111
cool-down 65
Cooper 12-minute run/swim test 41
coordination 39, 44
creatine phosphate 21

D
data 24, 41, 46, 75, 104, 107, 117-121
Decision Review System (DRS) 110
deep breathing (mental preparation) 96
dehydration 64, 80
delayed onset of muscle soreness (DOMS) 22, 65
deltoids 8-10
deoxygenated blood 14-16
depression 73-75
deviance 112
diabetes 72, 75
diaphragm 16, 25
diet 74, 79-81
diffusion 16, 24
disabilities 102
dislocation 66
diuretics 68
dorsi-flexion 6-8, 30
dynamic stretching 58, 63
dynamometer 42

E
eccentric contractions 11
ectomorphs 82
effort 30, 31
emotional benefits of exercise 73
endomorphs 82
endorphins 73
energy balance 83
EPO 68
EPOC (oxygen debt) 22
etiquette 111
exercise 36
  benefits of 72, 73
  long-term effects of 25
  short-term effects of 22-24
expiratory reserve volume 17, 18
extension 6-10, 30, 32
external intercostals 16, 25
external obliques 8
extroverts 97

F
fartlek training 55
fats 21, 79, 81
feedback 94, 95, 118
fibre 79, 80
fibres (muscle) 11
fitness 36, 72
  components of 37-40
  data 46, 119
  testing 41-46
fitness classes 59
FITT 51
fixators 10
flat bones 4, 5
flexibility 38, 44, 58
flexion 6-10, 30-32
fractures 67
fulcrum 30, 31

G
gamesmanship 111
gastrocnemius 9, 10, 30
gender divide 101
globalisation 107
gluteals 9
gluteus maximus 9, 10
goal line technology 110
goal setting 91, 121
golfer's elbow 66
graphs 24, 75, 104, 107, 117-121
grip dynamometer test 42, 46
growth hormones 68
guidance 94

H
haeomoglobin 15
hamstrings 9, 10
hand-eye coordination 39, 44
Harvard step test 41
Hawk-Eye 110
health 36, 72, 73
heart 14
heart disease 72, 74, 75
heart rate 23-25, 45, 52, 63, 65, 121
  anticipatory rise 24
high-altitude training 58
high-intensity interval training (HIIT) 56
hinge joints 6
hip flexors 8, 10
home-field advantage 113
hooliganism 113
hydration 64, 65, 80, 81
hypertrophy 25

I
ice baths 65
Illinois agility run test 43
imagery (mental preparation) 96
individual needs 50
information processing model 95
injuries 38, 51, 63, 66, 67
  preventing 63-65
inspiratory reserve volume 17, 18
insulin 72
intensities of exercise 51, 52
interval training 56
introverts 97
inverted-U theory 96
involuntary (smooth) muscles 8
irregular bones 4, 5
isometric contractions 11
isotonic contractions 11

J
joints 6, 7, 10
  injuries 66

Index

L
lactate accumulation 22
lactic acid 17, 21, 22, 65
latissimus dorsi 9, 10
levers 30, 31
lifestyle choices 74
ligaments 7, 25, 63, 66
line graphs 118, 120, 121
load 30, 31
long bones 4, 5
lungs 16, 25
  capacity 25

M
macronutrients 79
massages 65
maximum heart rate 52
mechanical advantage 31
mechanical disadvantage 31
media 107, 108
mental preparation 63, 96
mental rehearsal 96
mesomorphs 82
micronutrients 79, 80
minerals 80
minute ventilation/volume 22, 25
mobility exercises 63
motivation 97
multi-stage fitness test 41
muscle girth 25, 83
muscles 8, 9
  antagonistic pairs 10
  attachment 4, 5
  contractions 10, 11
  cramp 22, 80
  fatigue 22, 80
  hypertrophy 25
  injuries 66
  repairing 79, 81
muscular endurance 25, 37, 42, 55-59
muscular system 8-11
musculo-skeletal system 8, 9, 25, 59

N
narcotic analgesics 68
nutrients 79, 81

O
obesity 72, 74, 75, 83
officials 64, 108, 112
one-minute sit-up/press-up test 42
one rep max 42
optimum weight 83
osteoporosis 72, 75
outcome goals 91
overhydration 80
overload 50, 51

overtraining 51
overweight 75, 83
oxygen 16, 17, 24
oxygenated blood 14-16
oxygen debt (EPOC) 22-24, 65
oxyhaemoglobin 15

P
Paralympics 102
PARQ 45, 63
participation rates 101-104
passive stretching 58
pectoralis major 8
PE lessons 103
peptide hormones 68
performance 36
performance-enhancing drugs 68, 112
performance goals 91
personal exercise programme (PEP) 50, 51, 74
personality types 97
physical benefits of exercise 72
physical literacy 103
pie charts 120
Pilates 59
pivot joints 6
planes (of movement) 32
plantar-flexion 6, 7, 9, 10, 30
plasma 15
platelets 4, 15
plyometric training 57
PNF stretching 65
positive self-talk/thinking 96
posture 38, 72
power 40, 56, 57
practice 90
principles of training 50, 51, 63
progression 50
progressive overload 50
proteins 79, 81
pulled hamstring 66
pulmonary
  artery 14
  veins 14
pulmonary circuit 14

Q
quadriceps 8, 10, 57
qualitative data 117
quantitative data 117

R
racism 101
reaction time 40, 44
recovery 51, 65, 74

recovery position 67
recreational drugs 74
red blood cells 4, 15, 25, 58, 68
rehydration 64, 65, 80
reliability of fitness tests 46
reps 56
residual volume 17, 18
resistance training 56
respiratory system 16, 17, 22, 24
resting heart rate 23, 25, 45, 119
reversibility 50, 51
RICE 67
role models 101, 102, 108
rotation 6, 8-10, 32
rotator cuffs 9, 10
ruler drop test 44

S
sedentary lifestyle 75
selective attention 95, 96
serotonin 73
short bones 4, 5
sit and reach test 44
sit-up bleep test 42
skeletal system 4-7
skills 88-90
  classification 89
  movement characteristics 88
skinfold test 45
skin injuries 66
sleep 74
SMART 91
smoking 74
social benefits of exercise 73
socio-economic groups 102
soft-tissue injuries 66
software (movement analysis) 110
somatotypes 82
specificity 50
spectators 108, 110, 113
speed 38, 43, 55
spine 5
Spinning® 59
spirometer traces 18
sponsorship 107-109
SPORT (principles of training) 50
sports drinks 80
sportsmanship 111
spotters 56
sprains 64, 66, 67
sprint tests 43
stages of learning 88
stamina 37
standing jump test 43
standing stork test 44

static stretching 58, 65
steady-state training 55
stimulants 68
strains 66, 67
strength 25, 37, 42, 56, 59
stress 73, 74
stretching 58, 63, 65
strokes 72, 74, 75
stroke volume 23-25
sweating 23
synovial joints 7
systemic circuit 14

T
technology in sport 110
tedium 50
Television Match Official (TMO) 110
tendons 7, 25, 63, 66
tennis elbow 66
testosterone 68
tibialis anterior 8, 10
tidal volume 17, 18, 25
time-wasting 111
trachea 16
training methods 55-59
training seasons 59
training target zones 52
trapezius 9
trends 75, 107, 118
triceps 9, 10
type-2 diabetes 72, 75

V
validity of fitness tests 46
valves (heart) 14
variance 50
vascular shunting 23
vasoconstriction 23
vasodilation 23
veins 15, 25
vena cava 14
ventricles 14
venules 15
vertical jump test 43
violence 112
visualisation 96
vital capacity 17, 25
vitamins 80
voluntary (skeletal) muscles 8

W
wall toss/throw test 44
warm-up 63, 96
weight training 56
well-being 36, 72, 73
white blood cells 4, 15
work/rest/sleep balance 74

Y
yoga 59